THE CITY IS OUR FARM

THE CITY
IS OUR FARM

Seven Migrant Ijebu Yoruba Families

Dan R. Aronson

G.K. HALL & CO.
70 LINCOLN STREET, BOSTON, MASS.

SCHENKMAN PUBLISHING COMPANY
Cambridge, Mass.

Library of Congress Cataloging in Publication Data
Aronson, Dan R
   The city is our farm.

   Bibliography: p.
   1. Yorubas — Social conditions.   2. Ibadan, Nigeria —
Social conditions.   3. Detribalization.   I. Title.
DT513.A74   1978   301.36'1   78-16796
ISBN 0-8161-8252-3

This publication is printed on permanent/durable acid-free paper
MANUFACTURED IN THE UNITED STATES OF AMERICA

TO NINE FAMILIES . . . .

To the seven of this book, who must remain anonymous
To the memory of my father Jacob S. Aronson and to my
   mother Pearl B. Aronson and my brothers Joel and Carl
And to my wife Gerry and my children David, Jennifer and
   Joshua

Looking toward the new central business district of Ibadan from Bower Tower near the center of the old residential area

PREFACE

More than most other social sciences, anthropology is an individual enterprise. Along the way, however, the anthropologist piles up debts to teachers, supporting agencies, family and colleagues, and particularly to the people among whom he works. I am no exception to this pattern.

As an undergraduate at Wesleyan University, my teachers David McAllester and David Swift introduced me to the humanistic study of culture. Lloyd Fallers, Sol Tax, Edward Shils, Aristide Zolberg, and my doctoral supervisor, Robert LeVine, trained me in social science and in African studies at the University of Chicago. This study tries to mediate both the humanistic and the social science backgrounds that I have.

This book is based upon research carried out in Nigeria from January, 1966 to May, 1967. In particular, the family studies were done between November of 1966 and the following May. Fieldwork was made possible by the Foreign Area Fellowship Program of the American Council of Learned Societies and the Social Science Research Council, and by a supplementary grant from the Committee on African Studies of the University of Chicago. The Nigerian Institute of Social and Economic Research provided help in a variety of ways before and during my sojourn in Ibadan.

Among my colleagues and students it is difficult to record the names of all those who, knowing it or not, contributed to the preparation of this material. Professors Robert LeVine, Robert Mitchell, Olu Okediji, Philip Foster, James O'Connell, and especially Akin Mabogunje encouraged my thinking during the fieldwork. Philip Salzman, Myron Echenberg, Lawrence Nwakwesi and Judith Smith have stimulated my work at McGill University, and the students in "Anthropology 315" have served as sounding-boards for many notions incorporated here. Ade Kukoyi kindly read the manuscript and made many helpful suggestions.

My family gave invaluable personal support. One's work is distinguished only with difficulty from one's life, and this book is in fact a joint effort of, and a response to, my mother and father, my wife Gerry, and my children.

But the primary debts of the anthropologist are to the people among whom he lives and works, whose privacy he invades, and upon whose tolerance he depends. Without the norms of Yoruba hospitality I would never have been able to do as much work as I did in seventeen months. Ọlakitan Awojọbi and Ekundayọ Oduyoye and their families made mine feel at home. 'Yinka Craig and Marco Ojijoh were excellent research assistants. In Ibadan Chiefs J.E. Peters, J.F. Ọsọsami, and S.T. Ọsọba helped to provide the backgrounds to the family studies presented here, as did His Highness Ogbagba II, the Awujalẹ of Ijebu, Ọba S.L. Abimbọla, Ọba S.A. Ṣole, Balẹ Durojaiye Ariyọ, Imam Salami, Daddy D.O. Ṣegun and many others in Ijebu Province. For the sake of anonymity the seven families whose lives are outlined here cannot be thanked by name. They, and my teachers, colleagues and friends, are not responsible for the work I present here, but I offer it in gratitude to all of them and in the hope that in one way or another it will help to redeem the debts that I have incurred.

*The field work on which this book is based was carried out before the Nigerian civil war, before enormous increases in oil production and prices that have richly rewarded Nigeria's revenues, and before the reorganization of administrative structures in 1976 that created three states from the old Western Region. The epilogue to this book addresses aspects of the first and second of these events, which had few significant impacts on the lives of the people we shall meet. The third, by assigning the old Ijebu Province to the new Ogun State with an attendant redeployment of civil servants and a growth of "each state for its indigenous people" sentiment, may well be having a profound impact on social relations in Ibadan. This change is un-explored here, except in discussion of some of the historical and social roots of such strains.

CONTENTS

MAPS

TABLE

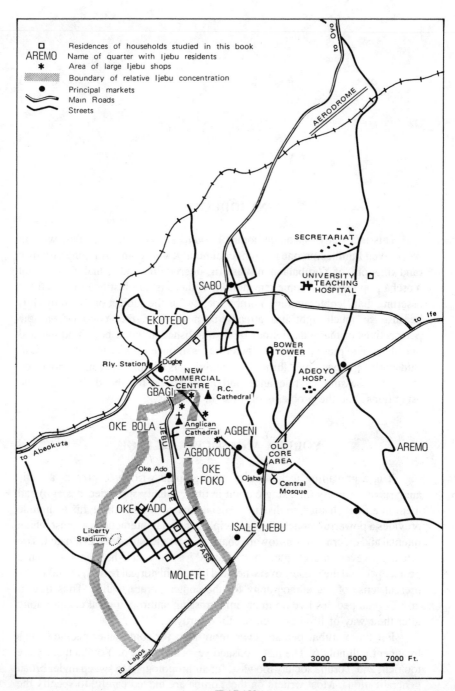

Residences of households studied in this book
AREMO Name of quarter with Ijebu residents
* Area of large Ijebu shops
Boundary of relative Ijebu concentration
Principal markets
Main Roads
Streets

to Oyo

AERODROME

SECRETARIAT

SABO

UNIVERSITY
TEACHING
HOSPITAL

EKOTEDO

to Ife

BOWER
TOWER

Rly. Station   Dugbe

NEW
COMMERCIAL
CENTRE

ADEOYO
HOSP.

GBAGI

R.C.
Cathedral

OKE BOLA

Anglican
Cathedral   AGBENI

to Abeokuta

AGBOKOJO

OLD
CORE
AREA

AREMO

Oke Ado

OKE
FOKO

Ojaba   Central
Mosque

OKE ADO

Liberty
Stadium

ISALE IJEBU

BYE

PASS

MOLETE

to Lagos

0   3000   5000   7000 Ft.

IBADAN

INTRODUCTION

This is a study of contemporary *Yorùbá*[1] society. In particular, we will meet seven families, in one migrant community, who come from one province (and kingdom) of Yorubaland in Western Nigeria. Fifty individuals from a total Yoruba population of some ten million! If there is any justification at all for asserting that "contemporary Yoruba society" is the subject of the study, it is because so much light has already been shed on the Yoruba from the perspectives of many disciplines by distinguished authors, both Yorubas and outsiders. The present attempt, therefore, is at once to introduce that work to students by approaching it through the individuals whom it concerns, and to add to it by assessing its relevance and implications for the daily lives, the aspirations, and the problems of those individuals.

YORUBA AND SOCIAL CHANGE

It is a prevailing technique of ethnographic writing to present a static analysis of a society (at a single point in time, usually some decades ago) and then, in a final chapter, to discuss "social change". At its best this technique provides a powerful model of the principles of social interaction, against which internal and external strains toward change can be measured and evaluated. Too often, however, the chapter on "change" is only half-hearted (or even a postscript), and the reader, overwhelmed by the ahistorical recital, mistakes the present tense of the ethnography for the contemporary reality. Thus freeze-dried, some peoples live on in an embarrassing anthropological elysium long after their way of life has been totally destroyed.

For the Yoruba, perhaps even more than for some other peoples, such treatment will not do. The last thousand years and more of Yoruba history are too rich, and Yoruba society too vast, for anthropologists to sweep under broad generalizations. Most writers on the Yoruba are indeed careful to specify the time period and the segments of the total population to which they refer. I will follow them both in limiting my focus, in my case to the *Ijebu* Yoruba, and in referring to "Yoruba" in general when I think that my statements may extend across the whole group.

The complexity of Yoruba society may be seen in two aspects, internal and external, which we may here set out cursorily by way of introduction. A bibliography at the end of the book provides directions to a host of excellent further materials.

The internal complexity of Yoruba society makes it one of the high points of refutation of those long-comforting Western myths of African primitivity. Perhaps from an original source area (Yoruba legend makes the city of Ife the cradle of mankind and the revered source of much of Yoruba civilization), speakers of what evolved into many dialects of the Yoruba language spread across forty thousand square miles of what has become southwestern Nigeria and parts of Dahomey and Togo as well. Either imposing their culture and government on autochthonous peoples or developing new lands of their own, the Yoruba built durable states with unique *urban* traditions. Whatever the real sources of the population, the whole area became culturally and linguistically Yoruba, with no distinctive strangers (other than migrant traders) living among them and with sharp boundaries between them and surrounding peoples. Nonetheless, probably no single city-state ever held sway over the whole land, though *Ọyọ́* created an empire throughout much of the north and west, including many non-Yoruba vassal states, from the seventeenth to the nineteenth centuries.

Each city-state elaborated its own internal structure, of course borrowing ideas from outside whenever useful. *Ọbas,* sacred kings, reigned over most of them, though often with more symbolic than actual power. Below the king patrilineal or cognatic descent groups, age sets, territorial organizations in wards and districts, associations of title-holders, religious cults, royal houses and enobled lineages, craft guilds and military groupings were combined in complex and variable arrangements to form the unique social order of each Yoruba state (Lloyd 1971). In each one the large majority of the population, both urban-resident and rural, was engaged in farming, so Yoruba city-states have been called city-villages as well.

The least powerful of these states comprised in fact only autonomous small towns and their surrounding farms. In places such towns came together as loose federations, mainly for defensive purposes. Elsewhere they were individually tributary to more powerful states. These latter again varied in the degree to which authority was centralized: some claimed practically independent areas as "parts" of the state only because they could sometimes exact tribute there, while others managed subordinate towns and regions through elaborate and sustained economic, administrative, and legal mechanisms. At its height Ọyọ

was far more than a city-state, and its military forces were pressing upon those
of the Ashanti far to the west. The rise and decline of autonomy and conflicting
claims of independence make it impossible to say how many Yoruba states have
existed: lists of twenty-one and of forty-one crowned ọba have been constructed
by Yoruba authorities, but there are many more whose claims have received
less confirmatory attention.

The conflicting claims to superior status among Yoruba states are
symptomatic of the second major aspect of Yoruba dynamism, the international
scale of action in Yoruba history. By this I mean to invoke both a language of
analysis and a perspective on change. Yoruba states were true states, not
"primitive tribes" or ephemeral chiefdoms. It is unfortunately still true that
much writing on Africa, especially at the introductory level, speaks for example
of "tribes" rather than nations or states, of "warriors" rather than soldiers, of
"feuds" rather than wars. All such language is pejorative, perpetuating
stereotypes of the inferiority of African achievements, positive or negative. To
the contrary, however, the Yoruba polities were clearly as serious about their
wars or their rituals as the states of Europe. Conflicts between Yoruba
kingdoms were international conflicts; and alliances, strategies, economic
policies, leadership, and the like were the consequences of attention to options
and obstructions, not the blind acting out of some hypothetical "traditional"
mentality. Indeed, the linguistic and cultural uniformity within Yorubaland did
not prevent individual states from competing with one another any less than
with their non-Yoruba neighbors. And when the European powers, especially
England and France, entered the political arena seriously in the nineteenth
century, they were seen as potential competitors or allies in current and future
struggles, not as exotic or overwhelming technical magicians.

Both the internal and the international aspects of Yoruba social complexity
are refracted in the modern self-consciousness that Yoruba have for their
society and culture. Yoruba politicians, administrators, and journalists, and
academics in every discipline, are involved in a continuous and profound search
for answers to a myriad of problems, some shared with part or all of humanity
and some unique. Of all the disciplines, however, it is anthropology which has
attracted least attention from contemporary Africans as a source of insight into
their society. Because of its orientation to obscure and exotic "custom", and
because of its lack of attention to change, the "first" discipline to study Africa
has been under heaviest attack.

Anthropologists have, nevertheless, indeed studied complex societies,
and their work is increasingly consulted by urban planners, health care delivery
specialists, and other students of current social conditions. In this work the
methods have been, by and large, the traditional anthropological techniques of
intensive observation — whether of small communities as representatives of

some larger problem (a slum, a hospital, a factory unit), of crucial situations as the keys to larger circumstances (a political campaign, a type of interethnic market transaction, a public encounter), or of individuals. The present study is of this third type, and it is offered to Yoruba and other Nigerian readers as well as to non-Nigerian students in the hope that anthropological intensity may still have value in focussing social debate, squarely on the ground.

"PERSONAL DOCUMENTS" IN ANTHROPOLOGY

Family studies like the ones presented here are part of a much larger body of "personal documents" that anthropologists have collected in the course of their work. Biographies and autobiographies, creative writing and dream reports, diaries and depth interviews have long served a variety of purposes within the discipline (Langness 1969). That these documents should exist is not surprising: in the last analysis anthropologists have almost always worked with a quite small number of individuals — key informants, interpreters, host families or cliques — whose statements and actions provide the bulk of the field notes in the anthropologist's files.

More surprising is that these personal documents have remained so far in the background of the discipline. However broad the humanistic goals of "understanding other cultures," the professional orthodoxy has long dictated that major anthropological research results be published in the narrow structure of a monograph, whether general or "problem-oriented," in which real people appear, if at all, only as illustrations or examples of some general proposition or its exception. Meanwhile the autobiography, the diary, or the family study is published later, in a remote and quiet corner, where it lies infrequently used in teaching or in research. I do not deny the power of the tools and formats that we have adopted. But one undergraduate's remark that "I decided to study anthropology because I was interested in how people live, only to find that *people* are never considered," leads me to question whether we have not been neglecting attention to possible alternative *genres* of anthropological communication. Recent growth in the number and quality of ethnographic films being produced, of anthropologists' accounts of their own field experiences, and of inexpensive editions of personal documents (some republished after many years), evidences increased experimentation with personalizing and vivifying other cultures. The present study aims to reconstruct the field experience by presenting the direct but informed observation of individuals which is at its core, and then by leading from observation to tentative generalization and discussion in the light of other cases and other materials available.

Among the various types of personal documents presented by anthropologists, family studies are of course most closely identified with the late
Oscar Lewis. In a series of superb narratives Lewis gave expression to the lives
of Mexican and Puerto Rican families in the "culture of poverty" (1959, 1961,
1964, 1965). Although Lewis' conceptualizations have been criticized and the
representativeness of "his" families questioned, there can be no doubt that his
methods of research and of presentation have had a profound impact on students
and on the general reading public. Lewis knew most of his families for several
years before he wrote anything about them, and then he did so only after
applying a battery of research techniques to them. Only in the fact that I have
also observed families and in the hope that letting them speak for themselves
also invites the reader to involvement and further inquiry can the present modest
study of Ijebu families in any way bear comparison with Lewis' distinguished
work.

Other family studies in anthropology are rare. Karve (1963) has written on
five Brahman families in India. Howell (1973) has described three American
blue collar families, while Laura Bohannan reveals a great deal of family life
among the Tiv in her novel of fieldwork (Bowen 1954). For the most part,
however, families appear in anthropological personal documents through the
prism of a single biography or autobiography.

In Africa, indeed, relatively few personal documents of any sort have been
collected. The bias away from psychology in British social anthropology has
conspired with the tradition of exemplary social structural studies done in
Africa to turn anthropologists to different tasks. While various biographies and
autobiographies of more or less exceptional characters (political leaders,
authors, converts) had been available for many years, it was only in 1954, with
the publication of M.F. Smith's *Baba of Karo* and of Laura Bohannan's novel,
noted above, that the lives of relatively "ordinary" Africans, in full cultural
contexts, began to appear. Winter (1959), Turnbull (1962), and Goldschmidt
(1969) have provided further studies of individuals in contemporary rural
contexts. Urban studies are even rarer, Epstein's brief account of his assistant
Chanda (1961) and Plotnicov's full-length and noteworthy *Strangers to the City*
(1967) being virtually the only exceptions. Of these African works, those by
Smith, Bowen, and Plotnicov are set in Nigeria, and the individuals and social
settings portrayed in them bear closest comparison with the Ijebu families of
Ibadan in this book.

Just as social structural studies rarely convey a sense of "what it is like to
be one," so personal documents may yield no sense for how general the
personal situations of the particular individuals may be. The problem of
interpreting idiosyncrasy is perhaps greatest when social scientists or lay
readers use the work of creative writers to "see" the society behind the work

itself. In this study it is the personal and the particular which is kept in fullest view. But as far as I can do so in limited space I try to keep the social and the general visible as well. For it is in balancing these two approaches that we can learn most how "real people" continually create and are continually affected by the no less "real" social and cultural forces around them.

METHODS

SELECTION OF THE RESEARCH SITE. For assessing the depth and significance of twentieth-century change in Africa, the societies of the "West Coast" (along the Gulf of Guinea) have special importance. West Africa was more "lightly" colonized, as we shall see in Chapter 3, than much of East, Central, and South Africa. It was left to its own devices more than elsewhere, and, relatively speaking, controlled its own destiny. Fewer laws circumscribed urban movement, residence and land-holding, or political or entrepreneurial activity. At the same time the much greater commercialization of the precolonial economies, the long history of non-colonial interaction with Europe (including, of course, the agony of the slave trade), and the denser populations in many areas poised West African societies for rapid and resilient experimentation with new ideas and new items (Hopkins 1973). Knowing all this, one could plausibly reason that whatever recent change had taken place in West Africa — the absorption of innovations, the rejection of change, or the abandonment of traditional culture — would speak more directly to the African condition and say more about African aspirations and possibilities than would changes in other areas which had seen more force, more external demand, or weaker internal capabilities of adaptation.

Thus I was led to look for a research site in West Africa. The depth of materials available concerning the Yoruba, including notably a flourishing literary and political expression, attracted my attention. A few other societies might have been just as rewarding, though, and to some extent my choice of the Yoruba was arbitrary. Among the decisive factors were the availability of facilities at the University of Ibadan for research assistance, and the fact that one of my teachers had done some research in Yorubaland a few years earlier and could thus provide advice on local arrangements. He also noted that among the Yoruba it was the Ijebu who had the most widespread, even notorious, reputation for involvement in and enthusiasm for "modern" life. So, with the knowledge that rural Ijebu were farming and trading in ongoing village communities and small towns while migrants born in those places were among urban Africa's dynamic "new men," as Hodgkin had called them (1956), I set out to study social change among the Ijebu Yoruba.

FIELD METHODS.   The family studies reported in this book were one part of
the larger research plan. Before I began them, I had started by carrying out a
hundred interviews with Ijebus resident in the city of Ibadan in order to learn
something of the range of migrant life histories, work experiences, and current
social positions. In the course of this interviewing I met briefly one member of
each of six of the families in this book. The seventh I knew much better, since
its head worked for me part time as an interpreter and assistant in this beginning
phase of the research. The second major phase of the research involved social
surveys and other data-gathering in five communities in the home province of
the Ijebu. I was interested in determining migration rates, the impact of
migration on home towns, and the dynamics of urban-rural relationships among
Ijebus. The five months I spent working in small towns assured that I would
have my own understanding of rural life, not just perceptions of it acquired
through the eyes of urbanites.

Then I returned to Ibadan, anxious to comprehend in detail the social life
of Ijebu migrants. I knew little about the relation of work and urban family life,
about interethnic contacts and residential arrangements, or about the actual
behavior of urban residents with respect to their kinsmen at home. I had the
interview data that could tell me what urban Ijebus *said* on these matters, and I
had seen some out-migrants when they came home to the towns I worked in, but
I did not know much about how urbanites *acted*.

Intensive observation of a diverse set of families afforded a means of
securing this knowledge. In each rural town that I worked in I had met relatives
and friends of one or two of the people I had interviewed in Ibadan. In fact, my
being acquainted with a fellow townsman sometimes eased my way "in" to the
rural community, or part of it. Now it seemed worthwhile, if I could, to use my
detailed knowledge of a few rural communities as background for further urban
research. Thus at least one member of five of the families in this book came
from the rural towns I had worked in, though in two cases I had met none of their
kinsmen because the town involved was so large.[2]

More than by their town of origin, however, what determined my choice of
families was my desire to include as wide a range as possible of family
structures and points in family development, economic and occupational
situations, education and life style differences, and areas of urban residence.
From the original interviews, therefore, I selected additional respondents for
approaching as possible subjects for these family studies. To test the feasibility
of the whole idea I asked my first assistant, with whom I had maintained close
ties, whether I could observe his family. If the methods did not work with
someone I knew, they would work nowhere. When they did, I went on
successively to six other families, with no refusals to cooperate with the study.

An eighth family was begun but for reasons extraneous to the study itself was never completed.[3] In every case I offered a small payment for permission to make what I considered to be a distinct invasion of privacy. None of this money was refused, but neither did the payment ever become a sole inducement to continue nor even a matter of discussion. To the contrary, each family was open and willing, within certain limits, to welcome the researchers and to honor our requests.

The methodology was weighted strongly toward observation rather than interrogation. My research assistant spent an average of six hours each day with one family for a continuous three-week period. Occasionally I was present, but, as a white foreigner, I was usually the subject of a great deal of curiosity on the part of non-family members visiting or passing the compound. The consequent abnormalcy of compound life made me reduce my days of observation to about one a week, with frequent but brief visits between.

Each study represents over 120 hours of observation, and over half as much time again in writing up notes and discussing them. The six-hour day was varied, sometimes from 6:00 a.m. to noon, other times from 4:00 p.m. to 10:00 and so on. On some days we remained close to a wife, at other times followed the husband to work or watched the children at play. Dull hours provided time to write up notes immediately, to catch up on notes falling behind, or to write out descriptions of rooms and neighborhoods. Each day I conferred with my assistant to read notes, raise questions for more acute observation or discussion, and to set the likely course of the next period of observation. Only after several days did we begin to ask questions concerning background events we had not witnessed, work and friendship relations we could not observe, and the like. Eventually we got brief life histories of each household member.

The research assistants were obviously crucial to the study, and it is well to describe them. All the studies but one were carried out with the same assistant, a Yoruba secondary school graduate whose English was fluent and who had a flair for writing (and art) which he has since indulged further. For the remaining study, that of Chief Ogunkọya, a second assistant proved more useful than I imagined, because he was a much older man to whom the Chief clearly unburdened himself in a way he might not have to a twenty-year-old. Neither assistant had social science training, but the second had worked previously as an interviewer and had demonstrable research skills. I had known and worked with both prior to the family studies they carried out.

I asked each assistant to act as much as possible as a camera and tape recorder. It was not always easy for them to be as naive as I wanted them to be — to write down the *behavior* of "punishing," "joking," or "quarreling," instead of those highly abstract words themselves. And even though their notes became more purely descriptive as time went on, there can be no doubt that the chapters to follow are reflected through the optiques of both my assistants and myself.

WRITING UP.   The process by which any writer in any field selects the data that he presents is rarely deliberately discussed, perhaps because the writer himself is not fully conscious of it. The materials I have had to work with are my own and my assistants' notebooks full of information on each family. Each of the major chapters in Part II of this book is taken from one such set of notebooks, but of course there was far too much material to use. After excerpts from daily life are recorded, I narrate briefly the life histories of the central household members and describe the current material conditions in which each household lives. Finally I discuss a few themes in contemporary urban life which arise in these narratives. The people involved recognize some of these issues, but do not reflect upon others. Here, too, the choices are mine, and it is therefore well to set out some of the criteria I can identify which underlie my own selectivity.

First, I have been concerned to convey a sense for the commonplace, the familiar, and the repetitive aspects of Yoruba family life, in order to help correct an unfortunate result of much anthropological writing. For in our legitimate and long-standing efforts to portray the uniqueness of human cultures, we have tended to overdraw the exotic, the unusual, the "otherness" that stands out in our field notes amid the humdrum of daily routine. This specialized selective process has made people seem stranger than they are, and the reaction has been that members of those cultures who read the work of anthropologists often resent their "anthropologization," that non-members who visit the society in question are often shocked by its routineness, and that students-at-a-distance find no basis for empathy with or even comparison of the human condition that is described. In this study I have tried to represent and discuss something of what *is* unique about life in Ibadan for the Ijebu families involved, but repetitiveness and ordinariness are to be found as well. Concretely, in some of the study periods a great deal of very revealing behavior took place, while in others "nothing" (i.e., nothing out of the ordinary) happened. My editing process remains faithful to these differences.

Second, I have let the family life speak for itself as far as possible. There is no attempt here to match "illustrative" data to some pre-set overview of "typical" family or uban life. Such a procedure, even were the "overview" possible, would inevitably have required a great deal of manipulation of the material to make it "fit" properly. Rather, I have presented episodes from the total study period in order, with as little artificial smoothing of transitions as permits coherent reading. But within each case itself, the material presented covers the full range of that household's activities — there was, for example, little consumption of other types of foods beyond those mentioned, little discussion of ideas outside the range of those reported. This limitation to the integrity of the data themselves further means that the generalizations that I discuss at the end of each chapter are to a large degree discrete, not meant to be summed for a balanced or fully integrated view of urban life because they were not derived from such a view. Nonetheless the discussion of themes does go well beyond the vignettes of daily life, not by overinterpreting the small episodes presented, but by drawing upon other aspects of the fieldwork and the large amounts of other literature available.

Third, as I have already noted, I have written with two audiences in mind. For those readers with no first-hand knowledge of Yoruba culture I have "translated" items of Yoruba, or sometimes of British, culture (recipes, monetary terms[4], idiomatic ideas and expressions) in footnotes, parentheses, or descriptive asides. In a larger sense much of anthropological communication is the translation of culture into foreigners' comprehension, and here my own North American middle-class origins are particularly likely to arise. If some Yoruba readers find my reportage or discussions tedious, over-simplified or "common knowledge," I beg their recognition of the special provincialisms of some of this foreign audience. With those readers who do know Yoruba culture well, I have implicitly raised questions of the significance and direction of social change, and of the interpretation of specific dimensions of urban and household behavior. There is, as I have mentioned, ongoing discussion of all these matters within the society itself: all a stranger can do is to remark on — hopefully sometimes to clarify — issues or ideas that may be hidden by familiarity or by emotion. If some non-Yoruba readers thus find me belaboring some points, it may be because the issue is particularly obscure in contemporary Yoruba life. Of course I can justify neither audience as sanctuary from the criticisms of the other, and though it is primarily seven families who speak in this book, in the final analysis the voices, and the errors, are mine.

Notes

[1]Yoruba is a tonal language: in the first occurrence of Yoruba words, syllabic tones are marked ` = low, ´ = high, or unmarked for mid-tone. Syllables are of equal stress. Vowels have "continental" values, except ẹ as in English bẹt, ọ as in slang American English "gonna" (going to), and ọn as nasalized ọ. Consonants are generally as in English, except ṣ is like sh in English shoe, gb is a double stop and therefore articulated simultaneously, and p is a double stop "kp", also articulated simultaneously. Ijebu is pronounced in English as if it were i-jeh-boo, and the ẹ is undotted in the text.

[2]Even some of the "small" towns of Ijebu Province have as many as 16,000 or 20,000 inhabitants, and nowhere are Yoruba towns closed communities where everyone is kin to everyone else. For a synthesizing work on Yoruba urbanism see Krapf-Askari (1969).

[3]The family was that of an insurance agent and his school-teacher wife. Material on their and their educated but sub-elite friends' values and life-styles would have thrown interesting light on the discussions at the ends of Chapters 9 and 10 below.

[4]Monetary exchange values are those operating at the time of the field study, when the Nigerian pound was worth U.S. $2.80.

Ijebu Traders, living above their shops, moved to Ibadan to mediate between the new commercial sector and the old city

Dugbe Market, with its long sheds divided into hundreds of stalls and its aisles full of shoppers

At dusk in Dugbe Market the perishables sellers crowd the aisles

PART ONE

BACKGROUNDS

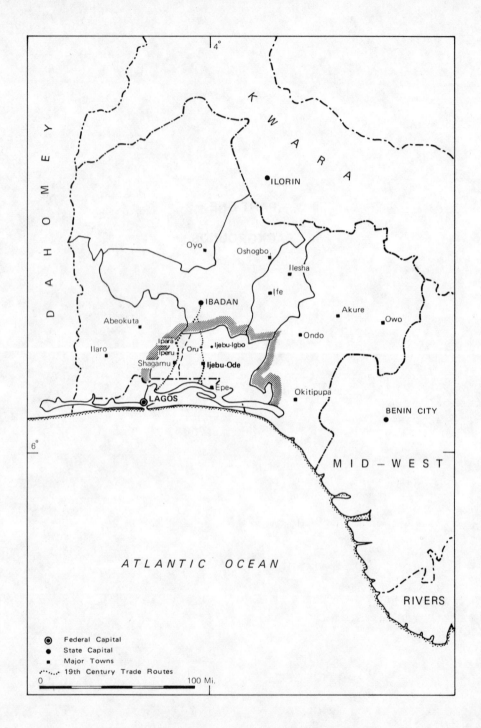

YORUBALAND IN THE EARLY NINETEENTH CENTURY
(With modifications, from Crowder 1962:109)

CHAPTER I

A Baseline: The Ijebu Kingdom

In May of 1892, using three cannon, rockets, and a Maxim gun, a British military expedition terminated the centuries-old independence of the Kingdom of Ijebu.[1] Until then, neighboring Yoruba states and European merchants and missionaries had held the Ijebu to be an exclusive, dangerous, inscrutable and treacherous group of thieves and monopolists, more likely to make a human sacrifice of an intruder than to let him through their country. Yet within twenty years of conquest the Ijebu were recognized as the most responsive of all Yoruba to the new appeals of Christianity, Western education, and commerce, surpassing other subgroups whose exposure had been up to fifty years longer. It became clear that behind the curtain of hostility which Ijebu had generated around itself earlier lay not a stolid or reactionary savagery but a self-reliant and politically aware citizenry as ready to assert itself in the reality of the new era as it was to defend itself in the old one.

The Ijebu families whom we shall meet in this book continue the heritage of determined response to their perceptions of opportunity. With considerable discipline they have pursued their culture's and their own goals and values, which are described in detail as they arise in the chapters to follow. If self-interest were all there was to social action, we might begin immediately to present the strategies by which these individuals and families seek their own advantage.

The social anthropologist, however, looks both for greater explanatory breadth than is contained in the notion of ''self-interest,'' and for sharper insight than (s)he finds in generalities such as suggest that ''the Ijebu'' — as a whole — responded with ''avidity'' to the new commercial opportunities or ''phenomenally'' to the missionaries. Opportunity, and the perception of opportunity, are rarely distributed evenly in a population, so the anthropologist tries to build up an image — a model — of the society with which (s)he is dealing by describing both external constraints on and internal variability of possibilities and actions. Then, if (s)he is concerned with changes that are taking place, as we will be here, (s)he can show what parts of the society are affected more or less, what conditions in the society affect the rate or depth of change, and what ramifications a particular stimulus is likely to have. (S)he cannot, of course, predict what changes may be attempted, nor by which particular people. But even the localization of cause and effect that (s)he can provide yields an understanding of society that would not be as deep without his/her method. With this aim of contextualizing the lives of the Ijebu families in this book, therefore, I will in this chapter sketch Ijebu society *as it probably existed in the third quarter of the nineteenth century,*[2] and, in the next, outline the major new institutional structures of *this* century.

Geography and Settlement

Covering an area of about 3,500 square miles (cut to 2,500 square miles in the modern Nigerian Ijebu Province), the precolonial Kingdom of Ijebu included diverse economic specializations based in part upon a varied geography. Along the southern edge, the marine lagoons encouraged fishing, reed weaving, and creek trading. The large dense forests in the eastern third of the kingdom and along part of the northern boundary stood as a defense against outside intrusion, or as a no-man's land; they remained virtually uninhabited until the middle of the twentieth century, when they began to fall to a modern timber industry. In the southwest, the very easily drained and sandy marine alluvium discouraged food crops except cassava but, again in the twentieth century, provided the locus of a prosperous trade in the caffein-rich nuts of the kola tree (see Cohen 1966).

The remaining central area of the nation bore nearly all of the population. It was divided into two agricultural subareas by the sedimentary escarpment which passes from northwest to southeast four miles north of *Ìjẹbu Òde,* the capital city. North of this line, the pre-Cambrian rocks support excellent soils for the cultivation of the northern Yoruba staple, yams of several varieties, and recently for cocoa. To the south, the "dissected margin" of sedimentary soils slopes gently from the scarp at 350 feet above sea level down to the lagoon. Here yams (and cocoa) grow quite poorly, but the easily-worked soil is well-suited for maize and cassava, the latter being the traditional Ijebu staple. The margin has been largely cleared of forest, and the bare, even topography supported a relatively dense population long before colonial advance.

The whole kingdom, north and south of the escarpment, is drained by several rivers flowing from the north into the lagoon to the south. The *Ṣàṣà, Ọ̀ṣun, Owà* and *Yẹmule* Rivers drain several minor watersheds and provide water for the human settlements dispersed throughout the area. Their flood plains have also been used for fishing and the growing of leafy vegetables (Onakomaiya 1965:18-20).

On this variegated geographical base lay a fairly constant type of human habitation. Like other Yorubas, Ijebus lived in large, densely nucleated settlements populated primarily by farmers whose lands were sometimes as much as twenty miles from home. Temporary shelters or small houses stood on the more distant farms for those who could not commute by day with ease. For everyone, though, the town was home; sleeping on the farm was tolerable, mainly because it was necessary only at peak periods of work in the agricultural cycle. This firmly-valued indigenous urbanism and urbaneness antedate European contact five centuries ago.

Ijebu was unlike other parts of Yorubaland, however, in the *patterning* of its settlements (Lloyd 1962:53-58). Usually Yoruba states consisted of a centrally located "metropolitan" town surrounded by hamlets on its own inhabitants' farm lands, with a number of much smaller subordinate towns with their own hamlets in turn in the outlying areas of the kingdom. In contrast Ijebu has a capital city with very little farmland of its own, and has many large outlying towns and villages (not hamlets), each with its own farm land. The reasons for the divergence of Ijebu from the more typical Yoruba pattern are not well understood, though they parallel other differences in descent group structure and economic development. In any case, the permanence, size, and legal status of the Ijebu towns outside the capital imposed a particular set of conditions on precolonial "national integration" which were to have their own effects on twentieth-century change.

The Precolonial Economy

Again in common with other Yoruba, the precolonial economy of Ijebu depended upon agriculture, craft production, and extensive trading. More than any other group, though, the Ijebu emphasis within the shared set of cultural elements was upon trade. The earliest historical records relating to the Ijebu, written by Portuguese at the beginning of the sixteenth century, mention the briskness of trade in their area. Succeeding references in the eighteenth and nineteenth centuries repeat and elaborate reports on Ijebu enterprise:

> The Jaboos . . . are a fine looking people, and always seem as if they came from a land of plenty, being stout, healthy, and full of vigour. They are a very industrious people, and manufacture for sale an immense number of common Guinea cloths: besides raising cattle, sheep, poultry, corn, and calavancies [calabashes], with which they supply their neighbours . . .
>
> It is these people who send so much cloth to Lagos and Ardrah, which the Portuguese traders from the Brazils purchase for that market . . .
>
> (Adams 1823:108,97).

As this note indicates, Ijebu trade was based in its own agriculture and craft work. Foodstuffs were produced in the small towns outside the capital, using the widespread African techniques of hoe agriculture (with hoe and machete the primary tools), mixed cultivation (crops efficiently interplanted for mutual nourishment and protection), and bush-fallow rotation (fields used for several years, then left to fallow for several more). Surplusses were brought into Ijebu Ode in return for imported goods and local craft objects (tools, cloth, jewelry, etc.), services (of the itinerant goldsmith, embroiderer, or blacksmith), and the specialized primary products (fish, cattle, kola nuts, etc.) of other areas in and beyond Ijebu. This exchange was carried on in complicated linked "rings" of rural markets, using cowries as currency. Small-town traders were forbidden to engage in foreign trade on their own, just as foreigners were excluded from internal Ijebu markets and from transshipping through Ijebu territory. Control was exercised by the authorities in Ijebu Ode, who ran the international markets at *Orù, Itọ́ Ikè, Ejìnrìn,* and *Èpẹ́,* and had overseers and toll-takers at the internal markets. The concentration of trade through hands in Ijebu Ode both enriched the capital relative to its hinterland and fostered jealousy on the part of outsiders, especially of Europeans in the late nineteenth century, anxious to take economic control themselves.

Craft production was also concentrated in Ijebu Ode. Some crafts (of musicians, e.g.) were practiced by lineage groups attached, sometimes as slaves, to the royal court directly. Others, such as dyeing, weaving, or pottery-making, were also carried on by particular families and compounds because of the amount of capital invested or the ways in which skills were taught. Since many crafts required long training and profited from full-time application, small towns could not support some crafts on their own, and so economies of scale encouraged the location of craftsmen in the capital. The goldsmiths, female weavers, dye makers, and indigenous doctors of Ijebu were justly renowned among the Yoruba for their expertise.

Numerically, of course, farmers were still the vast majority of Ijebus. Yet the proportion of the population engaged in non-farm occupations, we may reasonably conclude, was probably higher than elsewhere in Yorubaland a century ago, as it was (except for one other place) in the one reliable census in Nigeria done in 1952. The economic differences between Ijebu Ode and the outlying areas of the kingdom in the precolonial era also had effects on subsequent types and rates of change.

Politics and Government in the Old Kingdom

The *Awùjalẹ̀* of Ijebu, like other Yoruba ọba, was sacred and sheltered. Chosen from among the eligible candidates of each of four branches or "houses" of the royal lineage, the Awujalẹ was cut off after his coronation frcm direct access to most political resources. He presided over rituals intended to guarantee peace and increase in the state, but otherwise remained secluded within the palace, forbidden to go out by day. He was not supposed to see his sons and other close relatives. His deputies sat on various political bodies, but he could not himself attend. Many decisions were taken in his name but without his participation. Symbolically, in audience he was screened from view, and at state ceremonies the beaded fringe of his crown veiled his face.[3]

Real power was dispersed widely. Towns outside the capital were internally largely autonomous, and their political composition reflected that of the capital albeit in simpler structures. Some of the towns had ọba themselves; others had uncrowned chiefs. Capital cases, final appeals, and intercommunity disputes were referred to Ijebu Ode, which also knit the towns together economically, as we have seen. Except for some towns in *Rémọ* (the western portion of the kingdom) which periodically asserted their independence of Ijebu Ode, however, the whole kingdom acknowledged its unity under the Awujalẹ.[4]

Power in the capital, and therefore indirectly in the kingdom, was divided between two hierarchically arranged men's associations. One of these represented the interests of the populace, the other the large palace organization. Each expressed, made decisions, and took action on matters it found important. Sometimes the interests of the two collided, as in the revolution of 1882, when the leaders of the populace succeeded in forcing the abdication of the reigning Awujalẹ. No more than any other society was Ijebu a place of perpetual tranquillity and integration.

The *Òṣùgbó* (called *Ògbóni* elsewhere in Yorubaland) was the political instrument of the populace. While every free-born male was eligible to join, no one could rise in it higher than his own father (or his classificatory fathers) if the latter were alive. Thus the senior grades, achieved by spending lavishly on incumbent leaders in order to "take titles" from them, included the wealthiest and most powerful family heads in the town. The *Iwarefa,* an executive committee of six men led by the *Olíwo,* took final decisions for its membership that could include the death penalty. A deputy of the Awujalẹ, a slave known as the *Olúrin,* sat at meetings with no authority.

The palace organization of Ijebu was more complicated than anywhere else in Yorubaland. First, there were many separate groups of slaves. Some were lineages of craftsmen, while others were messengers and servants known as *odì*. Second was an association of free-born men known as the *Ifọrẹ* Society, led by the *Olótú-ìfọrẹ*. Why some men joined Ifọrẹ rather than Oṣugbo is not known. But some odi could also attain the senior ranks of Ifọrẹ, gaining their freedom in the process. Beyond all these groups was the office of *Ògbéni Ọja,* though whether he led them all or had distinct functions is disputed. At any rate, some of the senior chiefs of Ifọrẹ, the head of the odi, the Ọgbẹni Ọja, and three hereditary lineage chiefs closely allied to the crown — the *Olísa, Àpẹbi,* and *Ègbò* — all together constituted yet another society, the *Ilámùrẹn.* This most senior group of palace chiefs served as a cabinet for the Awujalẹ and arbitrated legal and political matters in his name.

The sources of power in this system were multiple. The king had one means of influence, since by using his key position in the communication system he could mediate competing interests or play them off against one another to his own advantage. The palace chiefs controlled the commercial economy through the craft lineages and supervision of the markets. And the populace chiefs, speaking for the citizens whose younger ranks provided the state's soldiers, had the force of superior numbers to see their will done. In fact, by the third quarter of the nineteenth century the increasing commercial power of the citizenry created by the booming trade with Lagos and Ibadan led the Oṣugbo to stand for free and open trade, while the palace guarded its historical prerogatives of royal control of the economy and national borders. It was this issue which culminated in the 1882 revolution. The Ijebu were straining toward the wider opportunities that came, in altered form, with British conquest.

Precolonial Ijebu Society

People were born, in precolonial Ijebu, into a society pregnant with change. Yet, like their counterparts in another turbulent age a century later whose lives are recorded in this book, most of them led lives of unextraordinary routine.[5]

The basic discipline of that life for Ijebus was imposed by the compound, the "flock of houses" *(agbolé)* in which most daily rights and responsibilities lay. Within its walls was the arena in which play groups formed, in which all the wives shared chores and child-watching, and where men, mostly close kinsmen of one another, formulated their plans and shared ideas about the property and other resources they jointly owned. The boundary between private life and public was between one compound and another, rather than between nuclear family and compound.

The compound included a number of categories of personnel. At its core were families related agnatically (through males) to the living "father of the house," the compound head or *balé.* In contrast to most other Yoruba subgroups which were overwhelmingly patrilineal and patrilocal, however, Ijebu compounds also counted as full members a relatively high proportion of households related to the core through women, usually the households of adult sons of a female member.

Living as well in the compound might be households of affinal relatives (through marriage), of domestic slaves, and of unrelated strangers who might be given surplus land in return for token rent but real political and economic support. Pawns *(ìwòfà,* whose labor was the interest on loans made to the pawn's family) and fostered children might be attached to individual families. Furthermore, the membership of the compound included deceased ancestors, buried inside their houses in the earth floors of the very rooms they occupied. From there they played an active part in overseeing the affairs of the living both as immanent "consciences" and by being consulted supernaturally through religious divination and possession.

Few but the largest compounds had all these categories of membership present: some were quite simple extended families. Villages in Ijebu contained from five to fifty or more compounds, and from a hundred to several thousand inhabitants. Lloyd reports (1962:136ff.) that in Ijebu Ode in 1952, with a total population of 28,000, the twenty-five or so quarters of the town consisted of from two to seven compounds each.

The basic resource controlled by the compound, or more exactly the descent group which was its core, was land, for houses, kitchen gardens, and fields. In addition, various titles and political and ritual statuses in the town — quarter chief, ward head, cult leader, counsellor, village chief — were the property of individual lineages. Houses, ritual paraphernalia, occupational skills, rights to resources such as wild indigo plants, rock and clay pits, trees used for medicinal purposes, and the like were other resources of descent groups.

To understand the organization of Ijebu society more precisely, it is necessary to look again at the fact that links through females as well as through males enabled membership in particular groups. The Ijebu descent system (Lloyd 1966c) was cognatic, meaning that a person *might* belong to any group to which he could trace blood relationship (for example, his father's, mother's, or any of his four grandparents' descent groups). In a cognatic system there are potentially as many groups as there are people with descendants, since a group can coalesce to manage the inheritance (of status or prestige as well as material property or rights to property) of any ascendant. In actuality, however, not nearly everyone's inheritance was worth forming a group to manage. Thus many rights were allowed to revert to the groups from which they were claimed. Similarly, pressing an individual claim to membership in a particular group involved time and money. Thus both the number of groups and the number of memberships that any one person held were severely restricted. For many people the compound in which they were born and lived contained the only descent unit in which they had actual as opposed to potential membership. There was a need to be present and active to assert and maintain one's rights, and a constant pressure to join forces with close kinsmen to anticipate and capture resources from those who would leave large inheritances. These two constraints had the double tendency over time to distribute people relatively evenly among compounds and to foreshorten lineages toward the point at which actual coresidential and co-owning units contained all the lineal kinsmen that one was prepared to recognize. It is for these reasons that, among the Ijebu, compound and lineage are roughly coextensive at least for the full members of the compound.

There was a further correlate of cognatic descent. By putting a premium upon the assessment and manipulation of potential access to a variety of resources, the system encouraged skill and risk-taking in kinship relations. This effect accorded well with the possibilities of personal achievement in economic and political affairs. Further, the institutions of pawning, fosterage of children, and clientage provided more costly mechanisms of access to occupations or resources otherwise unavailable.

In short, the social structure of precolonial Ijebu was essentially fluid. Through kin ties, political associations, and a diverse occupational structure, individuals could rise far beyond the conditions of their birth. It is no doubt true that the son of a chief in Ijebu Ode had more opportunity than the son of a farmer in a rural village. Even so, a number of powerful figures in nineteenth century history came from simple rural homes. It is difficult to gauge whether the reward of achievement in the kingdom was matched by a high rate of psychological motivation toward achievement, or how far these nineteenth century patterns account for twentieth century Ijebu achievement in the broadened context of the colonial structure. Perhaps it is only safe to say that there was, in Ijebu, no discouragement of personal initiative and no tightly ascriptive system of social status to hinder individual Ijebus from setting high goals and working boldly toward them as their world changed.

Footnotes

[1]For an account of the invasion and conquest, see Smith (1971).

[2]It is important to note that the model built up captures society at a brief moment in time. It is not meant as a substitute for history, though anthropologists' descriptions have often been misunderstood to imply that a given society was "always" in the state described in the model. Certainly in the Yoruba case no such misunderstanding could arise, for the dramatic changes of the nineteenth — and earlier — centuries are matters of rich historical record (e.g., Biobaku 1957; Ajayi and Smith 1964; Ajayi 1965; Ayantuga 1965; Ayandele 1966; Smith 1969).

[3]For discussions of the Ijebu kingship see Lloyd (1954) and Ayandele (1970). The interpretation here differs considerably from either of these.

[4]Some sources distinguish Rẹmọ as a separate "province" of old Ijebu, and in addition designate a vaguely defined northerly area as a third province, "*Igbó.*" No legal or administrative arrangements have been recorded, however, which would evidence that these geographical areas were actually "provinces."

[5]For general accounts of traditional Yoruba society see Forde (1951), Lloyd (1965), Krapf-Askari (1969), and Bascom (1969). For a general account of twentieth-century social change in Nigeria see Lloyd (1967a).

CHAPTER II

Social Change: Colonial Institutions and Migration

As the nineteenth century wore on, Ijebu policies were increasingly constrained by its powerful neighbor Ibadan on the north, and the growing commercial port of Lagos to the south. Trying to monopolize the middle position finally failed, as Lagos merchants and missionaries, and Ijebu entrepreneurs as well, saw greater advantage in one large arena for their activities which would be unhampered by internal boundaries and policy conflicts.

Thus, the most immediate effect of British conquest in 1892 was the breaking of the power of the Ijebu state authorities to enunciate and pursue their own international and domestic policies. Symbolically, the ramparts around the core of the kingdom fell into disuse. Importantly, the king and several senior chiefs of the kingdom were given annual stipends to replace the resources they formerly controlled, while royal toll-takers ceased to oversee the economy. Breaking the power of the state also dislodged those judicial and religious institutions which provided high-level sanctions for state activities.[1]

Voluntarism and Ijebu Social Change

In some states this blow to the head might have produced chaos in the years which followed. In Ijebu, however, the apparatus of the state was imposed upon relatively self-sufficient and self-directed families and communities. When, therefore, it was dismantled, a variety of social forces at lower levels than the state — in small towns, within occupational groups, and in descent groups — were given freer rein for individual initiatives.

Such initiatives were quick in coming. It is vital to an understanding of the resilience and optimism of the village-derived families in this book, and indeed of modern Yoruba society as a whole, to see how much of twentieth-century change for Ijebus has been voluntary rather than forced, rationalistic rather than reflexive.

The evidence for this voluntarism, this eager enterprise and adaptiveness, is abundant. For example, there were Christians in Ijebu before there were missionaries. When the missionaries moved into the countryside before the turn of the century, in town after town there would appear a small band of citizens claiming to be Christians already. Either they had become Christians, they would say, during repeated trading ventures to Lagos or Abẹokuta, or they had been instructed by Lagos Christians who had come to Ijebu, or they had had contact in some indirect way. Prevented from meeting openly by local pressure until the Europeans arrived, such groups formed avid nuclei for both the religious and the educational aims of the missionaries. There is little evidence that Ijebu were experimenting with western education before the conquest, but within a decade after it the British thought it necessary to curtail the import of books to Ijebu for fear that other areas would get none at all!

We have already seen that there were active Ijebu merchants long before commerce became a central pillar of the colonial *raison d'être*. Trade in West Africa clearly predates European contact; perhaps as early as the sixteenth or seventeenth century Yorubaland had not only an extensively monetized market economy but also a well-developed set of credit, mortgaging, and savings institutions. In the nineteenth century Ijebu traders were in the front ranks of those who found further possibilities in the newly-developing economies of Lagos, Abẹokuta, and Ibadan. Before British conquest, Ijebu merchants were exporting plantation produce to Lagos. Indeed, seeing which way the wind was blowing, one of the most powerful of the war chiefs made his own peace with the British just before the invasion, stood aside in the battle, and was rewarded with an annual stipend and a post as sole agent in Ijebu for a British importing firm. Midway through the nineteenth century the ports of Ijebu had brimmed with palm oil and foodstuffs; within five years of conquest wild rubber was being collected, smoked fish and sleeping mats were being exported, and Ijebu craftsmen were plying new markets.

With much more voluntaristic than coerced activity, in short, the Ijebu launched themselves into the new colonial era. It is true that they had fought a battle in 1892 to retain their independence, but they had already begun to include themselves in the expanding British "sphere of influence." Further, while that "influence" became actual domination, it is also necessary to note how relatively brief and light colonial rule was for ordinary Ijebus. British rule lasted from 1892 to 1960 — at Nigerian independence there were many old men who had grown up in an independent Ijebu. Indeed, though British intervention in Yoruba politics began before actual conquest, there was little direct impact on local Ijebu communities until head taxes and local administration were introduced after 1918. By then Nigerians had begun staffing the lower levels of the administration, and in 1954 all supervision of internal affairs in Western Nigeria passed into Yoruba hands. Certainly there was not the wholesale disruption of family life, markets and production, values and worldview that was the lot of many longer or more deeply colonized peoples in the New World, parts of south and southeast Asia, and North and South Africa.

Ijebu found it possible, then, to begin rapidly to take their own benefits from the colonial subjection they could not, in any case, avoid. As we shall see in the discussion of migration below, it was the relatively advantaged segments of old Ijebu which began to move, not the relatively downtrodden who might have been forced to do so. "Moved" is more than a metaphor here: in view of the fact that few colonial institutions were physically located in Ijebu, the way to jobs and opportunities lay in migration.

Colonial Institutions

Society exists apart from its members insofar as it presents to each of them a set of norms, institutions, and historical situations within which they must act. Choices are open at every moment — scientific anthropology has long since buried the myth that there are "primitive" peoples who simply act out, as robots, a single set of unambiguous customs. Culture is, then, a complex set of constraints which inform and guide choice-making by presenting sets of alternatives and their consequences in varying light. For a full view of any particular society, we thus obviously need to understand both the constraints and the individual actions taken with respect to them.

In twentieth-century Nigeria the dominant constraints have clearly been the three fundamental institutions of British colonialism: private commerce, governmental administration, and religion and religiously-sponsored education. In each institution it was Britishers, often in Britain, who made basic policy decisions, the three sectors collaborating with one another where necessary. The effects of those decisions upon Nigerians were always secondary to the advantage they yielded to British interests, although sometimes it was argued that benefits accrued to both parties. In an earlier day African merchants, clergymen, and officials had risen to high positions (Kopytoff 1965; Hopkins 1964), but it was the essence of colonialism that it displaced local achievements. Quick and sustained nationalist politics, spontaneous disorders, and rebellious or prophetic religious movements attest to the fact that Nigerians did not simply submit passively to the colonial situation. The situation itself, however, remained beyond their control. For Ijebus, like other Nigerians, the apparatus of colonialism was a set of "givens," around or in response to which they built their lives. It is from *their* point of view, then, that we may here briefly note some of the concrete aspects of those institutions, leaving their roots and the causes of change within them beyond our present scope.

Commerce. The British came to Nigeria, as Mabogunje says, "to exploit the resources of the country in a way most remunerative to their imperial interest" (1968:143). The primary resource of Yorubaland was agricultural labor. After an early ascendancy of cotton and palm products (oil and kernels), in the twentieth century southwestern Nigeria became one of the world's most productive cocoa-growing regions. As we have seen, however, Ijebu Province lies largely outside the so-called "cocoa belt." As a result, no substantial class of export-oriented farmers has arisen in Ijebu. What agricultural growth has taken place has been based upon the production of foodstuffs, notably cassava and kola nuts, which are shipped to the large markets of western and northern Nigeria. The one important niche in the cocoa economy which Ijebus did find was as buyers and transporters from small farms to the major entrepots where the foreign firms took over the export process. Especially in the two decades prior to 1939, when the prices payable to farmers began to be regulated by the government, many Ijebu fortunes were built as middlemen in these operations.

A new transportation network was built by the British to facilitate their activities. Precolonial transportation units were the head-load (or sometimes the canoe-load) and the day's march, and markets and hostelries were closely spaced to reflect this technology. The new system was vastly different. First, after consideration of a route through Ijebu, a railway line was constructed northward from Lagos via Abẹokuta instead, beginning in 1895. Motorable roads came much later, after the first World War, and then as feeders to the railway line. One major effect of these developments was to enhance or diminish the importance of towns, villages, and markets according to their location with respect to the new transport grid. Second, it provided a new field of employment (but probably not overall increased employment, since jobs in the old system were lost) for clerks, mechanics, telegraph operators, laborers and others. Indeed the transportation and communication systems remained among the major sources of wage employment for Nigerians until the general expansion of the civil service after 1946. As in cocoa production, however, from the Ijebu vantage point these jobs also required migration and residence away from home.

From these resources and with this system of communications, the colonial commercial economy was established. A small group of European firms came by the 1930's to dominate Nigeria's trade, having driven out prior competition both from foreign and African businessmen. By ten years later six firms handled a total of two-thirds of all the country's imports and an even larger share of her exports (Bauer 1954:69). This "oligopoly" operated throughout the country, controlling shipping, importing, exporting, warehousing, wholesaling, some retailing, and, later, manufacturing as well. Economic opportunities afforded to Africans in this situation were of two types: wage employment in the stores, yards, workshops, offices, and vehicles of the companies on the one hand, and related independent enterprises in retailing, processing (as of cloth into clothing), and services for both the firms and their employees. These jobs, too, were in the growing urban centers, and hence outside Ijebu. Vivid examples of the ways in which Ijebu responded to these opportunities may be seen in the next chapter on the growth of the Ijebu community in Ibadan, and in the chapters on the Odusanya, Ọnadele, and Bankọle families.

Government. Imperial Britain acquired what became Nigeria by fits and starts from 1861, when Lagos was annexed, to 1922, when portions of the formerly German Cameroons were mandated to Great Britain by the League of Nations. During that long period, government and military officers were sometimes deliberate and calculating of their expansionist goals, sometimes more concerned with quelling local resistance than with what they might "do" with the new conquest, and sometimes even reluctant to get entangled at all in particular areas or issues. Some historians call the Ijebu Expedition the "missionaries' war," implying that the missions, whose policies were being impeded by the Ijebu, provoked the conquest of Ijebu by otherwise indifferent British authorities.

In any case, after Ijebu was conquered in 1892 (a separate protectorate treaty was made with Remọ in 1894) it was "administered" at first by a military officer and then by a travelling "commissioner" headquartered elsewhere. Having decapitated the kingly authority and having assured free access to Ijebu for the merchants and missionaries, the British found it adequate to maintain only a slight governmental presence. By 1906 the Awujalẹ and his chiefs complained that they had been left to administer the territory on their own, but with no sources of revenue to finance their work. In British legal terms, it was indeed unclear who ruled Ijebu.

The amalgamation of the Northern and Southern Provinces of Nigeria in 1914, with its attendant administrative reforms, put Ijebu into a clearer status. Ijebu became a division of *Abẹòkúta* Province, then a Province in its own right in 1921. A British Resident, with a small staff under him, ruled Ijebu "indirectly," according to Lord Lugard's colonial model. The Awujalẹ and his Council, as the legally-constituted "Native Authority," collected the poll taxes and were responsible for a variety of public works, local courts, licensing, and later on some schools, dispensaries, and a hospital. My purpose here is not to trace the administration of Ijebu under colonialism, however, but only to point out that Ijebu as a province was quite removed from the direct presence of British overrule as compared with other areas. Indeed, in 1921 — nearly half-way through the colonial period — there were only twenty-four Europeans in all of Ijebu, including five missionaries and several teachers. The government agencies, and especially the Public Works Department of the

Native Authority, provided jobs for a few scores of people. The changes that had come to Ijebu were profound, but they were largely in the hands of Ijebu, and they went on against a background of considerable continuity in the daily lives of individuals. This situation was a far cry from the plantations, colonial settlers' farms, mines, and occasional industrial establishments of other parts of the continent.

Outside Ijebu Province governmental operations grew at a much more rapid pace. The Railway, the ports, the communications facilities, the higher courts, the local administration of Lagos, and other institutions each hired hundreds of Africans at lower and middle levels. Some of this employment existed in outlying governmental or transport centers, but the bulk of it was in Lagos, the bridgehead of colonial influence since the 1850's. Reflecting the importance of the city, its population quadrupled between 1891 and 1930, by which time over a thousand Britishers oversaw its variegated activities. It was a powerful magnet for immigrants, from all over Nigeria and elsewhere in West Africa, who made up three-fifths of its population in both the censuses of 1931 and 1950.

Africans had their "places" in the British colonial system, especially at lower and middle levels in government, where hiring the "natives" afforded real economies to administration. There was no rush, on the other hand, to provide the means for Nigerians to achieve positions commensurate with their abilities. Nigerians accepted the inferior jobs but immediately began to fight, at first for the higher places and soon for total political sovereignty in order to control the entire system. Nationalism in Nigeria was born before the country itself was pieced together into a single unit. The political history of Nigerian colonialism is a story of constant tension between the claims of the nationalists and the early hostility and later reluctant collaboration of the British (Coleman 1958). The institutions of colonialism, thus, were always under pressure from Nigerians to adapt and grow responsive to Nigerian needs.

At first the reactions were slow. Schools for medical assistants and engineering technicians were started only in the 1930's. The worldwide economic depression had dulled whatever appetite there was in the government for industrial or infra-structural development. After the second World War, however, the expanding forces of nationalism, both in Nigeria and in the world at large, precipitated first the period known as "welfare colonialism" and then internal self-government and final independence. Government services at all levels were vastly expanded, as were the bureaucracies to provide them. In southwestern Nigeria *Ibàdàn* had become capital of the Western Provinces in 1939. In the post-war years it probably expanded more quickly than Lagos as a new center for employment, its dynamic accelerated by the decentralization of power as separate Yoruba, Ibo and Hausa-Fulani nationalisms were embodied in the powerful Regional governments of successive Nigerian constitutions in the 1940's and 1950's.

Independence in Nigeria was declared in 1960. By that time national political parties had deep roots in Ijebu Province. Politicians from Ijebu at home and in urban centers were pressing the claims of those they represented, and Ijebu civil servants were spread throughout local, regional, and national administrations. *Within* these institutions, the end products of colonialism and nationalism, they competed toughly, sometimes bitterly, with other political interests. We cannot here narrate the details, but it is important simply to point out that Ijebus were full participants in the party split, election crises, institutional politics and finally the civil war which rent Nigeria in the mid-1960's. And they continue to be overrepresented among the major actors in current Nigerian events. Many of these large political and social forces lie beyond the lives of the families we are about to meet, but they impinge upon them in many ways, as we will observe.

Missions and Education. The work of the missions has been a vital third force in the development of modern Nigerian social life. In the nineteenth century missionaries were often the first Europeans to visit, or at least to reside, in many Yoruba towns. They often initiated trade in imports to support themselves, and other traders followed them. Some actually fought in nineteenth century Yoruba wars, while most became strong partisans of the town in which they lived. To promote their own interests and to protect themselves they frequently intrigued with political groups in their host communities or beyond, or, alternatively, called upon the power of British authorities on the coast. Anglican missionaries helped provoke the conquest of Ijebu, while Ijebu themselves at the last moment, tried to contact French Catholic missions in Dahomey for strategic alliance. Summarizing perhaps too simply, the flag followed trade, which in turn followed the cross.

The role they played in the extension of empire notwithstanding, the missions were enthusiastically received in many areas. Missionaries brought material imports like metal roofing sheets, but Yoruba were attracted at least as much by the offers to teach language and literacy skills, sharp instruments for dealing with the changing environment. Education in English was obviously the major qualification for advancement in the commercial and governmental institutions of colonial Nigeria. With some diminution as time passed, English language education meant broad exposure to and at least nominal adherence to mission Christianity. Many schools forbade attendance past a rudimentary level unless adherence to the sponsoring sect was strong. And entry into higher levels of schooling, available to only a handful of aspirants, was dependent upon both adherence and selection for favored treatment by a schoolmaster or pastor. The biography of Dr. Falujo in Chapter X makes this point clearly.

So, missions and the education they provided were thus a powerful agent of recruitment to colonial institutions and to Western (or, more specifically, Victorian British) manners and morals. Within a few years of conquest unpaid evangelists were teaching the reading of the Bible all over rural Ijebu. By 1921, a far higher proportion of Ijebu was Christian than of any other Yoruba province. At that time there were 138 local churches, 107 schools, and 227 teachers in Ijebu, and more children were in Ijebu schools than in any other Yoruba province outside the Colony of Lagos. By 1931 there were a few less schools, but the number of teachers had risen to 487. By 1965 3,210 teachers in 478 schools taught over 86,000 pupils, and Ijebu had both a significantly higher percentage of all its children, and a *much* higher percentage of its girls, in school than was true of any other province of Western Nigeria. Primary schools exist these days in virtually every Ijebu community over a few hundred in population.

Two-thirds of the schools of Western Nigeria are still run by Christian agencies, although direct ties to the churches have loosened, almost all receive government financial assistance, and there are many other schools sponsored privately, by government, and by Muslim groups. The constriction of educational opportunities at the post-primary level also remains, though entrance examinations have in large part replaced missionary favoritism as the mechanism of entry. Within Ijebu in 1965 there was but one pupil in secondary school to every ten in the primary classes, even though the number of post-primary schools in the province had grown from one before the second World War (Ijebu Ode Grammar School, founded in 1913) to 23 in 1965. But it is clear, though no statistics are available, that many Ijebu children have gone outside their province for further education, especially to Ibadan and Lagos where there are large concentrations of secondary schools.

Victorian manners have certainly declined throughout the educational system, to the dismay of some Christian parents! Schools now recruit for the contemporary Nigerian urban society that has replaced the colonial order. This is not to say that they recruit for Nigeria, for many would argue that they overproduce youths who will not farm but cannot find urban jobs, either. Questions of educational curricula and their relations to manpower needs continue to receive much attention by scholars and planners in Nigeria (see e.g., Abernethy 1969).

Compared with the relatively ordered growth and change in the Western educational institutions, the history of the church presents a much more complex picture. The established European churches agreed to divide the Yoruba countryside for more efficient and less competitive proselytism. Thus central Ijebu became an Anglican field, and Remo went to the Methodists. But as early as 1891 the racism and cultural imperialism of the European churches had produced a secessionist reaction. Besides, various American missions, small evangelical bodies, and the Roman Catholic Church moved in where they could. Thus competition for adherents grew anyway, even in small towns. By 1921 138 churches stood in Ijebu Province, claiming one of every eight Ijebus, some 22,000 in all, as converts.

Meanwhile Islam was also expanding, especially in Ijebu Ode, where by 1926 at least half of the population was Muslim. By that time, too, the general lines of religious differentiation had been drawn, in most places: the subsequent growth of all the sects was principally in communities, families, or districts in which they already had primacy. Thus today about two thirds of Ijebu Ode is Muslim and one third Christian, while the proportions are reversed elsewhere in the province. Few people admit not to be attached to one of the two world religions.

Yet even this picture is too simple. Beginning in the 1920's a wave of prophetic Christian and syncretistic movements spread across Yorubaland. Some now have large church organizations of their own. Other prophets, less successful or only more recent, ply their special visions and messages on foot across the countryside or in houses and tiny churches of their own. Many Yoruba are non-exclusive in their own religious life. They may take their successes and troubles in turn to an "established" church, a prophetic congregation, or a traditional cult, or, if they are not Christian, to a Muslim sage and then a traditional cult or healer. They see all these possibilities as specialized but overlapping means of religious expression and solace. At the same time both Christian and Muslim organizations are continually reworking their orientations and services to their respective communities, in ways that sometimes enter the lives of the families we will meet.

The major effect of the missions has been the production of a largely Christian elite through the Western educational system. Muslims at first shunned (and were shunned by) the schools, but later developed Westernized schools of their own. The close association of Christianity with the larger colonial presence has meant, though, that in Nigeria at large there will be no supplanting of Christian forms and idioms by a modernized Islam for a long time to come.

Migration from Ijebu

It was these institutions of colonialism, together with the indigenous institutions of Yoruba society which both modified and were modified by them, that provided (and still provide) the framework for individual actions. The voluntarism of the Ijebu provided an orientation to that framework. The result was an ever-increasing migration of individuals from their home towns to new centers of wage employment or entrepreneurial opportunity. Without Ijebu enterprise there was nothing inevitable about this migration — in other places and circumstances, a group faced with the same external possibilities might have refused to participate (for some examples see Diamond 1967; Gulliver 1969; Turnbull 1972).[1]

In colonial and post-colonial Africa, migration has been extensive. Millions of persons now work in rural and urban settings far away from home for at least part of the year. The motivations, patterns, and consequences of their movements vary greatly. In some places men trek hundreds of miles to sell their labor on rural farms during slack periods in their own agricultural cycles. Elsewhere families settle permanently in distant lands following the lure of trading opportunities. The better to understand the Ijebu among the many types of migrants, and the families in this book among the thousands of Ijebus living away from home, it is worthwhile to summarize data on the scale, dispersal, incidence, and mechanisms of Ijebu migration.

A Migration Survey. To secure reliable information on Ijebu migrants, in late 1966 the author and one assistant carried out a survey of migration from five localities (three small towns and two quarters of the capital city) representative of Ijebu Province. In each place maps were updated to allow drawing a random sample of houses, in which data was gathered on all migrants currently living away from home. Questionnaires were completed on two hundred and forty migrants.

Scale. The migrants in the sample came from a total of ninety-four houses sampled. Since other figures indicate that there are about ten current residents per house in Ijebu Province, the average of 2.6 migrants per house indicates that there may be up to 25 per cent as many Ijebu migrants as there are Ijebus left at home. Basing an extrapolation on the 1963 census, which counted nearly 600,000 Ijebus at home, we thus estimate that between 120,000 and 150,000 Ijebu migrants live away from their home towns. It is interesting to note that Ijebu Ode has a higher migration rate than the rural towns, reflecting the historically greater outward orientation of the capital and other factors we shall mention below.

Dispersal. The Ijebu migrants in the sample are spread over half the world. There are Ijebu students and teachers in American universities, Ijebu businessmen in England, Ijebu religious pilgrims working their way across the Sudan toward Mecca. As in other Yoruba areas, some families or communities have historic ties to specific locations — the Cameroons, the Niger Delta fishing villages, or to Dahomey, for example. But the greatest numbers go to the employment centers of modern Yorubaland. Over one third of all the migrants were in Lagos, one sixth in Ibadan, and one twelfth in the cocoa-growing areas, while nearly one fifth were in other areas of Ijebu Province itself. In numerical terms based on the extrapolation above, the Ijebu community of Lagos may total nearly 50,000, the Ibadan community over 20,000, and the ''cocoa-belt'' migrants 11,000, while nearly 25,000 may be intra-provincial migrants. Other smaller groups are scattered all over Nigeria, and in the markets and service trades of much of West Africa from the Upper Volta to the Zaire Republic.

Incidence. Analysts of modern African migration have followed Durkheim's work on suicide in distinguishing between *rate* and *incidence*. The rate refers to the proportion of the total population involved, the ''scale'' discussed above. Incidence has to do with the patterned ways in which the rate arises within the total population. That is, it refers to the particular categories or types of individuals who decide to migrate. It asks the question, ''who migrates?''

For Ijebu it is well to separate pre- and post-World War II migrants in answering this question. Rapid expansion of the civil service, of the educational system, and of major industries such as construction and transportation during and after the War have altered the conditions to which Ijebu responded. In the following notes, therefore, we distinguish those early migrants who left their homes before 1940, who number thirty-one (12.9 per cent) of the total sample, from the rest.

It is important to note that contradictory hypotheses suggested themselves as accounting for ''who migrates.'' One held that it would be the oppressed or weak in the traditional kingdom — slaves, marginal personalities, losers in economic or political fortunes — who would find, or even be driven to, the new opportunities. The other suggested that those with some advantage already would see further advantage in the new order. It is the latter hypothesis which is supported by the evidence.

For example, inhabitants of Ijebu Ode, the capital and commercial focus of the kingdom, tended to migrate earlier than people from the rural, subordinate towns. The average length of time that 73 migrants from Ijebu Ode have been away is 16.0 years, while 132 migrants from rural towns average 12.6 years each. More striking, only 9.8 per cent (13) of the ruralites left before World War II, while 24.7 per cent (18) of the Ijebu Ode migrants have been away that long. The greater economic complexity and social centrality of the old Ijebu capital are clearly reflected in this earlier movement of Ijebu Ode migrants.

Second, in the early days the children of parents with non-farm occupations were much more likely to migrate than those whose parents were farmers. Up to World War II perhaps as many as 70 per cent of all Ijebus were farmers. Yet of the 28 pre-World War II migrants whose parents' occupations were recorded, 61 per cent had non-farm fathers. As time has passed, the percentage of non-farmers in the province has grown steadily, but only 56 per cent of the fathers of post-1940 migrants had non-farm occupations. In effect, growing numbers of farmers' children were able to migrate, as kinsmen or townsmen paved the way for them. At all times the percentage of migrants with non-farm mothers has been very high — 71 per cent of the early migrants and 74 per cent of the later migrants have had mothers who were traders or craftswomen. These general findings probably reflect the greater intensity of knowledge of and contacts in the world beyond the home town that non-farm parents have had and have been able to use to their children's advantage. While the ''headstart'' has been reduced over the years within Ijebu, it still marks them off from other, more farm-oriented peoples in Nigeria.

A third characteristic of early migrants is that most had reasonably high skill levels before they left home. Nearly half had been to school at least through (primary) Standard IV, by which time they would have known how to read and write English fairly well. Others were often older people setting out to apply an already-acquired craft in a newly-developing market. More recent migrants have been younger, less highly educated or trained, and more dependent in their new surroundings.

Finally, religion as a variable is quite interesting. Predictably, eight of the eleven early migrants who were Christians went to Lagos (and one or two other major centers of western influence) as a first destination. Pre-conquest trade connections between Ijebu and Lagos may have disposed them or their families to become Christians in the first place, and thus their Christianity and their migration may have the same source. Second, however, Christians went to schools, and schools led to western employment, available at only a few centers in those days. We might have expected that Muslim trade connections to Ibadan and other northerly points would have led them to migrate in that direction. Nevertheless, eleven of twenty Muslims went to Lagos, reaffirming its primacy as *the* field for new opportunities. On the other hand the Muslims did spread to a larger number of destinations than the Christians, reflecting the indirect stimulation of demand for their craft and trading skills in towns and cities well beyond those where ''clerks'' could find much work.

In general, all the correlations have weakened in recent years. Free primary education has enabled nearly everyone to gain skills that they may potentially sell in urban labor markets. More and more people including farmers have some relative or friend ''abroad'' (i.e., outside the home town) whom they can call upon to aid their migrating children or themselves. There are jobs for the relatively educated in a wider range of places. Muslim as well as Christian Ijebu are going to school and then to employment requiring skills gained there. Finally, in the past few years the job market has been tightening, and Christian primary school graduates are apprenticing to craftsmen or assisting traders, dropping an older disdain for such work.

The upshot of these changes is that migration has taken on a great degree of normalcy. These days, children finish primary school and leave town. Some head for secondary schools, others for jobs or apprenticeships. Rural Ijebu communities appear drained of adolescents, though the published results of the 1963 and 1973 censuses are not yet detailed enough to document this point. Of our own sample, a total of 63 individuals migrated during the sixteen years from 1940 through 1955, an average of about four per year; from 1956 through 1966, 107 migrants left home, a steep acceleration to almost ten per year. These figures suggest an annual migration of nearly six thousand people a year in the Province as a whole. Such an estimate must remain only informed speculation, but it indicates the general magnitude of the many problems of housing, jobs, financial support, maintenance of family property, economic redistribution, and communications that individual families (like those in this book) and African economies must face.

Footnotes

[1]For an account of the Ijebu kingship in the twentieth century, see Ayandele (1970).

[2]Recent discussion has concluded, more simply than my argument here, that the rate of migration is determined by economic factors, ''in terms of a comparison of economic opportunities as perceived by [a potential migrant] in his rural home on the one hand, in [migrant] employment on the other'' (Gugler 1969:137). But this comparison can be drawn only *after* ''felt needs'' for cash, consumer items, educational or entrepreneurial achievement, and other goals have first been established, and after a definition of the situation as involving ''opportunities'' has in fact been made. There is, thus, still room to consider ''psychologistic'' arguments as to variables like ''voluntarism,'' ''receptivity to change'' (Ottenberg 1959), motivation levels (McClelland 1961; LeVine 1966a), and cognitive maps.

CHAPTER III

The Setting: Ijebus in Ibadan

Ijebu migrants to the city of Ibadan constitute one of its major groups of "strangers." Yet there have been Ijebus in the city from the time of its birth. To resolve this apparent paradox one must understand something of the intertwined growths of both the city and its Ijebu community.

Ibadan: From War Camp to Metropolis

The history of Ibadan is one of dramatic achievement.[1] In the first quarter of the nineteenth century the Yoruba states of Ọyọ and Òwu, and then the loosely-federated towns of the Ègbá forest, were successively destroyed and sacked. In the dust a collection of refugees and armed adventurers settled on the site of an Egba village. Thus Ibadan — now the home of a million people — was born humbly around 1829. By the 1850's, when the first missionary came to live in the town, continuing wars to the north and northeast had swelled its population to sixty thousand or more. In the meantime the erstwhile war camp was becoming the center of an empire of its own, built by military conquest. By 1890 most of central and eastern Yorubaland was under its sway.

In 1893 the British negotiated a disengagement of the sixteen-year-old Èkùìparapò War, and posted a Resident and an occupying military force in Ibadan. At that time the city had perhaps as many as 175,000 inhabitants, the vast majority being farmers like the people of other Yoruba towns. Over the next seven decades of colonial rule further functions were added to the city, each one stimulating additional growth. In 1901 the railroad was built as far as Ibadan, and soon established the city both as the major transshipment point for the cocoa-growing areas which stretched eastward, and as the commercial center of all Yorubaland. In 1939 Ibadan was made the capital of the Western Provinces of Nigeria (later the Western Region, and now, with somewhat diminished boundaries, the Western State). In 1948 the first Nigerian university was sited there. As a center of commerce (but not industry), government, education, and cultural life, Ibadan is second among Nigerian cities only to Lagos, the capital of the country ninety miles south.

The Growth of the Ijebu Community[2]

Each impulse in the growth of Ibadan brought Ijebu settlers to the city. It is useful to distinguish four "waves" (the early ones quite small) of Ijebu immigration, for each group had different motivations, settled in different areas, and had different relations with the non-Ijebu citizenry.

The first Ijebus in Ibadan were, indeed, among the original settlers in the city. Like the others they were led by armed adventurers, veterans of the Owu and Egba wars. They settled at the southerly extremity of the new town, in the direction of their origin, and in time the area was named *Isàlè Ìjèbu* ("Ijebu Lower Side") after them. Like the other settlers as well, they retained what became increasingly symbolic relationships to their home towns (most were from Rẹmọ), but were fully citizens of Ibadan. They farmed, made war, and participated politically with their fellow Ibadans. Over the next century they gave a series of distinguished military and political leaders to the city. Their descendants continue to define themselves as Ibadan men, not Ijebus.

The second "wave" of Ijebu migrants arrived later on in the nineteenth century. They were traders, forerunners of the vast influx of newcomers which began after 1900. As European missionaries and merchants increased their penetration of the interior, opportunities arose for indigenous entrepreneurs and intermediaries. The new group of Ijebus, whose core was a set of four brothers, had contacts both with Lagos traders and the missions. At first they speculated in the several currencies that were being used in the area, but later they sold hardware, stockfish, and other imports.

It was their attachment to the Anglican missions, however, that "located" these Ijebus with respect to Ibadan society. Adherence to Christianity in those days was a deviant choice, and Ibadan Christians as well as others were largely ostracized by their fellows for joining the church. Many, including the Ijebu group, chose to live in or adjacent to the church compound itself. Thus the "second wave" came to live at the eastern perimeter of Ibadan, near St. Peter's Church, where many of its descendants still reside. The Christian community, estranged as it was, in turn was sect-like in its exclusiveness. Members spent all of their leisure time in church activities. Within the group, bounds of ethnicity softened: the first marriage at St. Peter's was that of the youngest of the four Ijebu brothers to the daughter of one of the earliest Ibadan Christians. In the years that followed, this second group of immigrants neither interacted intensively with other Ijebus nor farmed and participated in Ibadan sociopolitical life. Their basic social identities remained focussed by the church, and neither they nor others could clearly categorize them with the ethnic labels "Ibadan" or "Ijebu."

Had the second group of Ijebus not become detached from the ongoing migration to Ibadan by the consequences of their religious choice, it and the next "wave" might well be inseparable. For in fact all through the latter half of the nineteenth century and continuing beyond, traders and craftsmen of various sorts had been coming to Ibadan as part of the old commercial economy of Yorubaland. They traded in food, livestock, cloth, metal and other items. At the beginning they were itinerant, staying with trade partners in Ibadan for a market day or longer before moving on. They travelled on foot, sometimes in large parties protected by men at arms.

As the safety of trade routes and the size of their Ibadan trade grew, these traders began to settle in the city, or to leave an agent there. They usually found permanent lodgings with old trade partners scattered through the town, where here and there their descendants have remained until today — or until 1965, when the deepening hostility between Ibadan and Ijebu forced many such longstanding relations to be broken and the Ijebu were, sometimes reluctantly, driven from their old Ibadan hosts' homes. Up to that point, however, a mutuality of interests had produced a set of Ijebu craftsmen, laborers, and traders, often Muslim and uneducated like their hosts, distributed widely but sparsely throughout the Ibadan community. Incidentally, this dispersal of Ijebus all over the city is one of the factors which makes any full count or sampling of Ijebus difficult to carry out before a total census of the city.

In 1900 the first European commercial house opened in Ibadan. The following year the railroad reached the town, passing to the west of the old city walls where a station was built outside the *Iddó* (Lagos) Gate. There a new commercial nucleus took root. Inside the town wall, between the gate and the built-up area, lay about two miles of farm land and bush. This interstice in the physical structure of the city was matched by a gap between the social and economic organization of the old and new centers, since for example, the foreign stores would not extend credit or sell their goods in small quantities to local consumers. Into both these openings, therefore, flowed thousands of migrants, in a wave that has not yet stopped running.

This fourth wave consisted at first of employees of the railroad and the foreign stores themselves. They were relatively well educated, usually Christian, and in most cases had migrated to Lagos before being transferred "up the line."

Soon some of these men and women left their salaried jobs to risk trading on their own. By the early 1920's the shops and often imposing homes of wholesalers and retailers of imported hardware, building supplies, haberdashery, patent medicines, bicycle parts, shoes, and many other items lined the once-overgrown footpath through *Ògùnpa, Àmúnigun,* and *Agbeni*. Although other quarters, notably *Èkó Tẹdó* and *Òkè Bọlà*, were developing near the railway station, and were absorbing migrants of diverse ethnic origins, these three took the majority of Ijebu migrants, and nearly only Ijebus, until after the Second World War.

As more and more housing was built by migrants in these areas, the craftsmen and traders of the continuing third wave, who came directly from Ijebu to Ibadan, began to find homes there, too. With the spread of education and the improvement of transportation facilities the distinction between the third and fourth waves blurred. Simultaneously, the cleavage between migrants, especially the Ijebu, and the indigenous Ibadans grew. In the Ibadan stereotype, Ijebus were seen as uninterested in farming or permanent settlement in the city, grasping, arrogant, and growing wealthy at the expense of Ibadans themselves. When specific issues arose, such as those over freehold tenure of land, the location of urban amenities, or the autonomy of the old cities vis-a-vis the Regional government (whose reins passed from European to African hands in 1954), the Ijebus were seen to have interests in direct opposition to those of the Ibadans. Although we cannot further trace it here, conflict between Ibadans and Ijebus has continued to be a major theme in Western Nigerian politics up to the present day (see, e.g., Sklar 1963:284-320).

In the 1950's and 1960's, the expansion of the city's economy brought ever greater numbers of Ijebus to Ibadan. The older quarters could no longer contain them, and they spilled into the large area on the southwesterly side of the city known generally as *Òkè Àdó* (though it is differentiated by its residents into several named neighborhoods). At the same time Ijebus have to some degree moved out of the aging areas of first settlement. Thus it is Oke Ado which is today first identified as the place where the Ijebus live. Of the seven families in this book, four live in Oke Ado. After a brief summary of some characteristics of the present Ijebu community in Ibadan, we will therefore return to describe the general setting in which these families live and work.

The Ijebu Community Today

There are, in short, several categories of Ijebu in Ibadan. However, the relative sizes of the third and fourth waves of migration, taken with the facts that these two have merged in residence and occupational diversity and that they are still receiving newcomers, mean that for many purposes they, and not the Isalẹ Ijebu "Ibadans of Ijebu extraction" or the old Christian group, are the Ijebu community there. All the families in this book are from the two later migration waves.

Technically, a proper use of the word ''community'' might be even narrower than our use of it to refer to this large category of Ijebu migrants. This is so, first, because the Ijebu population in Ibadan is not *organized* into a single body. Formal associations are those based on individual towns ("improvement unions" and migrant aid groups), churches (literary and mutual aid societies), or work (merchants' and craftsmen's groups). Some of the latter two types have memberships entirely Ijebu; others are not ethnically homogeneous. In many cases migrants are more closely tied to their home towns than to other migrants in Ibadan. There have been fleeting attempts to organize pan-Ijebu associations, but no equivalent to the hierarchical and inclusive Ibo State Union has been constructed by Ijebus. The Ijebu "community" is one of interests, current circumstances, and consciousness of origins, not of interaction.

Second, some of the political interests of Ijebus, alluded to in the foregoing section, are shared by other migrants to Ibadan as well. Lebanese, Hausa, Egba Yoruba, and Nupe have been in Ibadan since at least 1900. Ibos, Italians, Greeks, Urhobos, Edos, and Ijesha Yorubas, among others, have followed. Despite common interests, relatively heterogenous residential distribution, and the multiplicity of cross-cutting links at places of work and leisure, however, Ijebus continue to be self-conscious of their own special characteristics.

Within these limits, common to migrants around the world, we then may speak of "an Ijebu community" in Ibadan. What are the social and economic characteristics of that community? Are the seven families in this study representative of it? Answers to these questions are, unhappily, not easy to find. In the first place, there is no detailed census for Ibadan after the 1952 Nigerian Census, carried out before the major expansion of the Regional civil service in final colonial and early independence days, before free primary education became available and gave vast new numbers of youths some basic skills to try to capitalize on as migrants, and before the greatest activity in the housing market in Ibadan. Worse, even the 1952 Census made no distinction between indigenous and non-indigenous Yoruba, although it counted the non-Yoruba groups. In short, there has never been an enumeration of Ijebus in Ibadan.

On the basis of our rural surveys, at least twenty thousand Ijebus were estimated to be in Ibadan (though this figure may exclude many children born in Ibadan who were not mentioned as migrants in the rural surveys). Since they are spread across the whole city (even if concentrated in some areas), to draw an accurate sample for statistical purposes would have required far larger resources of staff and time than were available. Nevertheless, at the beginning of fieldwork I interviewed over one hundred Ijebus in Ibadan. They were drawn at first from among the many and varied acquaintances of a research assistant, and later from categories (women and civil servants) thought underrepresented to that point. There was no particular attempt to diversify the respondents by age, place of origin, religion, education, or migration experience. The overall

TABLE 1
Selected Characteristics of 108 Ijebu Migrants in Ibadan[a] and (in Parentheses) of the 15 Resident Adult Members of the Seven Households in this Book

1. Age		2. Sex		3. Religion	
20 or under	3 (0)	Male	86 (6)	Christian	78 (12)
21-30	30 (5)	Female	22 (9)	Anglican	45 (6)
31-40	25 (4)			Catholic	7 (1)
41-50	17 (3)			Methodist	5
51-60	18 (3)			Independent	7
Over 60	15 (0)			Other or	
				unspecified	14 (5)
				Muslim	30 (3)

4. Education		5. Occupation	
None	7 (1)	Professional, High Civil	
Literate in Yoruba	2 (1)	Service	9 (1)
Some Primary	11 (1)	Religion	2 (0)
Full Primary	41 (6)	Trader/Landlord	19 (1)
Some Secondary	27 (3)	Teacher, Midwife, Clerical,	
Full Secondary	12 (0)	Technical	24 (3)
Higher Education	8 (2)	Craftsman, Small Business,	
Unrecorded	(1)	Moderate Trade	35 (5)
		Petty Trade	6 (2)
		Student, Apprentice	7 (0)
		Unskilled Labor	5 (0)
		None	1 (3)

6. Origin		7. Years Migrant		8. Years in Ibadan	
Ijebu Division	87 (11)	0-1	0 (0)	0-1	8 (0)
Ijebu Ode	26 (6)	1-5	10 (3)	1-5	19 (3)
Other	61 (5)	6-10	11 (0)	6-10	20 (3)
Remo Division	15 (3)	11-20	30 (4)	11-20	33 (5)
Colony Province	6 (0)	21-30	21 (4)	21-30	18 (4)
Other	(1)	Over 30	36 (3)	Over 30	10 (0)
		Unrecorded	(1)		

[a] Non-randomly selected. No population statistics exist for the city of Ibadan or for its Ijebu population which would allow a comparison of these migrants with the total community around them.

range was wide indeed, from wealthy landlords to unemployed school-leavers, from the Permanent Secretary of a major ministry of the regional government to the proprietress of a dance hall and illiterate petty traders. Although it is not to be mistaken as a statistically accurate reflection of the Ijebu population in Ibadan, the accompanying table summarizes some of the major characteristics of the set of Ijebus interviewed.

Perhaps because my assistant stood to gain prestige from introducing me to his higher-status acquaintances, this group probably has a higher proportion of older and more highly educated people who have been resident in Ibadan longer and have better jobs than the Ijebu migrant population as a whole. The large number of males and of craftsmen and small businessmen in the sample is also likely to be a function of my assistant's circle of acquaintances. Nonetheless, the diversity, the high accomplishments, and the relative permanence of the Ijebu community in Ibadan are reflected in this table. Ijebus are full participants in modern Ibadan society, not marginal laborers for others or performers of an ethnic occupational specialty (cf. Cohen 1969).

In fact, many Ijebus and non-Ijebus hold a stereotyped view that the Ijebu have pushed their way to the very forefront of commercial and political activity. Data to support or refute this popular view are hard to find, but there are scattered bits of evidence to suggest that Ijebu *are* substantially overrepresented in the political, commercial, intellectual, and other urban-centered elites of the country. In a thorough survey of small craft enterprises in Ibadan in the early 1960's, Archibald Callaway found almost as many shops belonging to Ijebus as to all other non-Ibadan proprietors combined (1967:159). Furthermore, Ijebus had "high proportions in printing, improved tailoring firms, mechanics" (1967:160), three of the most highly capitalized businesses in Nigerian private hands. Among larger-scale enterprises, too — printing works, bakeries, inter-urban transport, local taxicabs, and plastic products — Ijebus appear to predominate (see Mabogunje 1967:88-90).

Data are even more scant for the market stalls and shops of women, for the civil service and expatriate-owned private enterprise, and for teaching and the professions. Yorubas in Ibadan can point out one insurance firm, say, or a government office in which most of the higher-level office workers are Ijebu, but another firm or office may have mostly Ẹgba or *Ìjèshà* or *Ifẹ̀* Yoruba employees. In some ways the *belief* that the Ijebus control more than their "fair share" of the positions in and resources of the modern urban economy is more important than whether they do or not, since it conditions the prevailing attitudes of hostility and jealousy toward Ijebu achievements. A summary statement of the known facts of the situation could only suggest that Ijebus are distributed throughout the occupational range in urban Ibadan, are probably underrepresented at the lowest levels and overrepresented at the higher levels, are probably the single most successful migrant group in trade and commerce, but hold a monopoly nowhere.

Seven Families: "Typical" or Not?

It would be dangerous to suggest that the seven families whom we shall meet in the remainder of this book are "typical" urban Ijebus, let alone typical Nigerian or African urban dwellers. Even if all the dimensions of urban public and private life could be separated and reduced to measurement, a "sample" of seven, no matter how carefully selected, could never encompass enough of the variation to be described as "typical."

On the other hand, the families in this book are both highly different from one another and ranged widely along those characteristics of Ijebu migrants set out in Table 1 above. The figures in parentheses in that table refer to the resident adult members of the seven families. It can be seen that there is almost as great variation within these families as in the much larger set of Ijebu migrants interviewed. Moreover, they are all from a single ethnic group. The diversity of their origins and life histories is not very different from those of many other Ijebus in Ibadan. The relationships within their families and in the compounds where they live are similar in many qualitative aspects to styles of family life observed much more briefly in many other homes. These impressions and comparisons lend confidence to an assertion that the experiences and actions reported here, though they are real and therefore unique, are a reasonably accurate reflection as well of Ijebu life in Ibadan in the late 1960's.

The Setting: Oke Ado

Ijebus form the largest single ethnic bloc in the southwestern sections of Ibadan. Oke Ado, with its component neighborhoods such as Liberty Road, Ìmàlefà-láfìà, and Àpampa, and the adjacent areas of Oke Bọla, Mọleté, Òkè Fọkọ̀ are all identified as Ijebu quarters. In fact, although there has been a slowdown in the rate of expansion of the built-up areas since the boom years of 1955 to 1962 or so, the town continues to encroach steadily into the surrounding farmland. But for outsiders looking at the Ijebu, it is all "Oke Ado."

There are other residents, too. Most are also Yorubas, some indigenous Ibadan residents escaping the cramped and less well-serviced areas of the old core of the city, and the remainder migrants from all over Yorubaland, drawn by the new economy to the busy center of the region. As well, there are other migrants from all of southern Nigeria. But other areas of the city, to the north and west of the new commercial center, have larger communities of Ibo and other southeastern Nigerians. Few northerners — Hausa, Tiv, Nupe, or any others — live in Oke Ado at all.

In all but the oldest neighborhoods of Oke Ado, the streets are laid out in a rough grid, allowing for the interference of a stream, an old house, or a large tree. The major residential roads, and a few of the minor ones, are paved. All are serviced by open drains in various states of usefulness, and the weather and season also help determine whether they should in fact be called drains or cesspools. Opinions about the oppressiveness of the stench that issues from them are matters of cultural and personal relativity, but the residents are aware of their manifest unhealthiness, and they vigorously dissuade their children from playing too near them. Above the streets run electricity wires with connections to almost every house, and telephone wires to a few. As is true throughout Yoruba towns, greenery is meticulously eradicated except for a few large shade trees, the occasional lawn or garden of a school or Westernized private home, and the overgrowth of an undeveloped lot. But the newer metal roofs, increasingly brightly-painted house walls, and greater variety of clothing materials of passersby give much more color to the scene than is the case in older and poorer areas of the city or in rural areas.

There are three or four small markets in this section of the city, but none carries a wide variety of goods. The largest, Oke Ado market itself, functions mainly as a sort of corner grocery, where food and a few other items needed daily can be picked up at prices slightly above those of the main town markets. But it is not necessary to go to the major markets at *Dùgbè, Gbági,* or *Gégé* to purchase other supplies, either. For one thing, hawkers of meat, fish, vegetables and a great many other items pass up and down the streets on foot calling out their wares with a distinctive slogan or a tone of voice which is often passed from mother to daughter. In this way a great many commodities are delivered to the doors of a fairly regular clientele. Secondly, there is a vast array of goods and services available at small shops, doorsteps, and frontages all through the area except at the remotest fringes. Perhaps half of the houses have regular shops either included or attached; at almost every house the wives of some of the tenants ply their trade in the midst of cooking, washing, and taking care of children. In short, therefore, one need only go to the town markets for major purchases, when the pennies to be saved on each item will mount up.

About half the buildings in Oke Ado are two-story dwellings, with very few industrial establishments interspersed. Almost all the houses face onto the street; only a few are behind others within the same compound or building lot, and almost none have the *appearance* of traditional compounds, which faced inward to a courtyard with little but a doorway and a tiny window or two to the world. Instead, with shops, porches, large windows and signboards in front, the houses give a façade of outward orientation. And yet the focus of social activity is still the back "yard." Here are to be found the one or two common bath rooms (a pail in an enclosed room with a drainage outlet away from the house) and latrines (often a similar room with similar, not more appurtenances, although the use of and demand for water closets is spreading), the kitchens (one to a household, another tiny room with an air vent near the ceiling, sometimes but not always an additional room for storage of firewood and dried foods), and usually a single water tap for the compound. In the newest houses some of these facilities are duplicated on the upper floor; in the oldest only a kitchen hut — no latrine or bathroom — may be visible. In any case the yard, often walled-in and paved, is the place where women and children of all the households interact for much of the day.

The present owner of the house was very often its builder as well, since much of the construction has been quite recent — after 1955 — and since this form of investment has been one of the least risky and financially most rewarding. He is also the resident landlord in most cases, usually occupying the upstairs while he rents out the rooms on the ground floor. If he is not present himself, he or a kinsman acting as agent is not far away, often in another house that he owns. Even non-Ijebu feel that nearly all the houses are owned by Ijebu, but no figures are available. If the landlord is present, the house is often better-kept, since he either directs a rotation of caretaking duties among tenants or has members of his own family do the work. But with no heating, almost no plumbing, rare painting and durable construction materials there is relatively little work to do, and so landlords and tenants are not often in conflict over maintenance. The landlords do complain of the late payers and remark that as the housing situation gets looser rent-skipping is increasing. Tenants explain that they do their best with payments given the vagaries of employers and the rising costs of food and other items. A more frequent source of quarrels is the bill for electricity. If there are no separate meters for each room, and there usually are not, the landlord must try to divide the payments equitably. The result can be accusations that another tenant runs a radio and iron, or the flat upstairs runs their lights late into the night, or that the landlord wants to avoid paying anything himself. The tension produced is a not uncommon motivation for moving to a more congenial compound.

The household itself is an easily isolable unit. Every man strives for a "room-and-parlour" for his family, sleeping in one and eating, entertaining, and studying in the other. If he cannot afford the £3 to £5 ($8.40 to $14.00) per month rent for two rooms, he has at least one: I never saw two conjugal families occupying a single room. Polygynous husbands usually have a bedroom for each wife, although men who keep two wives in the city and do not yet own a house are rare. Even in monogynous unions, the children often sleep on mats on the parlor floor rather than in the bedroom with their parents.

In the other rooms are people who may be from one's town or may be from a linguistic and ethnic group several hundred miles away. In Ibadan most non-Yoruba speakers quickly learn the language, however, and communication with co-tenants is rarely impossible. Kinsmen rarely live in the same house, even when they could do so if they liked. Since so much work has to be done in the rear of the house, and so much business transacted in front, doors are often open, but a curtain hangs in the doorway to guard privacy. One knows all one's neighbours, and those in the next house if they share the same rear courtyard, but the people in the next yard may often be only nodding acquaintances.

Finally, the bustle of the area is in part due to the constant activity of the seemingly always-pregnant goats, the muscular chickens, and occasional ducks, dogs, and sheep, all of which are far less common than in older areas of the city, but ever-present just the same.

Footnotes

[1]For a summary of early Ibadan history, see Awe (1967).

[2]Mabogunje (1967) describes the Ijebu community in Ibadan, and the summary here draws in part on his account.

PART TWO

SEVEN FAMILIES

Carriers bring lumber to Michael Odusanya's furniture shop (Chapter 4)

Bread hawkers near Tade Oyebanji's house (Chapter 5)

CHAPTER IV

Struggling Together: The Odusanya Family

Cleaning the Compound

Michael *Odùsànyà,* his wife Florence, three of their four children, their nurse girl, and five young relatives live in[1] a single room in a faded yellow two-story house on a busy footpath in one of the early areas of migrant settlement. A six-foot wall encloses a rear yard which slopes down away from the house. In the middle of the yard stands a cemented row of stalls, two used as "kitchens" (for storage and for cooking if it rains), two as bathing rooms and two, with buckets inside, as latrines. From behind this building paved gutters lead down through a hole in the back wall, but this rear area is cluttered with trash.

"*Adùnní!* Adunni, O! Come down here and let's start cleaning out this place. Maybe you don't think it's dirty enough yet, but I do." Florence Odusanya, called "Ma *Dejì*"[2] in the neighborhood, has taken it upon herself to clean the yard this hot afternoon. Her co-tenants are not eager to help. "Brother Tisa [Teacher], Brother Tisa, come to the window for a minute."

"Brother Tisa" says vaguely that he's coming, but Ma Deji persists, "Do you see this dirty corner? It's your wife's doing. Before she goes to Molete every Saturday, she piles up these things. Now please tell her to find somewhere else to put this stuff, or I'll call the city sanitary inspector on her."

She takes off her cloth wrapper that stretches from underarm to knee so that she can work comfortably. Brassiere and half-slip are acceptable, if somewhat rustic, working clothes within the compound. She takes a hoe and goes on clearing the drain that leads from the house along the side wall, muttering, "This stuff has been lying here three months now, and no one will raise a hand. They'd wait until the whole house begins to smell. . . ."

"Get your baskets," she commands the small children of the house who are watching her. "There's going to be big-scale cleaning here today."

Another woman joins her and the children. As they work, they find new culprits to blame for the mess. A downstairs neighbor comes in from work and smiles, "Hello! Working hard?"

"Ah, so you're home? What have you been doing? Let's go, help us clean up." When he hesitates, Ma Deji jokes, "You lazy, dirty man! If I call the sanitary inspector you'll squawk about what troublemakers the Ijebus are. OK, just let me hit you with this!" She brandishes a rusting frying pan, and he runs into the house laughing.

Still good-naturedly, she next assails a light-complexioned man nicknamed "Yellow." "Hey, Brother Yellow! Don't you see what we're doing?"

"I don't throw trash there. I burn all the sweepings from my room."

"What about things that won't burn, like the leaves they wrap meat in at the market?"

"Er . . . I leave it in my room 'til it's dry."

"But don't you know it's in your own interest to keep your room clean? Do you think all those women will want to take off their pants for you if your room is dirty?"

The second woman picks up Ma Deji's provocation. "The best thing for you to do is to tell her, as you roll off her, 'Please, darling, now won't you just throw away this rubbish for me'."

And when "Yellow" demurs, a third woman joins in. "What? You mean you'd just let them come use your power and go away with it? If anybody enjoys herself the least she can do is pay for it by cleaning up for you. Think of all the trouble you had to go through just to get her to agree in the first place?"

The attack soon switches. "And you, Adunni," Ma Deji exhorts, "Why can't you come out and help us?"

Adunni claims to be ill.

"Sure, sure, little girl! When it comes to a penis you won't complain about any sickness!"

"Ah, I don't know anything called that . . . and I'm going to tell our husband when he gets home." "Our" husband[3] is Florence's husband, "Pa Deji."

"It's only if you want something that he's 'our' husband. Well, if he is, then go make a fire and make us pounded yam[4] for supper. At least you're the *junior* wife."[5]

"No, no. It's my turn to 'sleep' tonight, and yours to prepare food." The three women laugh at their own sparring.

"Oh, so you're sick, but you'd still take your 'sleep' turn, would you?" Ma Deji plays on.

"Well, what would make you get well if not that?" Adunni responds.

"I guess you must know," says Ma Deji. "We saw your letters in the trash we were picking up. All those 'darlings' you promised kisses to. And we saw Sister Remi's letters, too."

Adunni denies that the letters are hers. But Ma Deji persists, and she confesses. "After all, you had your chance once, didn't you? Now leave me to mine."

"I will, sure I will. We'll soon become the same thing." Ma Deji cups her breasts. "Mine are 'slippers' now, and yours will take a shorter time to get like this."

All during the discussion Ma Deji has been going about cleaning, and the children have been carrying baskets of trash out to the public receptacle down the path. But now the cleaning is apparently finished.

Ma Deji catches her breath. "I must wash before I go upstairs to the room, or else my husband won't be able to get in for the smell."

Adunni uses the opening. "You have nothing to worry about," she says. "It's my turn tonight anyway."

"Go away," Ma Deji rejoins. "Who'd have anything to do with an Ẹgba girl anyway? Ẹgba girls — a thousand boy friends!"[6]

At this, Ma Deji goes to wash up, and then to rest before getting supper. Pa Deji doesn't get home from his shop until after seven.

Public Order: Without Law?

Two days later the "Freedom Furniture Shop," Michael's carpentry works, is buzzing more than usual. Pa Deji is in back of the ten-by-fifteen foot open-fronted shop, which serves as a showroom and office, giving directions to the three apprentices who are working at long tables under the rough plank roof that extends from the shop itself. He is having them begin to square the wood for a step-like display case. This time he plans to put the piece into the showroom for sale, although about eighty per cent of his work is done on specific order. Pa Deji is not working himself because of a painful bruised finger he got a few days earlier. Instead, he chooses the lumber, does the measuring, cajoles the apprentices into sawing and planing more quickly and more accurately, and deals with all the customers by himself. He is more animated than usual today, and when an acquaintance stops in to say hello, he immediately starts to tell why.

"Someone tried to steal my bicycle this morning," he begins. "I was in the bathroom when I heard a woman out in front shouting, 'Ba Deji, Ba Deji! There's someone running away with your bike.' I was lucky I was just undressing. So I ran out, and by the time I got there a bunch of people had grabbed the thief. Some had begun beating him quite severely.[7] He was an Ibadan man about 23 years old. And of course he said he'd wanted to rent the bike, not steal it.

"It costs a lot of money to report a thief. First I had to pay the shilling taxi fare to send someone to get the police, which was money wasted because another policeman came along before they got back. Then money for me and two witnesses to go to and from the station with the police. And the policeman begged to be 'taken care of.' I didn't even understand him at first when he said that — he said he wasn't asking to be bribed, but it's just that he's very broke and would like to borrow some money from me 'because I see you're such a nice man,' he said. So I gave him five shillings. But if they so much as hint about more money when I go to collect my bike after the trial, I'll go to the Special Branch, or to the Army Barracks, to report them.[8]

  "Anyway the case is now in the hands of the police. When the thief first got to the station he began begging to be let go. He said he'd just been released from prison a week ago, and his former landlord wouldn't let him return to the house anymore. So he was going to see a brother of his when he saw the bike and thought he'd use it to get there. The policeman in charge asked him if he could still remember the number of his uniform. The boy nodded glumly that he could. That was good, said the policeman, because he'd probably have it on for another ten years!"

  The morning's events keep Pa Deji excited all day. He sings and swears alternately while he works, and embellishes the story with further details as new customers come in.

The Family Routine

Later on in the evening[9] Deji himself, ten years old and lean like his father, arrives at the shop on his way home from extra tutoring that he stays for at school. An hour later, Pa Deji is ready to go. The apprentices are making piggy banks to show the people at home who are paying for their training that at least they are learning something. Pa Deji tells them to make sure they tidy up the place properly when they are done, and to put the unfinished display case inside. When he gets home, Pa Deji goes up to the room to pray for a few minutes.

  Ma Deji is on "afternoon duty" at the cigarette factory where she works. The nurse girl, an *Ìlọrin* Christian referred by a friend of Ma Deji, has been lax as usual in getting supper for the kids on time. At half past eight Pa Deji realizes that the children are falling asleep with no food in them, and yells to *Bọ́sẹ̀* to bring supper for everyone. The girl brings four plates of *ẹ̀bà* (cassava flour thickened with water to the consistency of mashed potatoes), along with a separate dish of oil-and-pepper sauce (or "soup") containing a few pieces of meat to be shared by father and children. After eating, the children play quietly and then drop off to sleep again. First beating Deji with a short switch for not remembering to clean a sore on his arm, Michael, too, lies down. Florence will not be home until nearly eleven.

The weeks when Ma Deji works on the second shift, from 1:30 to 10:00 p.m., are not really disruptive for the family. Deji stays at school for extra tutoring in the afternoon. *Wǫlé* and *Olú,* four and two years old, usually play quietly in the room or hallway, or in the back yard, and doze off and on through the afternoon. (The fourth child, *Ṣọlá,* who is seven, has been staying with Michael's mother in their small rural home for a year.) Bǫsẹ, the nurse girl, makes supper and Michael tries to get home by six or six-thirty. In the morning Ma Deji is free to clean, cook, go to market, and visit with neighbors and friends. When she works "mornings," from 6 a.m. to 1:30 p.m., breakfast for the rest of the family is more confused; the house is not as clean because Ma Deji is tired when she gets home, and the two young children get into more active mischief.

Moods

One afternoon Ma Deji is resting on her bed when Olu comes in crying that Wǫle has hit her.

"Go and bring him here — I'll beat him flat today," says her mother in an angry tone, exaggerated to please Olu. When Wǫle comes in she keeps it up. "So you hit my child, eh? All right, go get me the whip and I'll hit you back."

Wǫle brings an *ewédú*[10] stem stripped of its leaves.

"Put out your hand," Ma Deji orders. The stem goes up.

"Go and call Bǫsẹ, Olu," she adds, and Olu goes out. The stem strikes the bed post three times, and Olu rushes back in to watch the beating.

"There! I've taken care of him, Olu. Take the whip back where it came from."

Olu smiles as she goes out. She doesn't notice that Wǫle, his face buried in the bed, is smiling, too. Both are satisfied.

A few minutes later someone shouts from downstairs that Ma Deji should look out and see what is happening near the public water tap located a few houses down the footpath. Two boys in their late teens are dragging a girl about fifteen up the path. The girl is kicking and pulling furiously, but she cannot get free. Then her wrapper falls off, revealing dirty blue panties and ugly, fat thighs. The small crowd of spectators roars with laughter.

Ma Deji reports that the girl had run away from home because she wasn't being allowed to see her boy friend. She has been staying with the fish seller downstairs. Now her parents have discovered where she is and have sent two of the girl's cousins to bring her home. Ma Deji feels that it would be better to let her have her own way than to have all this furor, especially since there is little that can be done anyway to make her behave.

When the troop passes beneath her window, Ma Deji calls out to the "escorts" to let the girl put her wrapper back on before they get to the main street. Then she admonishes the girl.

"Don't struggle with them. It's a very bad thing if you fight like that all the way up to the road, with every boy looking at you! Just follow them home quietly, do you hear? And put your wrapper on. Everyone is looking at you."

But the procession moves on. One man in the crowd says that the girl's head has been turned back to front by too much sex.

"Rubbish," Ma Deji says. "Why can't some people keep their mouths shut?" And at that, she goes downstairs to prepare supper.

Downstairs she sits in front of her fire as she waits for the water to boil. Her mood is sour, and she finds fault over and over with the servant, Bose. She isn't grinding the pepper right; she hasn't put enough water into the pot; she hasn't done any work all day. Finally, for grinding the pepper too slowly, Ma Deji gives her a punch in the chest.

"I don't know what's wrong with you," she yells. "Five months here and no change yet. You're just plain stupid. When you have charge of a child you expect her to listen to correction, but not you! Ah, I'm not going to have a lazy good-for-nothing around me for long, do you hear? Now take this tray upstairs and bring me the package of *èlùbọ́* [yam flour] I bought this morning."

Ma Deji remains somber as she begins cooking supper for her family.

Freedom Furniture

The next day is a busy one at Freedom Furniture. A small-scale building contractor, who has heard of Pa Deji's industriousness and plain dealing, has placed an order for twelve window frames for a house he is erecting at the outskirts of the newer section of the city. A journeyman, no relation of Pa Deji, and the three apprentices, two of whom are brothers and all three of whom are the children of home-town neighbors, have begun work behind the shed. Only the overhanging roof shields them from the heat of the dry February sun. Inside, Pa Deji is showing a customer, whom he obviously does not know and who is not Ijebu, around the "showroom." She wants a standing clothes cupboard made.

"I'd like it like that, except taller, about six feet," she says, pointing to one in the corner.

"If I make it taller, it should be wider, too," Pa Deji responds.

"And that would mean more money!" the woman jokes.

"Ah, well," Pa shrugs, smiling. "Lumber is never given away free at Ogunpa market."

Then follows a great deal of haggling. Pa Deji's price is £18. The woman laughs out loud, and offers £15. Pa counts out a long list of reasons why it can't be done for so little, but at the end he agrees.

The woman's next question is whether "it will take £13." She is using the regular Yoruba bargaining technique of offering a price, getting interim agreement, lowering the offer, and continuing in this way until the seller cannot be moved further down.[11] Pa Deji speaks firmly. He describes how the grade of plywood he will use will insure against warping and joint separation, and notes how much the special spray coating the woman wants will cost. The deal is getting close now, and the haggling has the effect of verifying details. The woman says that one of her friends has gotten a cupboard just like it for only £12, but that is a weak offense in a land of bargaining. Pa begins another list of reasons that it should be £15. In the end, the woman offers, and Pa Deji accepts, £14.

"All right, fourteen pounds — but if anyone asks you how much you paid, say eighteen. And if it's a carpenter who asks, you ask him if he thinks I've cheated you. Then you'll know I'm doing this for you at a give-away price."

The woman nods agreement, and then another bargaining process begins over the terms of payment. Pa Deji wants half the total, but finally three equal installments are worked out, the last to be paid after the cupboard is finished. As the woman drives away, Pa remarks that indeed he does know her husband, an *Iléshà* man.

Though his bruised finger is still troubling him, Pa then pitches in on the several projects that are now at hand. Later in the day he goes to the Ogunpa lumber market, buys a dozen lengths of various sizes and discusses business in a provincial town with two acquaintances he meets. Finally he hires two Hausa "kaya" (carriers) to take the wood he has bought back to his shop. Headloading six boards, each fourteen feet long, almost a mile through busy streets is no easy task. Pa stores the lumber in the house nearest his shop, in the care of a woman who in return collects wood shavings and scraps for her fire. As usual the apprentices close up the shop near dusk at about 6:30 in the evening.

Chores and Errands

The following day is Saturday, and Ma Deji has gone to the market. Bosẹ is watching the two children eat their breakfast of rice and ẹwà, made from mashed cowpeas. When she leaves to clean up the kitchen, Wọle and Olu begin a contest of who can spray more of the remaining food from their plates onto the floor. When they finish, Wọle gets some water from a pot beside his mother's bed and begins to "wash" his plate. So Olu turns her cup of drinking water over onto her own plate and begins scrubbing away, dumping water on the chair and floor. Her dish cleaned to her satisfaction, she tries to pour the remaining water out the side window, as she has seen grownups do. Though she stands on her tiptoes, she cannot quite reach the open window, and so another mess is poured on the floor. Finally both children leave the room and go downstairs to play outside. When Bọsẹ comes up, she just grabs a rag and starts to clean up, knowing better than to let Ma Deji find the room in the condition it is in.

Ma Deji returns at eleven. She is going to work today on overtime. She wants to wash Wọle's boil-covered head before she goes, and so for lunch she tells Bọsẹ to heat up the left-over soup from the night before. She has Deji fetch the tin of "Sanitas" antiseptic from a neighbor (and co-worker), Ma *Akín,* down the hall, as well as a towel from their own room and the matted scrubbing fiber that Yoruba call "sponge."

Ma Akin advises her not to use the Sanitas because it stings too much and doesn't seem to do much good anyway. She says instead that there is a kind of plant that works wonders with this kind of "head trouble," and that she has seen some growing in the empty lot behind their own house. The two women walk over, ask a man who is working there for permission, and take some leaves from the plant.

It stings, too. Wọle kicks and yells when it is rubbed on his head. His mother shouts at him to stop, but needs Bọsẹ's help to hold him while she scrubs his head, breaking open the many sores with the sponge. After she finishes, she rubs a commercial salve on, but he continues crying. Though Wọle is nearly five, and years beyond babying, Ma puts him on her back to comfort and pacify him. A few minutes later she puts him down to get lunch ready.

As she eats she talks about her job. "They say people are not getting enough cigarettes to buy in the town, and that's why we have to do overtime today. Rubbish! It's because of Good Friday and Easter and *Iléyá*[12] holidays coming up next month. We have three days off within a week then, so they plan to make us sweat for it now. But it will be even worse if they want us to work the two days between the holidays — that would mean they don't want us to have any time off at all."

One of the other women cooking in the yard suggests that perhaps they will be given those two days off, and are working for them now. Ma Deji cannot carry the speculation farther, and goes to wash up for work. Ma Akin is already waiting, and since they want to walk to work today to save the taxi fare, they need to hurry.

They leave quickly, but Ma Deji cannot walk fast for long, and slows down to catch her breath every hundred yards or so. They remark that they have never been as late as this before, and it is the rule that workers must be in their overalls and head cover by 1:30 to replace the people who go off at that time. The two women run the last block; it is already 1:30 and the gatekeeper is locking the gate.

Sunday Reflections

The next evening, Sunday, finds the family together in their room. Ma Deji is still in her "Sunday" clothes, a head-tie, blouse, and wrapper of finely-woven maroon *aṣọ òkè*.[13] She has just returned from two meetings. The first, at noon, was a prayer meeting, the women's section of the "Light of God Society." The second, at two, was the *Ẹgbẹ́ Ìlú Lójú*, which is open to all women from Ilu-Ijebu and women married (as is Ma Deji) to Ilu-Ijebu men.

The second meeting did not go very smoothly. Only a small fraction of those who are eligible are actually members of the association. Many of those who are members were absent today; those who did come spent most of the time trying to decide what to do about the others' lack of enthusiasm. Ma Deji left early to be home to cook supper.

Pa Deji is figuring out, on his fingers and with a "Ready Reckoner" booklet of arithmetic tables, how much the window frames and other wood that were ordered by the contractor early in the week will cost. He is happy to see that it will come in materials alone to about £116 ($325), for although he has not negotiated the final price of the work yet, the size of the job will mean a large profit for him, especially if he can cut his expected labor cost by having journeymen who will work well but also quickly. When he finishes his calculations he puts on a clean white *agbádá* (over-gown) and leaves to visit the home of his senior apprentice nearby.

While he is gone, talk turns to marriage and children. Deji was already on the way when Florence and Michael were married. Ma Deji explains that, in some cases, you spend a great deal of money on a costly marriage ceremony, and then discover you are childless. This can lead to suspicion that some people are against you,[14] and to quarreling and divorce as well. Since there were cases like this in her family, her mother had advised her to marry only after she became pregnant. This did not mean that she was promiscuous. Michael's marriage intentions were known, and he had given the appropriate betrothal money and gifts. Only the marriage ceremony itself had not yet taken place. Their plans were to get married about two years later, but the quick pregnancy moved the date up.

In fact, both of them had wanted to marry "by the ring," that is, according to British law (and sanctions). But his relatives were opposed, saying that to do so would prevent his taking a second wife if he wanted one. There was a brief argument at the time, but the couple gave in.

"Not that I mind him having a second wife. It's good companionship — unless it turns out like the woman downstairs always shouting her head off at her junior wife. Anyway, there's no money for a second wife, and besides, the Ilu-Ijebu Young Brothers [Michael's church-affiliated town development association] doesn't want its members to have two wives."

Pa Deji returns while the others are eating. The meal is not any different from usual in content or service, but, because it is Sunday, there is enough meat in the sauce for everyone to have two large pieces.

At the end of the meal, the radio of the man in the next room starts blaring a church service. It is loud enough to hear clearly. Pa Deji makes notes of all the Biblical texts quoted, for later re-reading. On quiet evenings he sometimes reads to himself from his Bible. Still later, Boṣẹ makes Pa Deji's bed up with a fresh sheet, and puts Olu and Wọle on it to sleep. Later they will be moved to a double reed mat on the floor. Ma Deji retires to her bed early, and by 10:30 everyone is either sleeping, or dozing where (s)he sits.

Biography: Michael Odusanya

Michael *Adétọlá* Odusanya[15] was born in Ilu-Ijebu on April 21, 1933. His father was a Christian born around 1901, who had gone to primary school and then migrated to Lagos, where he became a railway clerk, but also learned and practiced English tailoring in his off hours. Before Michael was born he had returned home to marry, and while keeping up his tailoring trade he also became the Anglican primary school headmaster. Michael's mother, from the same town, sold dried fish and *gàrí* (cassava meal), and did well enough at it to support herself and her only living child, Michael, when the senior Odusanya died three years after Michael's birth. Although there was some pressure put upon her to marry her deceased husband's younger brother,[16] neither she nor the brother's wife would hear of it. She has remained in her husband's family compound to this day.

Michael started school late, in 1944, and his mother managed to pay his school fees right through to Standard VI (sixth grade). He took entry examinations for secondary school, but his father's brother advised him instead to go and learn a trade. At first he did not want to do so, and he taught primary school for a term. But his uncle persisted, and arranged to have Michael go to Ibadan, where he stayed with an older cousin on his mother's side.

This cousin discussed careers with Michael, and they decided together that he should learn carpentry. A friend from home was apprenticed to a carpenter who was from a small town not far from Ilu-Ijebu, and Michael signed on as well. His mother paid the five guineas ($14.70) "tuition" fee for the three-year apprenticeship. He finally stayed four years instead of three, gaining his "freedom" in 1956, at the age of 23. He was in his own room by then (in the house where his future wife was also staying), though his mother sent him the rent and he continued to eat with his cousin.

His own master was head carpenter for a large-scale Ijebu building contractor, and hired Michael on at the end of his apprenticeship. The pay was low, though, only four or five pounds ($11.20 - $14.00) a month. So he wrote an application to an Italian contracting firm operating in Ibadan, and was hired at £15 ($42) a month. At the same time he did odd work on the side, as he had opened a shop jointly with a friend after he got his "freedom."

Work at Palladino and Sons was eased by the number of machines for cutting, planing, drilling and the like. But it was also exacting in a human sense, with strictly kept hours, only two short breaks during a workday that lasted from 7 a.m. to 4 p.m., and little feeling of or hope for self-advancement. As soon as he had enough work to keep him going on his own, he dropped the salaried job entirely. Now, four years later, he thinks he makes a net profit for himself of about £25 ($70) a month, though he does not have a bookkeeping system which allows him to tell very accurately. He is sure, though, that he spends more carefully than when he was on a salary, since he is never sure when his next few pounds will come in.

Biography: Florence Odusanya

Florence *Ayòdélé* Odusanya is six years younger than her husband. Born in 1939 in a large village south of the Ijebu capital, she is also of a sturdily Anglican family. It was her grandfather who gave the land on which the village church was built. When Florence was a child her father had two wives, and he has added a third since she herself got married. In all there were nine children born to her mother, but only two remain alive. Her mother does some trading in rice and beans, buying in Ibadan (rice comes through a long-distance trade route from the north), and selling in small markets in the villages near her own. Florence's father farms, but also buys and sells a little cloth.

Florence finished the six grades of primary school when she was fifteen, and immediately went to Lagos, where she clerked in the shop of a male cousin of her mother's in return for room, board and £1. 5s. 0d. ($3.50) a month. She wanted to go on in school, but there was not enough money for her to do so.

At Christmas the following year she visited Ibadan and stayed with her father's brother. A friend of hers from home had a job at the Nigerian Tobacco Company, and was earning three times as much as she was. In those days the personnel man just walked along the lineup of applicants at the company gate and chose new employees by looking at them. Florence went one morning, and was selected. After ten years at the company she is earning £17 ($47.60) a month taking finished cigarettes off the machines for packaging. She is one of only a few hundred industrial workers in Ibadan, and considers herself lucky to have such a (relatively) large and steady income.

Michael was living in the same house as her uncle. He would come up to visit now and then, but was impressively reserved and soft-spoken. At the same time, she says, several much more active suitors were around, too. Thus, when Michael proposed to her, she was both surprised and overwhelmed. She didn't answer immediately, but communicated with her mother at home. In return her mother asked for the name of the boy, his parents' names and their home town. Next her mother came to Ibadan to meet Michael and, when they discovered that the two mothers often met at rural markets and liked one another, the young couple knew that family consent would be forthcoming. Many months, dowry payments, betrothal ceremonies, gifts, and promises later, they were married in a brief ceremony at Michael's paternal home and blessed at the church — three months after Deji's birth.

Biographical Note: The Children

After Deji, who was born at home in Florence's village, all the children were born at the general hospital in Ibadan. All four have been quite healthy, except for a case of chicken pox each, and various sores and· rashes like the one presently afflicting Wole. An only child himself, Michael is determined to have as many children as he can: he feels strongly the lack of immediate family. (In fact one reason for his family's rejection of a church marriage was the possibility that he might not have children who survived him unless he remained open to a second or third wife.) He does, however, claim to practice the Yoruba family planning technique of not resuming sexual relations with his wife until more than a year after each new baby. It is likely now that the Odusanyas will have six, seven, or more children before their family is completed.

The Compound

By that time they will have even further outgrown their present lodgings. Right now they manage only barely. With seven-year-old Sola away, five members of the family are only the core of the household living in, or out of, their one large room. Bọsẹ, the maid, sleeps on the floor with the children. Three boys, all brothers and the sons of Florence's father's younger sister, sleep in the hallway or on the open porch outside the room. Except for an occasional meal, however, they otherwise are rarely at "home." One has a job as a carpenter, having learned the trade from Pa Deji. The other two are apprentices, one to a barber and one to a mechanic. And two other boys, Pa Deji's kinsmen and apprentices, also sleep in the hallway and store their few possessions in the room. They eat with another relative who lives not far away.

While this residential density is extreme, the whole building is crowded. In the old cement-plastered brick building are sixteen rooms, four on each side of a center hallway, upstairs and down. At least sixty-six people live there, and, at that, four rooms are occupied by bachelors living alone. In no case, on the other hand, are two or more nuclear families sharing a single room. Of the fourteen heads of households (two households occupy two rooms each), ten are Ijebu and four are Ẹgba Yoruba. Only one marriage is "mixed" in the Yoruba sense, that of an Ẹgba Yoruba printer to an Ijebu Yoruba wife. The overall density (and the resultant difficulty in keeping the compound and the public ways tidy), and the density of Ijebus in this one building are typical of this old area of migrant settlement.

Despite the crowding, the down-at-the-heels appearance of the area, and the lack of amenities — there is one public water tap for a score of houses, the pathway is not motorable, and the hallways have no electricity — turnover in the neighborhood is low, because the rents are lower than in newer areas. Michael Odusanya pays only £1. 5s. 0d. ($3.50) a month for his family's large room, where they have lived for eight years. In fact they could afford better lodging, but prefer the convenience of the house to their places of work and the familiarity of old neighbors.

The Room

The room itself, though, shows its intensive use. Lining the walls are two single beds, Ma Deji's partitioned off from the room by a blue curtain attached to the ceiling. The third wall, which is the front of the house, projects outward, and has three windows, fitted not with glass but only with outer wooden shutters. One of these, nearest the bed, is never opened, and is darkened by three posters announcing the Military Government. Between, and partially blocking, the other two windows is a tall dresser in which most of the family's clothing is stored. Against the last wall are two soft-cushioned chairs, a small table, and two folding chairs. The open floor space remaining (where the children sleep at night on mats) is about ten by twelve feet.

Window sills, dresser and table top are covered with bottles of commercial remedies and cosmetics, packages of mosquito coils and margarine, shoes and more bottles, a few religious books and pamphlets, a notebook, photo album and writing pad, dishes and cups. Under the beds are the wooden boxes with the belongings of the young relatives in them, and the best clothing of the family, as well as a large can where the staple gari meal is stored. The walls are decorated with school-leaving certificates, Michael's certificate of apprenticeship, Ma Deji's citation for ten years' continuous employment, eight large calendars featuring advertisements for various merchants or pictures of town improvement associations, and framed pictures of each member of the family including Michael's mother. All of this is lit by a single red bulb in the center of the ceiling, and a long fluorescent bulb hung over the table for reading purposes. With the exception of Michael's bicycle, his tools at the shop, a few items in the kitchen stall in the yard, and a small chest of goods outside their door on the porch that the Odusanyas use, these are the family possessions.

Summary

Although their material circumstances are thus meager, their health, their excellent relations with townsmen in Ibadan and with their families and kin at home, and their steady jobs give them a strong sense of security and well-being. They are confident that Deji and his younger siblings will do well at school; Pa Deji sees his trade expanding despite the growth in the number of carpenters in the city; and Ma Deji looks forward to ten or fifteen more years with the company before she is given a watch, six months' retirement pay, and let go. With a humility that comes both from small-town origins and from a Victorian Christian commitment to modesty and manners, the Odusanyas are slowly building a stable and respectable future.

Discussion: Kin, Neighbors, and the Household

Family and Kinsmen. The Odusanya family is enmeshed in at least four separate networks of social relations, respectively involving kinsmen, neighbors, friends and acquaintances, and workmates and customers. In their home towns, as indeed in most non-urban societies throughout the world, the separability of these networks would not now or in the past have been nearly so great. There, the extended family compound, where other individuals were simultaneously kinsmen, neighbors and workmates, was the basic building-block of both the physical and the social structure of the community. Of course the closure was not complete, especially in the centuries-old Yoruba urban tradition. Political associations, trade and marketing, and friendship as well as warfare drew people together who were not kin. But modern migrants approach the other extreme: although *some* workmates, for example, may also be neighbors or kin (Ma Akin, or Pa Deji's apprentices for example), by and large the various networks consist of different sets of individuals.

Some works on urbanization or social change represent this situation as the "destruction of the old, solidary bonds of kinship," or some such negatively evaluative phrase. For migrant Ijebus the case is not at all so clear. On the one hand migrants could live among their kinsmen in the same city if they desired to do so, since the housing supply is great enough to permit choice. Significantly, however, neither the Odusanyas nor *any* of a hundred other migrant adults I interviewed lived in the same house as a close kinsmen — someone he or she would live with at home — unless one was a partially or wholly dependent widow or unmarried youth. One is tempted to turn the original assumption about the positive value of kin solidarity on its head, and to ask instead what it is in the traditional village situation that constrains kinsmen to live and act *together!*

On the other hand, moreover, the Odusanyas are still very much kin-oriented. Their own nuclear family is, obviously, very much intact. They have five young relatives presently living with them, of whom Michael has provided occupational training for three, and yet other relatives have stayed with them in the past. Meanwhile they themselves have sent first Deji and now Sola to stay ·with Michael's mother in Ilu-Ijebu in order both to be of help around the house to her and to gain for the child small-town virtue and discipline. Ma Deji's father cultivates a piece of land he bought for her, though she has now directed the proceeds toward her younger half-brother's education; in a return gesture Ma Deji sends home the two free cartons of cigarettes she is given at the factory every month for her grandmother to sell for pure profit. Letters and verbal messages, containing much advice or request, pass frequently through travellers to and from the rural area. And one or both the adults travel home as often as once a month to see to some family business, spiritual, or personal affair, often giving several pounds in cash to each of several relatives when they go. The frequency, the complexity, and the willing undertaking of these activities attest to a continuing vitality of kinship bonds despite the departure from the intensity of traditional kin group interaction.

Perhaps the dominant theme of contemporary urban kinship behavior is the relative freedom of choice that now underlies it. People *can* choose these days to ignore their kinsmen, though neither the Odusanyas nor most other Ijebu migrants choose to do so. We shall see other uses made of kinship in subsequent chapters.

Neighbors and Privacy. Neighborly interaction in the city evinces a strong

sense of living under public scrutiny. This second theme of urban life arises
vividly from the foregoing episodes in the Odusanyas' lives. It is a carry-over
from the intense interaction of the kinsmen and co-wives of the traditional
compound. The following description was given, by the late sociologist N.A.
Fadipẹ, of extended family life in the rural compound fifty years ago, but it
might apply almost equally to the Odusanyas and other Ijebu migrants today:

> A large part of the day is spent in the open . . . . everyone eats and drinks
> and talks in the full view of everybody else; and as the rooms are hot in the
> day-time . . . , most of the life of the compound has to be passed on the open
> verandah [now, in the yard]. . . . quarrels and rebukes take place within the
> full hearing of neighbors . . . each individual's weaknesses and vices are
> open to the observation of the other[s]. . . . People outside the immediate
> family are interested in its members and their welfare. . . . This makes
> exclusive family life in the Western sense impossible. Only a limited amount
> of privacy is possible . . . (1970:101-102).

There has always been, of course, an etiquette governing life in the
compound, and it continues with but minor adjustment. Husbands can
discipline their wives, and mothers their children, without the intervention of
neighbors — unless the punishment, in *their* eyes, exceeds the crime. A woman
who is sensitive to criticism of her children by others will be left alone, though
liked the less for her touchiness. A younger person of whatever age in the urban
compound will obey any elder without bridling, will tolerate his idiosyncrasies,
and may seek his advice, voicing disapproval only by seeking out another elder
to mediate on his behalf. When Adunni calls Pa Deji ''our husband'' during the
exchange recounted at the beginning of this chapter, she brings into focus
through her use of humor the tension between the shifting relationships of
neighbors (''our husband'' is the correct term of reference between traditional
neighbors, who were co-wives as well), and the continuing inter-familial
intimacy of the urban migrant compound.

Probably the major change in the interaction of neighbors parallels that
among kinsmen. It consists of the *possibility* of privacy, which is available in
the Odusanyas' house especially to those without families, and to other
migrants in the city who want to keep to themselves and can afford either to rent
an entire floor (four or more rooms) of a building, or to rent or build a small
house on the sparsely settled fringe of the town. Few avail themselves of this
potential secretiveness, in part because the personality characteristics that
would lead to it are discouraged from the outset of one's life. But the choice is
there.

Managing the Household. Within these two networks, of kin and of neighbors, the urban household is a discrete entity, which has relatively more solidarity (and the stresses that go with solidarity) than it would have in the home town. Men's and women's roles and activities there are more distinct than they are in the city (but much less suffused by values of male superiority than in many other cultures in Africa, the Middle East, and elsewhere). For example, if Ma Deji needed to be away from home in a village situation as much as she does, other female compound-mates would see to the children. In Ibadan Pa Deji adjusts his schedule of eating and shop hours to the demands of his wife's factory job, and looks after the children more directly. As well, the couple shares financial responsibilities more cooperatively than in the traditional situation, where their purses would have remained separate, the husband providing shelter, tools, medicine, school fees and major items of clothing, and the wife the food and the minor utensils, school items, and everyday clothing. The monogamous family has probably always implied less segregation of roles and activities by sex than the polygynous one, but the migrants blur the differentiation even more. Finally, while Michael and Florence attend meetings, go visiting, and sometimes travel home independently, they and other migrant couples spend more time with one another and with their children than do their counterparts at home: their own room structures more nuclear family activity in this sense than do the small, dark, sometimes windowless sleeping rooms of the rural compound.

The Odusanyas, thus, have a joint domestic venture. Michael's income pays for the rent and electricity, his own clothing, Deji's tutoring, meals at the shop, association dues, gifts and remittances to kinsmen, and reinvestment in his small business. In addition, he gives his wife £8 ($22.40) each month as "chop money," that is, for basic food supplies. Florence's £17 ($47.60) per month income covers: additional food expenditures, especially on ready-cooked food sold by itinerant hawkers and some neighbors for meals when nothing has been prepared at home, and for lunches at the factory for herself; Bose's salary, £1. 5s. 0d., or $3.50 a month; clothing and school needs for the children; other household items like soap, firewood, and cosmetics; her own gifts and remittances to relatives at home; and £4 or £5 ($11.20 to $14.00) in savings for major clothing purchases, or a trip home. Florence and Michael each supply the money for their own relatives, but they discuss mutually all the major amounts that they are planning to send or take.

They thus cover all their needs and have some discretionary income as well. But their comfort is only relative, and the sheer need for food dominates their budget. Like most Nigerian families, they spend more on food than on anything else. A consumer survey carried out in Ibadan by the Nigerian Federal Office of Statistics in 1961/62 indicated that low income households in the city spent more than 60 per cent of their total incomes on food, drink, and related items, while households of middle income (from £450-£1200 [$1260 to $3360]) wage earners spent about 40 per cent of their income on the same items.[17] (North American families, by contrast, spend only about 20 per cent of their income on food.) Though the Odusanyas, who would have been classified in this survey as being of borderline low to middle income, do not calculate their expenditures very exactly, it is probable that they spend about 38 per cent of their income, £16 ($44.80) per month, on food. If Ma Deji worked at some trade at home, she could save part of that expenditure, as well as dispense with her need for a nurse, but her steady and sizeable income makes these costs worthwhile.

Further, their gifts to relatives are not without relation to fairly basic needs of their own. Although they do not conceive it so in direct terms, their continuing contact and assistance provides them virtually the only potential social welfare insurance they can count upon, since they have no long-term savings. If anyone in the family, but especially Michael or Florence, had a serious illness, if Michael lost his business, if Florence were laid off, or if someone in the family were accidentally to die, the limited government medical service available for short-term care would be the only substantial assistance the Odusanyas would get from anyone besides their home-town relatives. Even in desperate circumstances they could find no relief from government or voluntary agencies, which simply do not exist except in rudimentary form. Seen in these terms, the network of kin ties is one that most urban families cannot easily afford to give up. Here, as in many situations in many cultures, people enjoy doing some things that they almost have to do in any case.

Footnotes

[1] Actually Yoruba families live not so much "in" their rooms as "from" them. Much of the daily routine takes place in the back courtyard, in front of the house, in the hallway or on an open balcony.

[2] The Yoruba system of personal address uses *teknonymy* to indicate the respect due parents. Ordinarily friends, neighbors, and spouses call one another "Mother (or Father) of (their oldest child's name)." For "mother" and "father" these days, either the Yoruba terms *"ìyá"* and *"bàbá"* (*"ba"* for short) or English "Mama" and "Papa" (or "Ma" and "Pa") may be used.

[3] In traditional Yoruba patrilineal (but see Lloyd 1967c) and patrilocal compounds, all the men (and sometimes their unmarried adult sisters) are formally "our husband" to the inmarrying spouses. The term of reference might be more accurately glossed, "member of the lineage we married into." Of course only legal form is signalled here, not behavioral reality, that is, no hint of group marriage is implied.

[4] The yam referred to here is the large white yam *Dioscorea rotundata*. Ma Deji suggests this particular food because preparing it requires very hard work. For Yoruba foods and cooking see Bascom (1951b and 1951c).

[5] The newest wife in a Yoruba polygynous family usually gets the heavy chores to do, and is at the beck and call of the senior wife or wives. To ensure least friction it is thus best to have the senior wives help select the junior ones.

[6]This is a stereotypical reference to the supposed super-sophistication of the Ẹgba people, who for various historical reasons have had the longest direct contact with European culture.

[7]Trust is an important principle in Yoruba society, where market stalls, houses, farms and other property are often left untended, unfenced or unlocked. Thievery is therefore a great threat. At one time a thief caught red-handed in a market might have been beaten to death on the spot.

[8]Pa Deji reveals a current belief that the army or the national police force will give service more impartially and with less petty corruption than the local police.

[9]The Yoruba division of the day is into four basic parts, morning, afternoon, evening, and night. The "evening" lasts from the first coolness of the afternoon, around four o'clock, until after sunset around eight.

[10]Ewedu is a leafy vegetable similar to spinach.

[11]Yoruba bargaining style is unusual, but only one of many in markets where bargaining is done. Transactions with Hausa traders, for example, follow a more widespread model, beginning with an initial price which is outrageously high, followed by an outrageously low offer by the buyer, and proceeding by steps toward the middle.

[12]Ileya is the Yoruba name for Id-el-Kabir, the Muslim New Year holiday.

[13]Aṣọ oke (literally "hill [i.e., up-country] cloth") is made on a narrow horizontal loom in strips up to fifty feet long by male weavers. Quality varies and patterns change in fashion.

[14]Ma Deji refers to the jealousy between co-wives and other rivals, and the fear of bewitchment or magical poisoning by them.

[15]Personal names, including surnames, follow a multiplicity of patterns among the Yoruba. Most have meanings related to situational or emotional circumstances of the family into which the child is born: hence *Ọlọ́runfúnmiláyọ̀*, "God gives me joy," or *Bàbátúndé*, "[The spirit of] father returns." A naming ceremony eight (in some places seven or nine) days after the birth is a major life cycle ceremony. At it anyone may ask for and be granted the privilege of giving the child a name, but the name that remains with the child is usually given by a parent or other close kinsman. Surnames, originally the father's personal name when they were first taken about a century ago, have now remained stable for from two to four generations, but people may still choose to use their own first name as their children's surname. Muslims use either Yoruba versions of Arabic names or Yoruba names; Christians are using fewer European first names now, as they earlier moved away from the taking of English surnames. Finally, nicknames, which are more frequently used than full versions both for children and adults, are halves of first names: *"Adétọ́lá"* may be "Ade" or "Tọla"; *"Yétúndé"* is usually "Tunde." (See also Johnson 1921:79-89.)

[16]This is termed the "levirate" technically. It operated regularly in Yoruba culture but was rarely forced on unwilling parties.

[17]Another survey showed that the percentage for Lagos low-income households was substantially lower than that for Ibadan, but in any case the pattern and the contrast with North America is clear. Further, the Nigerian surveys show that more than one-third of all food expenses go for staple starches and cooking oils alone. These calculations are based on the tables of the *Report on Enquiries Into the Income and Expenditure Patterns of Lower and Middle Income Households at Ibadan 1961/62 (UCS/1966/2),* and *at Lagos 1959/60,* published by the Chief Statistician, Federal Office of Statistics, Lagos.

CHAPTER V

Young Man on the Move: Tade Oyebanji

The Evening Routine

Tadé Oyèbánjí rests after work, reading a book entitled *Winston Churchill's Great War Speeches,* until six o'clock. Now he gets up to go to his older brother's house four blocks away. He selects a pair of white trousers and a gray turtleneck jersey from the closet, where only European-style clothing hangs. As he finishes, a bell on the campus of the Catholic girls' boarding school across the road sounds two weak notes.

"Sounds as if the bell man hasn't eaten for days!" he says. "That's six o'clock. Time for prayer. You can see all the girls running to the chapel as we go by."

On the way Tade sees one of the senior men in his department in the Ministry of Works and Transport drive by in his new white Peugeot. He remarks that the man has only the next certificate higher than the one Tade himself earned as a graduate, in plumbing, of the Trade Centre at Ijebu Ode. Yet he has a big salary while new graduates like Tade are making 13 s. 4 d. ($1.86) a day. It's because of this, he says, that some boys go into the contracting business on their own as soon as they graduate. They hope to get rich quickly, but sometimes they wind up with no patrons at all. So, Tade concludes, he's just as happy to start at the Ministry for now.

His brother lives in one of two buildings which are joined together by an arch and share a common yard. It is near the large tire retreading factory in the middle of the newer part of Oke Ado. On one side of the yard a small blackboard is propped on a stool against the wall. One of Tade's major jobs is to tutor several of the children of the compound — not only those of his brother — in their school work. And though he lives elsewhere, he is very much considered a member of this compound.

As soon as he arrives, therefore, two of the women sweep the area around the blackboard. After greeting the various people who are outside, Tade gets directly to the lessons. Today there are three pupils. A small girl learning English does an exercise on synonyms. A boy in the second grade is set to working on problems of changing shillings to pence and shillings to pounds. And another boy, who is going to try his secondary school entrance exams this year after fifth grade (instead of sixth), is given a series of long addition problems.

An Invitation Given

As Tade finishes assigning the work, a girl who lives in the house returns from the water tap down the street, sets her bucket down, and goes inside. Then a second girl, also sixteen or so, goes into the same room. Tade leaves the children and he, too, goes in. The second girl is sitting on a chair next to the bed.

"You said that I should be expecting a visit from you over the weekend," says Tade. "Not so?"

"Well, I came!" the girl replies.

"When was that?"

"On Saturday, and you weren't in."

"At what time?"

"It was about four o'clock."

"Ah," says Tade. "I was in then. If you had said five or six I might have believed you."

"Well . . . um . . . maybe I came at five or five thirty," says the girl, hesitating.

"Ha! So you were just guessing! I was out at four, but I came back right after that and I was home until seven! Well, all right, if you don't want to come there's nobody forcing you."

The subject is dropped there, and Tade goes back out to correct the papers. Then he eats supper, as he usually does, prepared by his brother's wife. It is gari with stewed meat today. Afterward he sets out toward home.

On the way he meets the same girl again, and he asks whether she is going to come or not. She says she can only get out between four and six. Tade tells her to name any day, and he will wait for her.

"What about your home lessons then?" inquires the girl.

"That can wait, but only if I'm sure you're coming. I don't want to wait at home for nothing."

The girl promises to come at six on Wednesday.

"OK, then. Goodnight," says Tade, remarking after she goes that he is sure now that she will come, and that he will be there. "It will only take a Seven Up to entertain her, and . . .," he adds, his thought trailing off.

Passing Time

The next day is Tuesday, and Tade changes his clothes as soon as he returns from the work site where he is supervising the laying of water pipes in a newly-expanding area of housing. He is going at once to the new Y.M.C.A., which has rented a small house with a large field behind, a few blocks past his brother's.

A few other youths are there when he arrives, some putting up a volleyball net, others playing table tennis inside. As soon as the net is up, the young coach, who has just been transferred from Lagos to this branch, calls everyone to play. During the game one of the oldest players, who is about twenty-five, cracks a joke in Ijebu dialect. Somebody asks if he is Ijebu, and he says yes. At that, others begin speaking Ijebu, and soon most are doing so. Tade, for some reason, doesn't join in.

"Too many Ijebus here," he mutters aloud.

After the game there is a meeting inside, in a room which is to become a library. The coach, who is in charge of programs, wants to increase participation and membership. Only a few of the older youths attend, and even then they have little to say.

At about six fifteen Tade decides he has had enough. Next door a juju band is practising. Tade, who had heard them perform at school, goes to listen for a while. In fact he has become friendly with one of the guitarists. An hour later he leaves for his brother's house, where he eats only a small loaf of bread, with a little leftover soup. Then he remembers that he wants to settle his accounts with the cooked-food seller nearby, and goes back to his own room to get the money.

The woman is a neighbor of his brother's, and trades in several kinds of cooked foods (steamed in leaves and sold in small cakes, or fried in pieces) which she carries at mid-day to the worksite of Tade's crew. She allows them credit by the week, keeping track in her head while Tade keeps a notebook and collects from the men. When he gets to his room, he tallies up the outstanding sum, nearly four pounds ($11.20). He takes it from a box in the closet and goes to the woman's house. She checks the sum and says that there is still three shillings (42¢) missing. Tade promises to make it up the following week.

When he returns home again, a fellow tenant sticks his head in to say hello.

"How, *Adébáyò*!" he calls.

"Ojukwu, how!" Tade shoots back. The boy is Ibo, and they jokingly call one another by the names of the military governors of their respective regions.

On hearing this exchange, another Ibo man comes out of his room across the hall to discuss the month's high electricity bill. The landlord simply hands the bill, which is calculated from a single meter, to one of the older tenants and lets those who live in the house decide who owes what. Tade rebuffs him, saying that he has neither a radio nor any other appliance which consumes electricity.

Tade's roommate *Túndé,* who is from a neighboring town and was a schoolmate at the Trade Centre, has bought some new film magazines. Tade reads them until about eleven o'clock, when he retires.

The Invitation Accepted

The following day is Wednesday — the big day! At half past four Tade is sleeping, while Tunde is on his bed reading a letter from a friend who went to Northern Nigeria to look for work and has now found a job after only two weeks. An hour later the boy who collects the rent for the lawyer who owns the house comes in. Tade and Tunde share equally the £2. 10s. 0d. ($7.00) monthly rent. This is double what the Odusanyas pay, but the house is new, is on a major street, has a water tap in the yard and a flush toilet for each floor, and is airy and clean.

"Oh, you've come for your money? Well, your money is ready, but first you must do something about that," says Tade, pointing to a corner of the ceiling. "The toilet upstairs is leaking, and that's dangerous to our health. When you fix it, you can come collect your money."

"Last time you complained about something . . ." begins the boy.

"Yes, of course!" Tade interrupts, shouting. "We must! Don't you know that £2. 10s. 0d. is difficult to earn?"

There are two knocks at the door, and the girl Tade is waiting for comes in. She isn't surprised by the crowd in the room, nor does she get shy and wait outside, as some girls would. Tade gives her a picture album to look at and a place to sit on the bed while he finishes with the rent collector. Soon everyone else finds one excuse or another to leave.

About forty-five minutes later the room is quiet. It is hard to tell whether anyone is there. Then the girl says something about pictures — the goal is still a long way off.

Another hour passes, and Tade is just going back to his room after seeing the girl off.

"I don't care anyway! Let her go — I don't have to count on her. My girl friend is at Ifẹ." Tade anticipates the questions. He says he asked, but she said no, and he didn't press it. He will write in his diary that the first time she came, he asked her for "something" and she didn't give him that "something." His tone indicates that perhaps he was a bit afraid to try anything.

Road Work

A couple of days later Tade is at work supervising the trench-digging for the pipes. He himself is sitting in front of an unfinished building reading today's newspaper. A long line of about forty men, mostly from Ibadan though there are some Ijebus, Hausas, and Ibos as well, is stretched down the side of the road, working with picks and shovels. Tade goes down the line every half hour to correct their side lines and to make sure the trench is deep enough. He rarely shouts or quarrels. At one point he asks one of the youngest laborers, who seems about the same age — twenty-two — as Tade, to get him a drink from a nearby house. The worker goes immediately — Tade is the boss here — but comes back saying that the tap is dry.

"Ah, well," says Tade. "That's why we're laying these new pipes. Thank you. You can go back to work now, or do you want to rest a bit?"

The man readily agrees. Shortly, the owner of the house where they are sitting comes to see how his workers are doing. The house is being wired for electricity today, and the electrician's apprentices are calling one another by the various Nigerian military leaders' names. No one wants to take the unpopular ones' names, though, nor those of the ones who were killed in the second coup a few months earlier. So "Gowon," "Adebayo," "Ojukwu," "Wey," and others call to each other as they run the wires back and forth.

As the owner gets ready to go, Tade approaches him. "Sir, if you want the plumbing job here done soon, I think I can do it if you will try me. I would have the men open the trench right there, and it will save you problems later."

The man says that that is all right, but that he has a brother who is a plumber and to whom he has already promised the work. But perhaps Tade can do part of it. He will discuss it the next time he comes.

After he leaves, Tade remarks that obviously the man doesn't mean to see him again if he has someone already. In any case, he has tried, and will in this way gradually build himself a business outside his regular job.

Some of the workers finish before noon. "Baba Kano" inspects their work as they complete it. He is a Hausa man and was a moderately successful contractor, but he squandered his money on liquor and women, and lost his business besides. Now he gets an ordinary £14 ($39.20) a month as a foreman. "Money comes in a man's direction only once in life. If you don't make use of it that once, then you've lost your chance,'' Tade philosophizes on the case.

In the afternoon the men finish by about 3:30, and sit around until the end of their day at four o'clock. At ten to four they begin to go.

"It isn't four yet; don't go," Tade warns good-naturedly. "You know that guy from headquarters. He could leave his car way up the road and walk down here, and if he sees that you are gone. . . .''

Nobody takes any notice of what he is saying. Within minutes everyone is gone, and Tade, too, sets off for home. On the way one of the oldest of the laborers, a man about fifty, comes up and asks to carry Tade's record book and tape measure. Tade says that he can manage, but the man persists, and over Tade's objections takes the items from him. This inversion of Yoruba seniority patterns, while common enough in modern work situations where deference is a function of the relative statuses of the job, is nonetheless discomforting to anyone raised with proper Yoruba respect for the hallowed status that comes with age.[1] The older man walks ahead of Tade all the way home.

That evening Tade and Pa *Bólánlé,* an Ijebu produce inspector friend who lives upstairs, attend a spy film starring Dean Martin at the Lebanese-owned theater across town.

Turbulence

When they return, Tade doesn't feel like staying home, even though the radio is broadcasting the transcript of the Aburi conference, held in Ghana by Nigeria's military leaders to discuss the deteriorating national political situation. Instead, he walks over to his brother's. As soon as he arrives, his brother comes down from his room in an angry mood. Trouble between his elder daughter and her first cousin, who lives with them, has developed into trouble between his daughter and himself.

"Tade, good evening. *Yemi* has done something very serious today, and I won't forgive her for it. She says that her friend *Bisi* was insulting your friend here [the anthropologist's research assistant], saying that he watches things like he has never seen them before and then writes things down. Yemi told her not to say things like that, but Bisi wouldn't stop. Anyway, it developed into a fight this morning when they both went to draw water. When Bisi slapped her, Yemi grabbed hold of her dress and wouldn't let go. Everybody passing by begged her, but she wouldn't listen. Her mother went: same result. Now, if you were fighting and I sent my hat with someone to the place[2] asking you to stop, you would, wouldn't you? Well, I did even more, I went to the balcony and called 'Yemi, Yemi, Yemi!' At first she pretended not to hear, and when she did look at me she still would not let go of the girl's dress. That really got me mad. Does a child like that recognize me as her father? I beat her quite well afterwards, but it didn't smother all the anger in me. So I have decided what to do. I'll send her home to the village. Let her grow up there — I don't care what becomes of her. . . ."

"That I won't support," Tade cuts in. "If she goes, she'll only get wilder. And while her friends here get good training, she'll have nothing. And you know, whatever she becomes, she'll always be Oyebanji's daughter."

Pa Yẹmi emphasizes the seriousness of the offence, but Tade asks him to cool off, and says that he'll come tomorrow to help decide what to do. On Tade's way out, his sister-in-law (Ma Yẹmi) tells her version of the story. Part of the fight was over who had drawn less water, and Yẹmi wouldn't stop fighting because she knew she was in the wrong. Nonetheless, Ma Yẹmi does not think she should be sent away. Tade says again that he will come tomorrow, and heads home.

A Solution for Yẹmi

The next evening Tade heads for his brother's house with a plan. He tells Pa Yẹmi that Yẹmi should come to stay with him for a while, because he thinks she will obey him and mend her rebellious ways. Ma Yẹmi supports this idea, and after a long discussion, Pa Yẹmi agrees. He is quite serious about the degree to which he is upset by the headstrong behavior of his daughter.

"Let her go with Tade, then, but if she comes back here and repeats anything like this, watch out. Either I'll bundle both her and her mother out of here, or I'll stop the girl's schooling. OK?" He tells his wife to call Yẹmi and announce her punishment.

Just then the driver of one of the two taxis that Pa Yẹmi owns comes in with the day's earnings, just over £3 (around $9.00).

"Why this little?" crackles Pa Yẹmi, who has obviously been approached at a bad moment.

The driver, an Ibadan man with long "tribal marks" (actually lineage-related facial scars) on his cheeks and temples, begins to make excuses.

"All right, all right," says Pa Yẹmi. "I know you cannot do without taking some of the money. Just remember that I drive, too, sometimes, and I know how much I bring home when I do. They say the hunter who sacrifices after killing an antelope doesn't do it because of that antelope, but because of others he wants to kill later. I'm just telling you this because tomorrow I don't want to see as little as this. Do you understand me?"

Later Pa Yẹmi drives Tade home in one of his cabs.

Sunday Boredom

On Sunday Tade is getting ready for church. Though he does not much like Catholicism (he had run-ins with the priests at school and confided once that he would rather be an Anglican), he goes across to the girl's school nearly every week to attend mass. The service is a long one, in part because the priest's English is translated into both Yoruba and Ibo as he goes along.

Tade gets a newspaper on the way home, and prepares a big breakfast for himself, with the help of Yẹmi, who has now moved in with him. Though some people prefer certain foods at certain meals, most basic Yoruba dishes may be taken at any meal. Tade has rice and beans, with a meat sauce, remarking that he likes ẹwa (the bean dish) so much that he tries to have it for one meal every day.

After eating he lies down to read the newspaper, and soon falls asleep. At one o'clock he wakes, has a drink of water, and drops off again until almost six.

Youthful Fantasies

Three days later Tade comes home early from work with a headache. He lies down, checking over his men's attendance register rather vaguely. After a while a boy comes, inviting him to join Tunde for a meal at the home of a friend of Tunde's, a police force carpenter from the same town. There is pounded yam, and the two roommates are happy not to have to cook for themselves or to buy their food. In fact Tade prepares his own meal only about once a week, since he has breakfast and lunch at work and usually eats dinner at his brother's. The policeman talks about a large radio-phonograph he wants to buy, if only he can win something with his ''coupons.'' These are from the large-scale gambling pool operations, based on British soccer league play, that Levantine entrepreneurs operate out of store-front betting offices all over Nigeria. One policeman, he says, won £1,500 ($4,200) last week. He wore his uniform when he went to collect his winnings so that the proprietors would not swindle him somehow, as it is believed they often try to do.

After dinner Tade stops at a friend's house to pick up some exam question papers he will use in tutoring his pupils. On their way home the two roommates pass two Ijebu girls, cooked food hawkers, sitting at the side of the road. Tunde points to one of them.

''That one — they say she's a real horse. And that's true. Just look at her and you can tell. Of course I've never ridden her, but she's a horse anyway.''

Tade says he pities her mother or whoever it is who thinks the girls are out selling her wares, because they are obviously not getting anything done. The trouble with such girls is, he feels, that they think they are ready for marriage, but probably aren't. So they paint themselves ridiculously to attract men. And men are crazy enough to fall for such fakery.

"Of course, if I had anything that runs on gas," he continues with bravado, "I'd be a ladies' man, too. I would get a place on the outskirts of town, and once a girl follows you down there . . . well, that's the point of no return!"

At lessons later, Tade has six pupils. One lad about eight protests that he should be doing second grade work, not first. When he then spells every word from the harder list wrong, Tade sends for a cane to punish him. But the boy cries so hard before the cane even arrives that Tade relents. The lessons this evening do not end until 9:30.

Heading home again with a friend who comes to his brother's to meet him, Tade suddenly turns away to follow a girl up the road.

"She said she knew what I wanted to say," Tade relates excitedly when he comes back fifteen minutes later. "I said she couldn't have guessed. She said it wasn't any different from what other people like me rush after a girl for. I said perhaps men rush at her to ask her to marry them. She said no, they wouldn't do that all at once. So I said, 'See, you're wrong about knowing what I wanted. It so happens that I'm looking for a wife and I think you meet my requirements!' She laughed, and said she had to go inside. I said that that was too bad, because I could have shown her where I live, but then, as long as I knew her house I could come over another time to ask for her. She asked me where my house was — but in such a condescending way that I couldn't think of a better answer than to tell her that everyone's home is in heaven.

"Anyway, I asked her name. She told me so readily I didn't believe her. She said of course it was true, that you don't have to think for an hour before you remember your name! I saw where she lived, and said I'd see her tomorrow."

The full recitation lasts all the way home, where Tunde is washing some clothes. Tade is restless now, and decides to walk the few blocks to Oke Ado market to buy some fried fish to have with a late evening snack. It is after eleven when he returns. The next day there is no further mention of the girl.

Conversations

On Saturday Tunde's friend *Débólá* is listening to the afternoon sports news on the radio so that he can hear the pools results. Tade comes in from outside and asks how many tied games there were (picking the 'draws' is one method of playing the pools).

"I don't know, but you've won nothing," says Debola, smiling.

"How could I, anyway? I don't play the pools," Tade responds.

"Ah, you forget I got one ticket for you last time — I staked two and six [35¢]!" Debọla laughs.

"Oh, that, forget about that."

"Forget?" Debọla stops laughing. "What about my two and six?"

Tunde enters from the yard and also asks how many draws there were. They all go across the hall to check with the man there, who copies the results down carefully every week.

"Only eleven draws!" Tade exclaims. "Those Lebanese have their prayers answered this week! They'll go to Ọja Ọba tomorrow to buy goats — you know they always celebrate a week of low payoffs with goats' meat."

A few minutes later Tade decides to go to his brother's. He finds him just finishing a shower bath, about to go up to put some medicine on a boil.

When Pa Yẹmi comes back down, the conversation turns to politics. They note that the present military governor of the Western Region is now making tours around the countryside, which is what the first military leader of the country was doing when he was killed. They talk again of the civilian politicians who were toppled by the military men the year before, and are still awed by the excesses of their regime. Pa Yẹmi says that there was one useful thing that the sheer excess did — it destroyed such confidence in the government that the coup, and then the commissions of inquiry into the politicians' scandalous behavior, could take place. Now they've found one man who owned six private cars worth £6,000 ($16,800) each, and another who in one year put into his "savings" account at the bank three times as much as he earned.

Then they recall the story of how the Midwestern Region was formed in 1964.[3] It is said that the Prime Minister didn't want to give in to the movement to carve the Midwest out of the West, despite the entreaties of his good friend and minister of finance who wanted the new region created. So, the story goes, Okotie Eboh, the minister and a spectacularly flamboyant man, went to the North to see the premier of that region, who was held to be the power behind the national government. When he arrived he began to cry. He said he was suffering, that his people wanted a state of their own and the Prime Minister wouldn't let them. The Northern premier, the Sardauna of Sokoto, laughed, and asked if that was all. Okotie Eboh said yes. The Sardauna said if so, then everything was all right and Okotie Eboh should come to eat. The latter said that he could not, because his heart was heavy. The Sardauna again said not to worry, that the Midwest was being created at that very moment. And within a few minutes a call to the Prime Minister in Lagos turned a week later into the public announcement of a plebescite for the Midwest.

There is not much talk about current politics, but Pa Yẹmi thinks that Colonel

Ojukwu, in the East, is going too far in his confrontations with the national government, while he thinks that the military governor of the North is being so obstinate that he is hindering the military government from working out its internal disputes.

Tade eats supper and stays at his brother's until late in the evening. At home he finds Tunde lamenting the ''loss'' of the table fan he had hoped to buy with his pools winnings this week. Tade laughs, and turns in early.

Comic Relief

Yẹmi is still sleeping at Tade's, although she eats and plays after school at her own home. On Monday she takes the key to school with her, so ''Ojukwu,'' the Ibo boy across the hall, invites Tade in.

''Take seat, and come and chop [eat],'' he says in Pidgin English.

Soon Tunde and Pa Bọlanle also arrive home from work, and everyone crowds into ''Ojukwu's'' room. Pa Bọlanle is a naturally funny fellow, and he and Ojukwu start to mimic the popular radio comedians who are on every Sunday. In a multilingual situation like Nigeria, language — both communication and miscommunication — provides an endless source of humor. The subject this time is Pidgin English, the lingua franca in much of southern Nigeria of those without much schooling.[4]

''One time Baba Rebecca was talking about his barber,'' Pa Bọlanle begins. ''He said, 'This man came inside my room. I asked him what do you want? He said him be barber. So I told him, so? You be baba, make I run? I be baba, too, look Rebecca na me born am. . . .' ''

''Ojukwu'' takes over, repeating another bit.

''One time I just de see people for our office get leave [vacation]. I thought they get 'leaf.' I no know say na leave them get. So I went to my boss, I say, 'Sa [sir], I want get my leaf, too.' He said abi [what!], I demand? I tol' am make 'e siddown for there, na signature to make. He just hear yet and he done start dance, say when I play the 'real music.' So I play the 'real music' by going to nearby bush to cut one big leaf, come show am to boss as my own 'leaf'!''

A Crisis Defused

Tade gets up to go, as Yẹmi has come with the key. Later he visits the Y.M.C.A. briefly, then suddenly remembers that he wants to go and see Tunde's girl friend. She is probably pregnant, and has promised to tell Tade the whole story. Whether or not Tunde will be named as the father is still unknown. The house is not far from the Odusanyas.

There are two girls on the balcony. The younger, about seventeen and quite good looking, is the one involved. At first the conversation drifts aimlessly, the older girl doing most of the talking. When an abstract question about the proper age for marriage arises, the garrulous sister says, "Let's ask Mr. Tunde!" And indeed Tunde is on his way up the stairs.

Finally, since the conversation is getting nowhere, Tade and Tunde both decide to go. But once outside the girls call Tade aside alone, and stop next to a shed to talk secretly. It is an hour before they finish, and Tunde is waiting down the path nervously. As soon as he comes up, Tade says, "I was sort of chairman there, but there was no chair. . . ."

"Cut out the jokes. What happened?" pleads Tunde.

"Why didn't you come and hear it yourself?"

"Did any of you three invite me?"

"Who needs to invite anybody to a discussion about himself and his wife?" Tade taunts his friend.

"No, no! Don't start that, o!" cries Tunde.

Tade says it took a long time for the girl, Ṣọla, to get to the point. She talked of the times Tunde came, of what they used to talk about, of how he invited her to his place — and then, Tade relates, she went mute. The chattering girl suggested that he simply ask her if she is in fact pregnant.

And, to Tade's great surprise, Ṣọla said she wasn't. It turned out that it was her father who believed she might be, and started spreading the rumor to shame her. The older of the girls said she advised Ṣọla in any case that, if Tunde believed her father without seeing her, he must not love her and must only be using her for his own pleasure.

"I told them that there is a proverb that says you don't ask a farmer what he is planting, because sooner or later everyone will see it growing anyway," concludes Tade. " 'It's agreed, then, that you are not pregnant. Anyhow you haven't seen Tunde for two weeks, and that puts him in the clear if you do get pregnant.' Ṣọla said there was no need for all this deliberation. She simply wasn't pregnant and that was that."

Tunde is, of course, delighted, and thanks Tade for his help. The talk on the way home tonight is of all the ways girls use to trap men into marrying them.

Biography

Magnus *Olútadé* Oyebanji was born in 1944 in the small town of *Aiyégbàmí* northwest of Ijebu Ode. Aiyegbami is an old town which lies along the earthworks that formerly surrounded the core area of the Ijebu kingdom, and as one of the old "border" towns it has long had intense connections with the capital. Tade's ancestors gave a family from Ijebu Ode some land to farm seventy years ago or so; as we shall see in a moment the relationship is still useful.

Tade's parents are successful ruralites. His father is a farmer who spends much of his time at the small house he has built on his farmland about seven miles from town. He has been a Catholic since he was young, but never went to school, and is unable to read or write. Nonetheless, he is not economically conservative and grows marketable "cash crops" of kola nut, cocoa and a bit of coffee rather than subsistence crops alone. Tade's mother is a Muslim and the senior of two wives. She has a fairly large trade in cocoa, buying it from small farms and selling it to large-scale buyers. She has the additional fortune to have nine living children, of whom Pa Yẹmi is the first and Tade the fourth. Two of the others, a married sister and an upholsterer's apprentice also live in Ibadan not far away, but Tade does not often see them.

Tade went to primary school in Aiyegbami. There is no higher school available in the town. Taking advantage of their old relationship with the family in Ijebu Ode, Tade's family was able to secure free lodging for him there, in the home of the man whose grandfather had gotten farm land from them. For two years, while he went to "secondary modern" school,[5] he lived there. At that point he applied for and won entry into the new Government Trade Centre that had just been built in Ijebu Ode. His plumbing course lasted three years, and gave him a higher level of skills and qualifications than he would have had after five years of apprenticeship to an ordinary practitioner. Moreover, as is true of boarding schools at all levels, he made friends there in a variety of trade specialties that he will call upon all his life.

Both because his older brother was there and because the regional government — and its jobs — are there, Tade knew that he would go to Ibadan when he graduated in 1965. So he had Pa Yẹmi start looking for a job for him almost a year in advance. In the end he got himself his job simply by applying to the government when he arrived after graduation.

He is a bit disappointed with his job. Because of his relatively high general education, he has rapidly been moved to a supervisory position where he gets little chance to work under more experienced men on practical projects and problems. Since his education in trade school deemphasized "real-world" experience — compared to that of an ordinary apprentice — he feels all the less accomplished in the basics of his trade.

Eventually Tade wants to start up a business of his own, and to train, in the more advanced techniques that he knows, apprentices of his own "not fortunate enough to be able to pay to go to school for training" as he did. This is relatively far in the future, though, for he allows that it might take ten or fifteen years to build up sufficient trade alongside his regular job to go on his own entirely.

In the meantime he has a much shorter-range investment plan. From his

£17. 10s. 6d. ($49.07) monthly salary, he is saving £7 ($19.60) every month. His mother gives him £3 ($8.40) more, and the whole £10 ($28) goes into an esusu[6] which will come to his turn in November. He will then "take" £130. In the next round of the esusu his turn is second, so in February he will have another £130. The total will be a large down payment on a taxi, which Tade will give to his brother to manage. Pa Yemi, besides owning two taxis of his own, now manages two others, and all are profitable. So the money that Tade expects to make from that investment will in turn go into savings, towards a house after he is married.

Marriage is, of course, also on Tade's mind. A friend of his at the Trade Centre lived in the city of Ife, and Tade, while visiting his home, met a Ghanaian girl who goes to secondary school there. He has been corresponding with her for a year, and considers her his "real" girl friend. Of course many things may happen in the four years or so before he feels he will be ready for marriage. He does not, however, preclude marrying a non-Ijebu, although he would not marry anyone without seeking his parents' approval. He intends to take but one wife (although his brother may soon take a second), and to have "not more" than five children. He knows how much it costs to educate them.

Until his marriage, however, he is his own man. He rent takes only £1. 5s. 0d. ($3.50), and the electricity bill only a few shillings more. Before he joined the esusu, all the rest of his salary went for food, clothes, furniture, entertainment, and other personal expenses. He gives small amounts of cash to his old relatives when he visits home (which he does as little as possible, preferring to visit friends in Lagos but going to Aiyegbami if his brother sends him). And occasionally he buys special foods, such as meat or fruit, for his brother's wife. But everyone expects him now to spend his money on himself. His major savings toward the taxi, in fact, mark him as more frugal and more steadyminded than most of his friends.

The Room and the Compound

Tade's sobriety is reflected as well in the room he shares with his friend Tunde. The room is almost undecorated, containing only the two beds with a table between. Both young men have spring mattresses rather than the thick layer of reed mats of the Odusanyas. The table contains some books (almost all about plumbing), magazines, notebooks, and photo albums, but is also used for meals.

At the foot of Tunde's bed, in the corner, is a small kerosene stove together with some cups, plates and utensils stacked beside it. Opposite Tade's bed is the built-in cupboard, a closet above and four drawers below. All the frequently-worn clothes of both young men are hung there, and underwear, food, shoes, the electric iron and coil water heater, and other items fill the drawers. Above the cupboard are two small suitcases containing infrequently-worn clothes (neither Tade nor Tunde wears overgarments or pants cut in Yoruba styles, except to family affairs). On the floor next to the bed is a half-finished sack of gari belonging to Tade. The walls are bare, and the windows are shuttered but glassless and curtainless.

The general impression of less intense use of the room extends to the building as a whole. There are twenty rooms on two floors here, but in all only about forty-three people (versus the sixty-six in sixteen rooms at the Odusanyas). The figure is approximate here because Tade does not know the tenants in two of the rooms upstairs. Only five of the total of sixteen households in the building are nuclear families; the rest of the rooms are held by single men or women, often with a young relative to see to housework. Thus the competition for cooking and kitchen space, and the tenor of day-time activity, are much lower than in buildings housing more wives and children of more families. Only four of the sixteen households are Ijebu; others are from elsewhere in Yorubaland, from midwestern and from eastern Nigeria.

Summary

Both in his living arrangements and in his life situation as a whole, Tade Oyebanji is in a stage of transition. Between the obligations of childhood and of full adulthood, he is in a period of exploration — of social relationships with men and with women, of personal lifestyles and new leisure activities, and of a satisfying work role. If he can ward off the entanglements that can come all too easily from his increasing involvement with girls, if he keeps his job, and if his plans for the taxi come to pass, he will be ready for the further responsibilities of marriage with a self-assuredness inspired by having firm footing on the ladder toward success. Like the Odusanyas, Tade too is confident that he can convert his past and present opportunities into future security.

Discussion: Jobs, Leisure, and Social Obligations

Education and Employment. Tade Oyebanji was lucky to be among the first graduating classes of the government's new Trade Centres. Lucky, too, were university, secondary school, and other specialized schools' graduates — until recently. All of them, like the primary school leavers in the days before the expansion of advanced educational facilities, have been able to find jobs promising some rate of advancement and, barring personal or political vicissitudes, long-term security. In part the jobs existed first and created the demand for schools of one type or another (one of the major reasons colonial governments financed schools at all was that bringing minor clerks from the homeland was much costlier); in part the government has an interest in assuring that at least the first results of its plans are not hollow.

Nonetheless, the general expansion of jobs in the 1950's and early 1960's had slowed considerably by 1965 or so, while the numbers of children in all levels of schooling continued to climb. Craft apprenticeship used to be an alternative to any formal Western education; now so many primary school graduates are entering apprenticeships that master craftsmen like Michael Odusanya worry that the sheer numbers of competitors will drive down prices and thus reduce profits to the vanishing point. Secondary modern schools have already died. Youths who do not complete high school hope only for the most routine clerical work in stores or offices. University graduates are becoming teachers in larger and larger numbers, and driving down the competitive value of diplomas from secondary schools and teacher training colleges. It has been estimated that over 150,000 youths with at least a full primary education entered the labor force in southern Nigeria in 1965, but that at most perhaps 30,000 jobs became available to them (Abernethy 1969:196-203). Only the absorption of most of the rest into craftsmen's shops as apprentices, into commerce as street hawkers, or into urban families as domestic servants maintains the sense of activity for what are, in their own minds, armies of unemployed or unsatisfyingly employed young people. Whether their expectations are readjusted to the realities of their situation, or are nourished by those of the further thousands who will find even these ''occupations'' filled up and closed, only time and factors beyond their individual control can tell.

Meanwhile individuals and governments attempt to cope with the huge disproportion between supply of and demand for employment in a number of ways. P.C. Gutkind has called parapolitical activity by the unemployed ''the energy of despair'' (1967), and the phrase is only a bit too dramatic, perhaps, to extend to these coping actions. The feverish after-school tutoring that Deji Odusanya secures after school and that Tade Oyebanji gives to the children in his brother's compound gears even first-graders toward success in secondary school entrance examinations, a crucial passage since secondary school graduates earn two to three times what a primary school leaver can expect (Teriba and Philips 1971:99). In 1966 there were 673,687 pupils in Western Nigerian primary schools: but while 179,620 entered first grade in that year, only 67,915 were in the final (sixth) primary year, only 37,746 of these passed the School Leaving Examination, and only 11,893 of these won places in the next secondary school entering class (Western Nigeria 1971). In this context the

examination-oriented single-purposefulness of schooling is perfectly under-
standable, whatever its consequences for a broad definition of education.
Second, youths who have left school and are employed are very often studying
after work for further schooling. Only in their late twenties or early thirties do
many men and women give up the idea that their jobs are but way-stations
toward higher rewards. While their ambitiousness is admirable, the chances of
their success grow ever smaller. As well, the lack of commitment that many of
them display toward their present jobs gives rise to many complaints, for
example by older teachers, about their effectiveness. Third, governments,
moving to increase turnover, have lowered the retirement age to 60, and in
some cases to 55. Since job switching may have continued until they were 28 or
more, even if they have been working earlier, their regular careers may be
relatively short. Tade is unusual to be into his career at 22. Besides, many
parents will have heavy educational expenses for their own children when they
themselves are 55 or 60, and most will still have years of productive capacity
ahead of them. It is partly in view of these prospects that young workers like
Tade have incentive to build their own business and leave their salaried posts.
This spur to entrepreneurial activity, if resources are available to fund it, may be
a useful result of the loss of dynamic in the public sector of the employment
market.

In short, the formerly closer articulation of schools to the employment
situation has come apart: Tade Oyebanji was lucky to be among the *first*
graduating classes of the new Trade Centres.

Leisure and Recreation. There are striking differences between the
Odusanyas and Tade Oyebanji in the quantity and the use of "spare time."
Because their work and their family make heavy demands upon them, Michael
and Florence Odusanya have little time or money to spend on "recreation" or
"entertainment." While they do spend time together in the afternoon or
evening when their jobs allow it, most of their leisure occurs on weekends,
especially Sunday, and they spend it on prayer and association meetings, on
trips home to visit relatives, or on other forms of social gathering. Ma Deji has
never, she says, seen a film, although they have together been to one popular
play. Music comes from the radio or from groups playing at funerals or other
ceremonies; the Odusanyas would not consider going to one of the "night
clubs," open-air bars and dance halls, which dot the city.

Tade, on the contrary, utilizes all these forms of entertainment, though he
rarely goes to the clubs because he does not care for beer or liquor very much. In
addition he has discovered the Y.M.C.A., and sometimes goes to the stadium
nearby to watch a soccer game as well. He, too, does a good deal of visiting,
and in fact rarely stays in his room at some personal pastime like reading unless

he is too tired to go elsewhere. For him as for youths in small villages, the market and the roadside are still good spots to girl-watch and to while away the coolness of the evening. In short, Tade has a much more diverse set of leisure activities than the Odusanyas, especially in terms of spectator entertainments.

The range of the activities in which any given individual participates is not so much a function of age or of family status as it is of Western education and, to some extent, wealth. That is, Tade has learned to enjoy films, organized sports, night clubs and their bands, magazines and even the betting pools as he has gone through school in the early 1960's. These forms of leisure activities were simply not as available to earlier generations, except in the largest towns. In fact the arrival of a pool house, or a mobile outdoor film unit, or a portable tape recorder and generator-driven lighting arrangements for the purposes of a dance all mark the spread of scarce urban "amenities" to smaller and smaller communities across the Nigerian countryside. The diffusion of these new cultural forms and their associated behaviors is one index of the "urbanization" of the villages. As we have just noted, however, it is primarily a change in the forms of leisure pursuits, and does not imply that the new are of more value than the old. The latest addition to the list is television, broadcast from several points around Nigeria: few would argue that the spectacles to be seen on the "box" surpass in quality the older arts of sociability that are the mainstay of the Odusanyas' leisure.

Youth and Social Obligations. It is instructive to note the alternative interpretations that can be made of Tade's sense of social and financial obligations. Depending upon the perspective we take, we might characterize Ijebu migrant youth *either* as changing quickly and radically from the behavior of their older kinsmen and parents, *or* as changing only imperceptibly. Let us illustrate.

On the one hand, Tade appears much different even from his older brother, Pa Yẹmi. Tade dislikes visiting his home town. He spends most of his money on consumer goods for himself and redistributes little of it to his relatives (in fact his mother even gives him money). His tastes in clothing, his willingness to have girl friends who are not Ijebu, and his greater exposure to new values in terms of the diversity of co-tenants in his building or of his frequenting of movie theaters and night clubs all reveal a greater catholicity of interests — inversely, less involvement with kin and provincial culture — than is true of many of the older individuals in this book. His muttering that there are "too many Ijebus" at the Y.M.C.A. reflects his outlook.

Were we only to aggregate these facts, we might well conclude that Tade, or youth in general, are detaching themselves from obligations and expectations their elders value. But against such evidence is another reciprocal set of expectations about youth that we can only discover by asking about present attitudes and future hopes, by looking at older individuals of about the same education or occupation, and in general by taking a perspective concerned with the whole process of domestic life rather than with isolated facts. From that point of view we find that in the transitional phase to adulthood that Tade, for one example, is in, his elders *expect* him to do just about what he is doing.

During this period, after school is ended but before he marries, a youth's primary obligations are to himself. He should sow his wild oats, find a job that suits him and secure any equipment or special training required for it, build strong friendships that will endure the alternative demands of wife and children, gather a personal inventory of clothing, implements, furniture, and other durable possessions, and begin to accumulate enough money to pay for a wedding and to supply the new wife with initial trading capital. The parallels with traditional society are clear enough, whether or not we can speak of "continuity:" this was once the period when Ijebus formalized their age-sets, began to work full farms, served in town militia or public works duties, and also accumulated capital for their marriages.

Thus his obligations to himself are in fact to his own future, and to that future in terms of full membership of his society. In other words, there is consensus that the time will come soon enough when he should contribute more fully to the wider social groupings around him. Others have that duty now; his turn will come after he gets fully "established" (the word English-speaking Yoruba use), that is, when his work and family get firmly under way. Tade's present contribution of tutoring must therefore be seen as much more than a *quid pro quo* for food at his brother's house. It is an earnest of his full membership and of acceptance of his present and future statuses as well. Neither Tade nor most other youths we interviewed more briefly bridles at the thought of returning to others in the future the help that their families have given them (a few exceptions will be noted later). The record of the men a few years older than Tade, who are "established," indicates a routine enlargement of involvement with kin and community.

There is, to sum up, a cycle of statuses in the life of Ijebu Yoruba that has always included a period of detachment from family obligations. To some extent the content of such relationships has changed, as we noted. And there may be shifts going on over a longer time span — particularly when a generation born in the city gets beyond "establishment" — that are or will be significant. Whatever the complexities of the current position, however, baldly to mistake this youthly role for a permanent withering away of hallowed social bonds is obviously false. The urban youth of today is not yet dispossessed by or dispossessing of the social order in which he grew up.

Footnotes

[1]Technically, seniority rather than age per se is the quality deferred to by Yoruba (Bascom 1942; Fadipe 1970:114ff.). With such a disparity as in this situation, however, age is felt by everyone involved to override the inverse seniority of the job. See also Chapter VI, pp. 238-240, below.

[2]The sending of a token is a widespread custom for symbolizing one's intended participation in some occurrence. Here the intent is to stop the violence and await mediation.

[3]Nigeria began its independence in 1960 with three political Regions, North, East, and West, each of which had a parliamentary system of government led by a premier. At the federal level a parliament also operated, the governing leader of which was the prime minister. In 1964 a fourth region, the Midwest, was created. During this period the Northern Region dominated the federal government. In 1966 the parliamentary system was replaced by military rule, and in 1967, by decree, the four regions were further subdivided into twelve states.

[4]In fact Hausa and Yoruba are also common second languages for some. Compared with many Euro-American populations, a relatively high proportion of Nigerians speak two or more — not infrequently four or five — languages.

[5]Secondary modern schools, covering three years beyond the six of primary school, were conceived in the late 1950's as an answer to the devaluation of the primary school leaving certificate as a ticket to employment. By the time the first classes graduated, however, even some high school graduates were having a difficult time finding jobs. With little further utility, therefore, the modern schools began to disappear. Six years after they got under way, few remained.

[6]The Yoruba esusu is a classic "rotating credit association" (Geertz 1962; Bascom 1952). Briefly, a number of people put in a set sum each month (or week, or day). In turn, one of them takes the whole amount for whatever purpose he has. No interest is earned, but the forced savings program generates a substantial capital sum for each participant. The order for "taking" may be determined either by lot or by the participants' projections of when they will need the money. In any case the fact that they almost always have prior and ongoing social relationships provides the setting in which each participant continues to give his "contribution" even after his turn to "take" has come. In Tade's esusu each of thirteen people gives £10 a month, and each receives £130 when his turn comes. Swindlers in large cities start esusu for the unsuspecting, and abscond with the first deposits. But honest esusu men also have large operations going that function virtually as neighborhood banks.

CHAPTER VI

The Perils of Urban Life: The Ọnadele Family

A Day's Work

To get a full day's work done on any of the five houses he is building, *Bọ́lá Ọ̀nàdélé* must rise early. At seven o'clock his current foreman knocks and enters, ready to start for the casual labor market. Bọla goes into his bedroom to gather up a few tools that his men may need during the day, decides he also needs the building plan for one of the houses but then puts it down again, and makes a face at the baby in the crib as he goes out the parlor door. From the courtyard in the rear, where she is sitting over a wash-basin of clothes, his wife calls out, *"Ó dàbọ̀!"*

The two men walk down the street, passing Chief *Ògúnkòyà's* house (see Chapter IX) and on the next block a burnt-out building with the charred remains of two American cars in front of it. Bọla tells his assistant the name of the politician who lived there and describes the day at the end of 1965 when a crowd of youths came and set fire to the place in the violent aftermath of the rigged Regional elections. At the end of the street is the house and workyard of one of the major Nigerian contractors in Ibadan. A sign is up announcing work for carpenters and bricklayers, and about thirty men are waiting at the gate. Bọla notes that *Olíwo* is the richest contractor in the city, but is crafty, too. He says that the foreman will probably take a two pound ($5.60) bribe from each man waiting to be hired, and then, after a short phase of the project is done, will dismiss the whole lot so he can hire more. The main street through Oke Ado is full of taxis, trucks, and people on their way to work, and the two men stop talking because they cannot hear one another anyway.

Ten minutes later they are at the crossroads where perhaps fifty or sixty men of all ages in ragged workclothes are chattering in small groups, while five or six men go about bargaining with one or another of them over a day's labor. Bọla stops to say good morning to a printer whose shop is near the corner; one of the houses that he is working on belongs to this man. Shortly Bọla leaves the shop to find laborers, but for one reason or another none will agree to work for him. He reports that other boys around have urged everyone not to go with him, since they will not get paid at the end of the day. Finally his assistant goes to see what he can do. Bọla complains that there is neither money nor satisfaction in his business any more, and he thinks he should fold it up. But soon his man comes over with three boys in their mid-teens ready to work. Bọla asks who is spreading the nonsense about his not paying his workers. The boys deny having heard that, saying it was only that they will not work for less than four shillings (56¢) for the day. Bọla says that three and six (49¢) is all he can give, since he has their taxi fares to pay, too. Finally they compromise in the middle. Bọla hails a taxi, and the whole crew heads for *Félélé* layout. It is almost eight-thirty.

Felele is an area of quite recent development at the southern edge of Ibadan, and much of it is still either tall grass or farm plot. Bọla is building two houses there a few hundred yards apart. One is a small one for a transporter who lives upstairs from him now; the other (for which he is now building only the "boys' [servants'] quarters") is for Bọla's cousin, a lawyer who lives near him in Oke Ado. Two men, hired for the whole job, are already at work on the transporter's house when Bọla arrives. After checking their work, he goes through a corn field and comes out at a large thatched grass hut inhabited, it turns out, by Igbira people from central Nigeria. Bọla stores tools, bags of cement, and other material with them for a small fee. Two women, one working at a small loom, three well-dressed men, and five or six children wearing only waist-beads are inside. Bọla picks out some of his tools and gives them to one of his laborers to carry. On the way to the lawyer's site he talks about how much he would like to follow the wealthy contractor Chief Oliwo's "policy" and model, except that he has not capital enough to do so. Or else he would like to start a cement block plant that would be efficient enough to attract many customers.

The rest of the morning passes quietly, with Bọla's foreman directing the laborers in concreting the floor of the lawyer's boys' quarters, and Bọla moving back and forth between the two houses to check the work at each. Bọla himself works, in spurts of great energy, at repairing a faulty patch of plaster or at testing the levelness of the new floor.

Just after noon, Bọla decides to go home for lunch. He rarely eats any breakfast at all, so eats lunch earlier than most of the others we have met. On a bench in the passageway two-year-old *Jídé* is asleep. Ma *Lára,* Bọla's wife, is in back grinding pepper on a flat stone. She greets Bọla warmly, but adds, to the researcher, that he should make a special note that Bọla will not spend the money to have their pepper ground by machine. Everyone laughs.

Bọla wants to send his son *Ṣégun,* who is not quite four, down the street to buy some iced water, but Ma Lara protests that he is too young to be trusted on the road alone. A few minutes later Lara, the oldest of Bọla's four children, comes in from school, and she goes instead. Lunch consists of ẹba and a sauce of ground melon seed *(ègúsí)* with pieces of fresh fish in it. Everyone eats from a separate dish except for *Lọlá,* the baby, who finishes a bottle of orange juice and is then fed bits of ẹba by her mother. Bọla's dog, "Yellow," gets a plate of ẹba as well. Over the meal Bọla talks about his work, about the Ibadan man who owns all of Felẹlẹ layout, about the two plots of land he himself owns and his plans to build a house soon on one of them, and about the house he is building for the printer in a part of town between the indigenous and the migrant sectors that was never built up.

On the way back to work, the taxi drops Bọla off at the beginning of the dirt road into the area, refusing to go farther either out of fear for his car's springs or because he thinks he may be robbed after being led to the "bush." Bọla argues, but finally walks the last half mile. At the lawyer's site the men have done most of the floor. Bọla leads two of the laborers to get water at a stream not far away, and stops to point out where he says he saw a small alligator. Back at the transporter's site the men appear to have done very little that is noticeable, but Bọla says nothing. An hour later, around three, he pays off the day laborers, takes his tools back to the Igbira hut, and heads home.

Routine Problems

Bọla has a car, of sorts. It is a twelve-year-old gray Opel station wagon which has obviously seen better days. Battered on the outside and thoroughly worn inside, it is more often broken down than working. On Saturday morning Bọla is making another attempt to get it on the road. Scowling, he tells Lara and *Búkọlá* (Ma Lara's youngest sister, who lives with them) to stop gawking at him and sweep the house instead.

At the same time, Bọla's two permanent laborers appear to ask what they should do for the moment, since the transporter does not have money enough to buy more blocks and cement for his house. Bọla tells them to go start plastering the interior of the lawyer's. Bọla mentions that someone building another house at Felẹlẹ has accused him of stealing ten bags of cement. The laborers exclaim their disbelief.

"Haw!" says one, pulling a key from his pocket and placing it between his teeth. "This is *Ògún* — master has never stolen even a grain of sand from anyone as long as I have known him!"[1] After a few minutes of further discussion, and a mumbled request for "chop" (food) money to which Bọla does not respond, the young men leave for work.

"I'll probably get there before you," Bọla says optimistically, "because I'm coming by car today." At that he gets out a hand pump to pump up his flat front tire, since he has no spare. There is another car parked in back of his today — a sparkling Mercedes Benz. It belongs, Bọla says, to the son of a woman upstairs who is the separated wife of a rich Ijebu merchant. The son is an accountant for his father's many enterprises.

The tire seems to hold up, so now all is ready for pushing the car down the hill to try to start it, since the battery is dead. At the last moment before reaching the main road it finally starts, but then the air spurts out at each revolution of the tire. Bọla turns the corner and heads for a "vulcanizer's" shop where he can get the tube patched.

At home, meanwhile, the rest of the family is eating a breakfast of ẹwa and pieces of boiled yam. Lara and Bukọla are still in the shower, but they join the rest in a few minutes. Ṣegun is glum-faced, his mother says, because he wanted to go with his father to the site this morning. Ma Lara is the only "housewife" among all our families, having no sewing machine to pursue the trade she knows. After breakfast she has little to do, and sits in the parlor chatting. An Ijebu man and his Ibo wife vacated the other room on their side of the passageway this morning, she reports. The man came only last night to say they were going to Lagos. He did not say why, but Ma Lara thinks it may be that the wife wanted to be near some relatives if any further violence breaks out in the country. The Ibos have been suffering very much, she thinks, and the Yorubas are being too "quiet" about their position. All the leaders seem to care about is the amount of money that gets into their own bank accounts. One of the ministers in the last civilian regime in the West was a close friend of Ma Lara's family. He was a nice lawyer when he first came back from England, she says. She doesn't understand what "turned his head into the crazy business of politics." She hopes he is not among those rumored to have recently plotted against the life of the new military governor.

While she talks she plaits the baby's long hair. She goes on to talk about the time last month, at the age of only four months, when the baby got bronchial pneumonia. She had to spend all day at the hospital to feed her. The Ibo woman who left this morning fed the other children.

She is interrupted by the cries of Ṣegun, who has fallen into the shallow but putrid drainage ditch that runs along the street in front of the house. Ma Lara calls her young sister Bukọla to wash Ṣegun's clothing and Lara to wash Ṣegun himself thoroughly.

Just after eleven o'clock Bọla returns with a woman he has met somewhere along the way. He takes her out in back to show her the bags of cement he has for sale that his workers brought from the site yesterday. He never mentions where these bags came from originally. In any event the woman buys all four and promises to send someone for them that afternoon. Bọla goes into the room, angry that his wife has not watched him sell them so she might do so herself the next time. He appears to be in a bad mood, perhaps because of his car. He mutters that the tire was flat by the time he reached the vulcanizer, so he left it there and took a taxi to Felele. He is going back to pick the car up now.

III Feelings

The next week is not a good one for Bola. He has been fighting a light case of pneumonia, too, which makes him tired and irritable. He spends time at the worksite each day, and also attends to chores at home like the repair of his car. Both the battery and the tire need replacement, but he cannot afford to do so. So the car sits waiting outside the house, and Bola sits inside, hoping his luck will change. The only bright note in the house is struck by the older children Lara, Bukola, and *Jímòh,* Bola's distant cousin, a high school student, who is the eighth and last member of the household. They are making party hats to sell for the coming Christmas holidays, from cardboard, gleaming wrapping foil, ribbon and string. Jimoh is the entrepreneur, and even hires other boys in the compound, at four pennies a day, to work on the hats with them. Other than the novelty of this activity, however, the week passes dully, punctuated by minor quarrels between Bola and his wife.

On Monday at lunchtime Bola returns from the site sleepy. He lies down only for a few minutes, though, and then comes out again. In the passageway a new tenant and two men who are with her are talking with the goldsmith and his wife who live across the passage. The new tenant is a slim, well-dressed woman about thirty with pencilled eyebrows and polished fingernails and toenails. Bola knows the woman from somewhere, and knows that she has run away from her husband. In fact he was concerned when she moved in that her husband might think that he, Bola, had helped the woman to find the room here.

The woman and her two male "friends" go into her room for a while. Just as they come out Bola, who is standing in the front doorway daydreaming, thinks he sees the woman's husband turning the corner toward the house. He turns quickly and warns the woman. The two men race for the back yard, climb the wall, and disappear into the next compound. The woman leaps upstairs to hide there. Bola, meanwhile, goes outside to greet (and intercept) the cuckold, a tall man with a goatee. On learning from Bola that she is "not in," the man begins bewailing his fate, to have had his wife of nineteen years run away to be a prostitute.

"Some people are just so incomprehensible," he sighs. "I don't understand how she could come to a place like this. Imagine! I spent £42 on a bed for her, had two boys to wait on her, did everything for her, but she preferred to go around picking up useless men. I even opened a hotel [open-air night club] for her, but it got worse there. She would go sit on men's laps and beg them for beer. She's a fool. Now our son — he's in high school; these are his shoes I'm wearing — says he will deny being her son.'' He praises Bọla for listening to him so sympathetically, for being such a good man, for not falling into her "file" of customers himself. "God will reward you for your good deeds, sir." Finally he leaves, dejected even more by his confession.

When he goes Bọla walks back inside, where he and the goldsmith, whose shed is at the back of the compound, discuss the man's problem. His mistake, they agree, was to open a hotel which simply got her involved with more men. In any case, however, it is proof that one should be careful about women, and never trust them. Bọla also wonders whether the man who came with the husband dropped anything around the house. He says there is medicine the man could use that would make everyone in the house fall sick or die. The goldsmith refuses to believe that, but before Bọla can cite a story he knows that "proves" it can happen, Ma Lara walks in with Lọla on her back. She has been at the hospital clinic all day, from eight until two, waiting for the doctor to see Lọla for a penicillin injection and check-up.

Ma Lara is in low spirits, too. Besides the boring wait at the hospital, she reports that she and Bọla argued yesterday. As a result, he refused to eat the lunch she had prepared, and it is still sitting, in covered bowls, on low stools in the parlor. The incident was trivial: Lara had taken some clothes out back to wash but had forgotten a towel. Bọla called Ma Lara to take it, and Ma Lara called Lara herself. But Bọla insisted that Ma Lara should take it, because she should have seen it before he had to remind her. Since she didn't attend to it, she and only she should do so, he argued. Ma Lara refused bluntly, and Bọla refused to eat. In the evening he went out and presumably bought himself supper. There the argument stands, simmering.

Shortly Bọla gets ready to go to the building sites at Felele. Before he goes Ma Lara tells him that she has not eaten since yesterday (she had to leave too early this morning to cook), but that there is nothing in the house.

"What about the money I gave you last Saturday? The ten shillings?" Bọla demands.

"It's gone."

"What? Just since yesterday?"

"Saturday was the day before yesterday."

"Oh," says Bọla weakly, and fishes a shilling from his pocket. It will make a small lunch for Ma Lara and the five children (Jimọh eats lunch at school).

To be sure, at eight o'clock that evening when Bọla returns from work and a visit to his cousin the lawyer's house, the children have not eaten supper. A university lecturer in chemistry, the owner of the fourth of Bọla's five building sites, has stopped in to see Bọla, and Jimọh told him that he was at the lawyer's building. Bọla is furious — the boy should have simply said that he was "out," especially since he knew that Bọla has work to do on the lecturer's building as well. Now he feels he must go to the university right away, to see what Dr. Àyándéjọ̀ wants. And when Ma Lara now asks him for more food money for supper, he simply stares at her for two minutes in speechless disbelief that she dares raise so minor an affair.

Ma Lara turns to go inside, and Bọla sets out to find a taxi. But quickly each of the children (except for Ma Lara's sister Bukọla) comes up to him to ask for money to buy food. Realizing that Ma Lara has set them to this pleading, Bọla simply sends the children back, with a soft word about returning soon. To two-year-old Jide he gives a penny as a double sign of affection for the girl and defiance of her mother. Bọla is somber and silent as he heads across town toward the campus.

A Major Fight

By the next afternoon the Ọnadeles have had a major confrontation. At noon Ma Lara is dressed to go out. She quickly reports that there was a real fight in the morning. The goldsmith's wife, she says, gave the children a meal last night. This morning he gave them some money for breakfast, but none to her to buy any food. Instead, he said belligerently that she should ask her first husband for it. That got her angry, and she told him that if he couldn't be a proper husband he should not have married. They went on arguing until he told her to get out, and shoved her toward the door. Then they began fighting in earnest — she has a swollen cheek to show for it. Furthermore, he locked the door so that no one could get in to separate them. He only left a little while ago, when his cousin the lawyer, having been told what was going on by a neighbor, sent for him to come at once. Now, says Ma Lara, she is going to the lawyer's to report her version, and is then going to her mother's house at Mókọ́lá across town. She ties the baby onto her back and leaves. Lọla and Ṣegun look unflapped by the morning's events, and stay behind playing happily by themselves.

At the house of the lawyer — whose name is Táíwò Ọlọ́runṣọlá — Ma Lara learns that in fact her husband has not come there. She tells her story, adding only that he twisted her arm until it nearly broke. An hour later someone comes to say Bọla is now at home again.

Sitting sulkily in his parlor alone with the anthropologist, he refuses to see the lawyer or his wife. "You ought to know by now that if I say I won't go, I won't. If you don't know, then you've failed — you and your research!" He goes on to tell his version of events, interrupting to say how lazy and rude Ma Lara is. This is the first time their arguments have come to blows, he says, and it happened because she thought she could force him to do something he didn't want to do.

In the fight she tore his shirt and trousers and broke his Parker pen, worth two pounds. He has put all these things in a bag to show her parents, and he is headed there right now.

On the way he talks of "that woman," and how it is the goldsmith's wife, who is a typist at the university, who puts her up to this impudence. At Mokọla he sees Ma Lara's mother privately. When he comes out, Bọla decides he wants to buy a kind of duck sold only at the nearby market. He reports that his mother-in-law told him the best thing to do would be to come back tomorrow night, when her husband, Ma Lara's father, would be home. Bọla is angered by her cool response, saying it shows that she supports her daughter despite the "evidence" against her that he has brought. So, he says, he won't come back here tomorrow — or ever again if he can help it. And "that woman" can just "pack out" of his house altogether.

He buys the duck and takes a taxi for Oke Ado. Ma Lara is standing in the doorway. She gives just enough way for Bọla to slip by her. They exchange no greetings. After a few minutes lost in thought, he suddenly decides he will go to the battery charger's shop, where he has left his car for a day. But the man has not yet charged the dead battery, so Bọla heads, finally, for his cousin's.

Taiwo has gone back to his office. His wife, a trained nurse, is home with the children, watching "Rosemary Clooney" on television. For a long time Bọla says nothing, and everyone just stares, vaguely, at the screen. Finally Bọla starts talking, and again narrates the morning's events. He adds a new detail — that it was Ma Lara who locked the door and threw the key onto the floor, so that he could not go out. Mrs. Ọlọrunṣọla is persuaded slowly by his argument, and agrees that Ma Lara should not have barred his way. "She should have flattered you, asked you to forget it, and just said 'please' a few times. That's what you men need . . . ."

When Bọla sees he is winning a supporter, he perks up. He shows "Mama Laide" the marks where Ma Lara bit him on the arm. By the time he finishes, Mrs. Ọlọrunṣọla is ready to argue with Ma Lara herself.

Bọla heads home. It is nearly nine thirty. The children are all asleep on a mat spread on the parlor floor. They have not changed into night clothes, and they are not covered. Ma Lara is in the yard talking in low tones to the goldsmith's wife. Bọla puts his things down and goes out again immediately. He wants to buy a package of rice which, he says, he will cook for his children tomorrow.

The Pot Simmers . . .

The next day passes without further incident. Ma Lara, reviewing her plight and nursing her aches and bruises, adds to the details of the story. "Think of it! He shoved me and struck me and tore off all my clothes. If I hadn't had on pants and a brassiere it would have been terrible — when people saw that the door was locked they came down the narrow passage between the house and the compound wall to have a view of the struggle! And do you know he went to my father's house and told all sorts of lies?"

Later in the afternoon Ma Lara sleeps, stretched out on the children's floor mat. The three older children would probably remain in Bola's custody if Ma Lara really does leave, and she is giving him a taste of that future by paying little attention to them right now (though she makes sure they have something to eat). When Bola comes in from work he tells Segun to get a clean dress for Jide, and he applies some medicine to a sore that has opened on Segun's arm. The baby is sitting in the crib crying, and Bola takes her onto his lap to pacify her. A few minutes later she is crying again. After an hour of housetending, Bola gives up and goes out, saying he wants to go to his own building plot on the new Back Road, where he is having a carpenter build him a tool shed. If only he can start building a house for himself this year, he says, he can live his own life without neighbors butting in to his affairs.

Ma Lara's uncle, by profession a dispenser at a hospital in Ijebu Ode, is an influential man in her family, with powerful skills as a mediator and conciliator. The next day he comes to the house to talk to Bola and Ma Lara. On the one hand he is dead set against a woman being given sanctuary by her parents or relatives if she fights with her husband. On the other, he is offended by Bola's not having come to Mokola last night to discuss his case with them as Ma Lara's mother had asked. He apportions the blame evenly: Ma Lara has been extremely disobedient, but Bola has given unusual and unnecessary punishment. If Bola is not satisfied in the future to complain to his in-laws, he should send word to him, Mr. Àjàyí, at Ijebu, and he will come immediately. He has four wives with him in Ijebu, he says, and he has never gotten to the point of beating any of them.

After Mr. Ajayi leaves, Bola remarks outside that he was only feigning contrition in front of the old man. Yes, perhaps he will give Ma Lara money, but at the same time he will create a situation so unbearable for her that she will leave anyway. With that pledge, he goes inside to sleep.

Ma Lara is yielding, however. "Let him do whatever he wants," she sighs. "I'm ready to bear anything. I know it has become my lot to bear with him for the rest of my life. You see he hasn't given us any money for lunch even now — Lola's powdered milk is gone and she's just cried herself to sleep."

Lara comes in from school, crying, "Mama, I'm hungry. Very hungry."

"Tell your father that," says Ma Lara.

Lara goes into the bedroom. "Baba, I'm hungry." Bola mumbles "Hmm," and turns over.

Jide runs in crying with Ṣẹgun at her heels. Lara says he is trying to grab a piece of bone that Jide has been sucking at. Suddenly Ṣẹgun rushes at Jide again, grabs the bone, and takes two quick sucks at the marrow before his mother takes it away again and slaps him. Half an hour later Bọla gets up and, before he goes to check his workers at the site, he gives Lara money to buy each of the children some lunch from the cooked food seller in the next house.

. . . And Boils Again

On the next afternoon the whole compound is in an uproar. Bọla has gone out, and Ma Lara is in her room. But many of the other women, including those from the other house which shares the same yard, are standing around shouting and arguing. One of the two wives of the transporter upstairs comes to tell what has happened — Bọla appears to be carrying out his threat to make life intolerable in the house.

"Baba Lara" (i.e., Bọla) came over to the other house this noon, she begins, to thank the women there for coming to separate him and his wife when they were fighting on Tuesday. But he did more than thank them. He narrated the whole quarrel in great detail, and said that it was the goldsmith's wife who had been "lecturing" Ma Lara on what to do with her husband. He went on to say that these two women are starting "an association called 'what can husbands do,'" but that before it gets rooted he intends to send his wife away. The women then decided they had better go and see the goldsmith's wife simply to warn her not to get involved in the Ọnadeles' affairs. But the goldsmith got angry at them, saying that they were simply spreading lies about his wife who, he said, was not involved anyway. His wife joined him and they both shouted at the unwelcome delegation. Before long the landlord's wife came from a house nearby, listened for a while, and then told the group of women to mind their own affairs. So they started in on her, too. With nearly everyone cross at everyone else the resulting squabbles are still in progress.

In the passageway Ma Lara is talking quietly to the goldsmith's wife about the "decree" Bọla has issued that the two women have nothing further to do with one another. Jide comes running in, trips, and crashes to the floor.

"Imagine," says the goldsmith's wife. "I shouldn't talk to any members of his family again, so if I see this child about to kill herself like this I should still not talk?"

"Oh, he's crazy," replies Ma Lara. "Don't you know him? Everyone in the house knows what type of man he is, including those oversized women out there. As for me, I'm going to get out before he kills me or something."

By this time the landlord of the compound himself has arrived. "Keep to your own rooms . . . only the passage and back yard join you,'' he urges, as he tells everyone to calm down.

Towards Settlement

By the following week the dust is settling. If Bola and Ma Lara are not reconciled, at least they are not finding new bases for deepening the conflict. On Saturday, Ma Lara reports, they both went to her parents at Mokola and agreed to calm down. On Monday she spends the whole day at the hospital waiting for Lola's last injection and check-up. Meanwhile Bola takes Lara and Segun to register for pre-school lessons at the home of a former *Aládúrà* ''prophetess'' who has a high reputation for success with the children she teaches.

On Tuesday there is a small spat when Bola blames his wife for letting some bricks he has in one corner of the yard get broken by the children. But he is too busy to do much fighting. The university man, Dr. Ayandejo, has got enough money together to put up the ground floor of his house at Bodija Housing Estate, and Bola is busy finishing off the ground floor of the last house he has been working on occasionally, too. It is not that he has very much work really, Bola says, but only that it is all coming at once. In fact he is about to finish the current stages of three of the houses, and the fourth, the printer's, is inactive now anyway. So he must tell Dr. Ayandejo that ''it is up to him to see that I don't go hungry now,'' because it is only his job that Bola will be working on for the next couple of months.

The Autobiography of Bola Onadele

''I was born on July 10, 1928, at a village called *Ilétò Kéré,* about a mile from Ijebu Ode. My father was a rich cattle trader, but not the type that went to the North for their cattle. No, he stayed at Ijebu and had the cattle sent down to him in large numbers. Before that, I was told, he started as a palm wine seller, and from that he got more capital and traded in rice and beans from the North. His father's compound is at Iwade in Ijebu Ode. My father's father was a *babaláwo* [a diviner], and he died a pauper. But my father's grandfather was a very rich man — also a babalawo but a rich one . . . .

''My father had many wives but only nine of them had children for him. When Christianity first came to Ijebu he was one of the first people to become a Christian, but he turned Muslim when he learned that Muslim law allowed for many wives . . . .

''My mother had only one child for him — me. She is from *Ìkòròdú* [near

Lagos] . . . She never had any children when she wanted them, so she was told by a babalawo that if she could go back to where she originally came from [meaning where her ancestors came from], she would have children. So she came back to Ileto Kere, from where her ancestors had migrated long ago, and there met my father and married him.

"My father was not a very genial man. His wives had to endure his temper or find themselves out — especially the ones who had no children for him. So it wasn't very surprising that my mother got fed up soon after I was born. She went back to Ileto Kere, and that was where I spent my childhood.

"Then my mother started trading all the way to the river areas near *Òkìtìpupa* [the westernmost part of the Niger Delta]. Trade there was still mostly by barter then. She sold tobacco leaves, gunpowder, and some cloth, all bought in Lagos.

"She had a sister — not of the same mother — living in Lagos then. Her husband worked at the harbor authority. My mother took me to live with them. There were so many children there — kids of relatives, like me, and his own children, too. His eldest son was a sort of a leader for us then . . . The whole house was full of Christians then, and although this uncle had two wives, there wasn't any trouble at all. Or if there was trouble we kids couldn't hear it, not like my trouble with 'that woman' — she is a silly idiot, she doesn't know anything, . . . oh! But let's go on.

"I started school in 1936, and I soon became an expert at sharpening pencils. I earned a few pennies that way, and later I learned to ring the school bell . . . and gave other boys lessons to get my lunch money. But I didn't finish primary school there. It started this way.

"My father had died in 1933. In 1938 my father's sister came to take me out of the house where I was to take me back to Ijebu Ode. Her explanation was that if I wasn't brought back the family would lose me forever, and, being a male, that would count as a great loss to my father's whole family. But my mother didn't want me to go to Ijebu Ode; she was still going about trading then. So I didn't go, but my father's sister did see to it that my school records were changed to have my surname be Onadele. At the time they had me down as Johns, which was the surname of the family I lived with. Anyway, I didn't go to Ijebu Ode then, but two years later, in 1941, my mother's sister came again, and had her way.

"I only stayed a few months in my father's house, though, along with my mother, who was temporarily home. Then we both had to run off due to too many members of the house wishing to do us harm, since I had a full share of my father's inheritance though I hardly had lived there. My mother just got fed up and decided to quit. Up to this day I rarely go to my father's house, and when I do I am very careful — I will never take my children there. And they will use my name, *Ajìbọ́lá,* as their surname, instead of Onadele.

"We were given a room fortunately with one of my father's half brothers, so I started school again and finished primary school that year. I had to repeat the examination the following year, and in 1943 I passed an entrance examination to Ijebu Ode [Secondary] Grammar School. It was a very difficult time. I had to work to support myself, and my mother was away trading most of the time. The same people in Lagos, the Johns family, helped me, and that made me feel so indebted to them that later, when my mother had a big argument with them, I refused to take sides with her. I still don't agree with her on many things . . . She's a very strongheaded character but even so . . . she's my mother anyway.

"I left school again in 1946, mainly because I found it very hard to study, especially mathematics. I wanted to read what I liked, study literature and read about great personalities . . . When I got the money I started buying all those books I wanted very much to read — Shakespeare's plays, Winston Churchill's biography, Abraham Lincoln's and Gandhi's life histories, too. And these readings improved my [English] vocabulary a lot, and taught me some things about the world and how to go about in it that I'd never learned before.

"In Grammar School there was a teacher interested in photography, and I somehow impressed him, so he taught me about the solutions used for developing and many other things. I bought a small camera, but made a tremendous profit on each roll of film. When I was in Lagos visiting my mother's half brother, I bought a bigger camera. And soon I decided to quit school and devote full time to the photography business.

"I had a small shop for a while, but then I learned from my friend Mr. Omito that I could do a roaring trade among the Ijaws. I started making frequent long trips there, by hiring a canoe and taking pictures anywhere there was dry land! I did this for eight years, until 1956.

"At that time I got the idea that if I got a job as a newspaper photographer, they might send me to the U.K. for a training course — so many people were being sent there by the Action Group political party for various jobs, and coming back and getting fat salaries. I came to Ibadan and saw some of the big men of the party, but these people kept telling me to come back 'tomorrow.'

"Finally I got called for a job interview for a newspaper in Lagos, but I didn't get the job . . . I stayed with my Ijaw friend Mr. Omito then. Soon I got a job with the Development Corporation, but I stayed there only two weeks. I got into a training course with Singer sewing machines next. It lasted three months. But I got in the bad book of one Cypriot who was in charge of the trainees, and when the course was finished he wanted to send me to the Cameroons. I refused, and was sacked [fired]. Then for a while I repaired sewing machines on my own, and I also got some work touching up photo negatives for other photographers. But these things couldn't support me forever, and I went on thinking about what to do next." [Bọla was 28 years old by this time.]

"My mother's brother was a builder, and I remembered him then. I stayed with him from 1958 to 1960, when we came to Ibadan to build some houses for the government on Jericho Reservation. Then I decided I had learned enough, and I left him. First I went into the gravel digging business. . . . That lasted only a few months, though, until one day when I travelled to *Akúré* and the bus overturned. In fact I had dreamed that something evil would happen that day. I couldn't even walk for many months, and I had to have these four front teeth replaced. . . .

"It was during this time that I met Ma Lara. While I was convalescing I stayed with one of my friends near their house. Since I was home most of the day, I had enough time to get to know her and put my message across. There wasn't any big wedding ceremony. I paid about £25 to the parents and gave some other small gifts. Before her I had already married a wife during my days as a photographer, in 1954 or 1955. She didn't stay long enough to give me a child — ran away because she said she couldn't live with me if I let my mother interfere in our affairs so often. She was a nurse — I've never seen her since, and I don't know if she's alive or dead now.

"I got my first building job from the man I was in the gravel business with. I built a nice home for him on Freedom Road, and I've built some houses in Imale Falafia and at Fẹlẹlẹ. What I'm planning to do now is to begin again. That is, to get new workers and fresh tools. To start a systematic plan on how to go about this building business, or else chuck it off and start a new job — anything that can bring me some few pounds every day."

Biography: Ma Lara and Her Children

"Ma Lara" is ten years younger than her husband. She is not an Ijebu at all, but an Ẹgba Yoruba, from Abẹokuta. Her father owns land there somewhere, but her own family has lived in Ibadan since 1943, when she was only five years old, and so her knowledge of Abẹokuta is scant. Her father is a public health inspector for the government, and is often away from home posted to different towns. Her own mother is the senior of her father's two wives, and wholesales cement and other building materials.

Each wife has eight living children. Ma Lara is the second oldest of her own mother, and four of her mother's are all older than the oldest child of the second wife. Eight-year-old Bukọla is Ma Lara's youngest sibling *"ìyàkan"* (of the same mother), and has been living with Ma Lara both in order to help her with her own children and so that she will receive a discipline that their mother might not impart to the "baby" of her family.

Ma Lara's elder brother went to England to study architectural drawing.

Three of her younger brothers and sisters have attended secondary schools as well, with the financial support of the older ones. But for Ma Lara her father had no money for higher education. She finished primary school, learned to use a sewing machine, and continued to live at home, doing a great deal of housework and baby-sitting since she was the oldest girl in the huge family.

Perhaps out of the frustration or boredom of this routine, she fell for the charms of an apprentice mechanic "boy'friend" of hers in 1957. Whatever the motivation, she became pregnant, and gave birth to a baby boy the following year. Her parents warned her against marrying the father, though, and she simply kept the boy, who is the same age as Bukọla and is being raised by Ma Lara's mother.

After she had Akin, she found a job as an attendant at University Hospital. Two years later she again got pregnant, this time by Bọla Ọnadele. She says she did not like him at all, and even told him so. But, miraculously, one day she found herself in bed with him. It must have been some kind of special "medicine" he had, she says. Her parents again didn't want her to marry, but her uncle, Mr. Ajayi, said she must, or otherwise people "would start counting how many men she had had babies for." Besides, Bọla was begging her parents, promising to take care of her well. Two weeks after she finally moved in with him, in May of 1961, Lara was born.

Three more children have followed quickly. All were born healthy and have stayed that way, until Lọla got pneumonia. Ṣẹgun was born only seventeen months after Lara, in December of 1962. Ma Lara says that it is Bọla's "fault" that the theoretical three-year interval (produced by abstention) did not occur between the two births. Ṣẹgun, his parents admit, does not appear very bright mentally, but is enthusiastic about manual tasks. Jide is next, born in September of 1964: she is the bright one, able to find things, for instance, that Ṣẹgun cannot locate. Lọla was born in June of 1966. In a taxi one day Bọla agreed with the driver that almost all the children born these last few months have been girls! Bọla also mentions frequently how much he would like it if one of his children became a doctor and one a lawyer.

Ma Lara has plenty to do, obviously, in looking after her four children, even with her young sister's help. Nonetheless, most other women with families as large also manage some trade or other. Bọla, she says, wants her to spend full time as a housewife. When they first married he gave her a few pounds capital, but he took things from her stand without paying for them, and finally told her to sell everything quickly because he was broke and needed the money. Since then he has refused to give her any more capital. Another time she got three pounds ($8.40) from her own relatives in Abẹokuta and started to trade in small amounts of provisions, but Bọla said she should go carry on her trade where she got the money. So although she would like to earn some money, she cannot.

Meanwhile, her schoolmates and even her younger half-sister have better clothes and cleaner, better-furnished homes than she does. As a result, she is increasingly embarrassed and ashamed to visit them since she cannot reciprocate equally. Her problem, she says, is that she is an ọ̀dè (a "wishy-washy" person, a "sucker" or a "glutton for punishment"), and so she does not fight Bọla enough nor find a way to do what she wants. It is this personality trait, she says, that she must overcome.

The Room and Compound

The "room and parlor" that Bọla Onadele and his family tenant are bright and clean. The house is only six years old, and has amenities older buildings lack, including a flush toilet and overhead shower stall in back, higher ceilings and larger windows than was formerly the standard, and fresher paint. The rent reflects these differences — Bọla pays £2 ($5.60) a month for each of the two rooms.

Despite the potential comfort of the rooms, however, two factors make life in them difficult. One is the size of the family, two adults and six children (including Jimọh and Bukọla), occasionally augmented by long visits of Bọla's mother or Ma Lara's firstborn son. For this household the parlor must serve as the sitting room, dining room, nursery (a metal crib in one corner was bought for Lara in Bọla's more extravagant days), children's sleeping room (the thin reed mats on which they sleep on the cement floor are rolled up during the day), and study. Short stools, a small table, a cushioned sofa four feet long, and two folding chairs supply what space there is to sit, study, and eat. In the bedroom the only furniture is a large wooden bedstead covered with a pile of reed mats and a box in which Bọla stores all his Yoruba-style clothing. (He almost always wears European-style shirt and trousers because, he says, they are less cumbersome for working.)

The second reason for the closeness of the rooms is that every bit of left-over space is used for storage. Not only are there the usual utensils, clothes, books, medicines, and other household items, but also there is a large variety of building materials, tools, auto parts and other materiel that Bọla keeps whether or not it is usable. The resulting clutter is impressive: pipe fittings, a broken gas hot plate Bọla found in a field, a generator housing, a disused draftsman's board, the back bumper of Bọla's car and several pieces of lumber and tin roofing sheets fill the parlor, even the foot of the crib that Lọla is not yet big enough to need. In the bedroom are two tool boxes, a wire stretched across the room from which hangs Bọla and Ma Lara's clothing, two old bicycles, a number of boxes and loose tools, and a small table that Ma Lara used to use for trading. Altogether the bedroom is less crowded than the parlor, for as with other Yoruba families, it is primarily Bola's room, while the parlor is for the rest of the family. During their long argument Ma Lara slept on the parlor floor with her children.

The Onadeles occupy the first two of the three rooms on the left of the passageway through the house. Almost every other household head in the twelve-room house is Ijebu, but three of the wives — Ma Lara, the goldsmith's wife (also Egba), and the Ibo wife who moved out during the study — are not. In all only twenty-one people live in the building, of which total the Onadeles are eight. Upstairs a civil servant, his teacher wife and two children occupy all three rooms on one side, the rich merchant's wife has two rooms to herself, and the transporter for whom Bola is building a house lives alone in the sixth room because his two wives and five children have two rooms in the adjoining house. That house, which is part of the same compound and shares the common back yard, is simply a two-story row of four rooms, with an exterior stairway and balcony providing access to the rooms above. In the yard the occupants of both houses attend to cooking, washing, and other chores, competing with several chickens, two goats, Bola's two ducks, clotheslines, the goldsmith's shed, the water tap, four cooking sites, and childrens toys for a bit of space. There is every reason to believe that a few more years of such intensive use will take the remaining freshness out of the compound and make it yield to newer housing as a desirable place to live.

Summary

Whether or not the Onadeles are able to move out by that time to better housing is very much open to question. First, of course, they may not remain together as a family. But even if they do, the future is in doubt.

The sources of instability are many. Bola's querulousness probably has roots both in his early family life and in his present economic insecurity, especially since the building boom of the period around independence has subsided. Whatever its source, though, it works against friendships, enduring work relationships, and the support of family and kin. Bola is not a member of any town-based or other association at all, being cynically distrustful of most institutions including especially the church, which he never attends though he was raised as a Christian. His only good friend and *confidant* is Julius Omito, the Ijaw teacher he has known since his childhood travels with his mother to the rivers.

Second, Bola has a penchant for wildly unrealizable schemes, which he sees as devices to turn his dwindling finances back toward growth. Some ideas are related to his work; for some he has no special knowledge at all. During the study he spoke of getting a license to import gravel-digging machinery, of a large-scale cement block-making plant, of supplying sand and gravel to foreign contractors, and of becoming a land speculator. He had also bought two northern calves which he thought he might raise and sell at a good profit, but he had to keep them in a tiny storage stall, and both soon died. Even the building lot that he owns and on which he wants to build a house "this year" is a problem, because title to the land is in legal dispute between segments of an Ibadan family only some of whom signed Bola's deed. Bola is always extremely anxious to prove the quality of his building skills to his clients, but as he tries to cut labor costs and has developed a reputation for penny-pinching and reneging on wages, the enthusiasm of his workers and the grade of the work that they do declines. On any of these arrangements he has tried, Bola has lost money, not profited.

Finally, the general economic situation, over which he has no control, is a real enough threat. His present clients take longer and longer to accumulate money enough for a new phase of their buildings, and fewer people seem to be starting houses. The political insecurity in 1965 and 1966 may have been a contributing factor here, but no one is sure when, or whether, the climate will improve. Meanwhile the children are often mildly ill with coughs or colds, the periods without work are growing longer, and it is difficult for Bola or Ma Lara to see an end to the downward spiralling of their own relationship and their social lives.

Discussion: Authority, and the Meaning of Work

Seniority and Authority. A strict system of seniority governs normal interpersonal relations among the Yoruba. Though it originates within the family and compound, it extends far beyond it. The symbolic markers of seniority are ever-present: nearly every salutation indicates — by its duration, content, depth of bowing, and the pronouns meaning "you" — the relative seniority of the individuals involved. That seniority rather than age is the characteristic to which Yorubas attach importance is demonstrated by the instances when the two principles are in contraposition. For while many seniors are likely to be older than their juniors (elders in a family, master craftsmen or teachers, for example), there are instances where the senior in a situation is the younger person. Thus a child in a lineage is senior to a newly-inmarried wife even though she may be older, a band leader may be senior to an older man who has left his band to start another, and a supervisor may be senior to much older workers.

Any senior has a right to unquestioned service, deference, and submissiveness from any junior. In domestic chores children (and in rural compounds the younger wives) are on call for any senior, and should undertake even the heaviest work without having to be asked. The greater the disparity in seniority, the quicker to serve the junior should be. At the other extreme, when age and seniority are at odds, age mitigates the duty to obey.

The importance of seniority has not diminished in new urban areas like the migrant areas of Ibadan. To the extent that the separate nuclear families of an urban compound like Bọla Ọnadele's get along, a man may expect any woman younger than he is to attend to necessary chores and errands. Similarly any adult may send a child on an errand he or she knows is within the child's capabilities. It is not a question of "favors;" these are rights that seniors hold, in return for which they have their own obligations to lead, to teach, and to aid their juniors.

The system of seniority establishes a single hierarchy of reciprocal obligations in all situations. Within its strict framework, many acts of stubbornness, laziness, independence, originality, or idiosyncrasy may be interpreted as insubordination and impudence. These judgments were made of Ma Lara's behavior both by Bọla and by her own uncle. The uniformity that this code of authority imposes on wives, children, servants, and employees alike constrains the common language often used for all these relationships: Bọla and others speak in English of "sacking" (firing, divorcing) either a recalcitrant wife or a difficult employee.

Yoruba conceptions of seniority place a difficult burden upon juniors. Children often get less food, or less of the choice food, than their parents. Disobedience is severely punished (B. LeVine 1962). Yet seniors, too, are burdened by the system they control. With his social status in part dependent upon his ability to control juniors, the lenient or indulgent parent or employer is "abnormal," and not to be copied. A common way to insult seniors in arguments is to imply that they are senior only in name, or in body, but that no parallel respect is due them. By contrast, however, the senior who is most rigid about the respect due him by juniors is the most likely to become enraged when he suspects he is not getting it. Perhaps Bọla's anger at his wife reveals a deep doubt about his own self-esteem.

The Meaning of Work. When asked for information on his household budget, Bọla Ọnadele demurred. "Only an *àkòwé* [a clerk]," he said, would keep records of "how three-penny bits and halfpennies get out of his pockets." At first this rebuff was discouraging, and indeed we were unable to obtain a clear picture of his finances. Subsequent reflection on his and others' statements and actions, however, revealed the multiple significance of Bọla's simple remark. Anthropologists are often led to their insights by such unintentional probes and responses, and have learned not to force inquiry — for instance an interview schedule on budgets — down paths they alone select. In this case Bọla was saying a great deal about the meaning of work and income for contemporary urbanites.

First, by comparison with the recent Euro-American world, work is a more integral part of life, not a "world" of its own. In physical terms, a high proportion of the men and women of Yoruba cities do their work, or at least a portion of it, in their own compounds. Cooking, taking care of children, entering into disputes or resolving them, or chatting with neighbors during the course of the day may be "inefficient" in Western terms, but many Yoruba enjoy the opportunity to pursue such tasks while they are working. Part of the high value that Ijebu place on self-employment derives from the greater possibility, if one is one's own master, to work at home. There, one can spend time on all the people and problems, including of course those of work, that are part of one's life. Chief Ogunkọya, whom we shall meet in Chapter IX, has achieved this status fully. Similarly, the offices of most of the most prominent Ijebus — merchants, lawyers, and contractors — are at home.

Financially, too, "business" funds are not separated from "personal" funds. Neither Michael Odusanya nor Bọla Ọnadele keeps detailed records of his business. Bọla keeps no financial records at all. Like Michael he sets a price on a job — often a phase of a building — and then uses the lump sum agreed upon with his client to buy materials, pay his workers (he calculates no "wage" for his own time), and support his family. The amount that he can use for his family obviously varies with the corners he cuts on materials and labor and with the accuracy of his original calculations. For eight weeks prior to the study he had been living and working on a hundred pounds ($280) that his cousin the lawyer had given him for the construction of the boys' quarter of his house. As that ran out and a next large sum did not at first appear, Bọla became increasingly irritable. As he pointed out, he would next be dependent upon Dr. Ayandejọ. In the last analysis, unless Bọla's budget were examined in detail over a period of many months, no meaningful statement of his financial position could be offered.

A second insight into the meaning of work is indicated by Bọla's disparagement of the akọwe. The precolonial Yoruba economy was based on farming, craft production, and trade. Colonial institutions — government, mercantile houses, and the missions created a fourth broad class of occupations, all demanding, as a basic skill, literacy in English. Akọwe means "clerk" first, but catechists, teachers, communications and transport office workers, officials in banks, retail houses, and government enterprises are all akọwe. For migrant Ijebu like Bọla, then, urban workers are either akọwe or onísòwò, traders (who may only buy and sell some commodity, apply craft skills, or do both). Each occupational category includes both rich and poor — lawyer and messenger boy on one side of the dichotomy, industrialist and pepper hawker on the other. In this context Bọla's remark about the akọwe's concern with petty record-keeping is one indication of a wider fact of urban culture: the primary occupational distinction is not ranked. That is, akọwe are not any more prestigeful than onisọwo. There are no "blue collar/white collar" or "worker/boss" connotations here, for the occupations involved crosscut such an implied distinction of inferiority and superiority.

These two statements, that work is conceived as inseparable from daily life as a whole, and that urban Yoruba do not attach greater or less prestige to the basic distinction they make between kinds of occupations, come together in a third. In modern Yoruba society one's job is not held to be a particularly important guide to one's status in society at large.

In modern Western history what a man *does* has been seen virtually to indicate what sort of whole man he is. The question, "What do you do?," is second only to asking a person's name in seeking to identify his place in the social world. Responses like "student" or "car salesman" or "steelworker" are held to signify a great many things about him beyond merely what he does for several hours a day. Sociologists have shown how occupations can be ranked according to the "prestige" they confer upon the people holding them. It is, in the West, as if a man were some function of his job.

To the contrary, in Yoruba society men and women are judged not by how they earn their money but by how they spend it. Since a man's occupational role is less distinct from his other roles, which are more visible in any case, it is necessarily less important in assessing him. And since high income may derive from a great variety of careers, the occupations themselves take on less importance for the granting of prestige.

Instead, the *ènìà pàtàkì*, the "man of principle" (Bascom 1951a:493-497), is the most prestigeful role in Yoruba society, today as well as long ago. The ẹnia pataki is gentlemanly, fearless, and socially responsible. He is always followed by a large group of friends and supporters, whom he attracts partly by his personal qualities but especially by his organization of pleasurable redistributive events. That is, he either spends his own money entertaining lavishly, or mobilizes and spends others' resources in such a way as to be seen as the sponsor of the ceremony, funeral, feast, or some more minor bit of hospitality. His prestige allows him to be outspoken, to take liberties with others' property, and to preen in his public behavior. Finally, in personal terms, he himself will have *àláfìà,* a quality to be described later, in the discussion of Chief Ogunkọya.

There are many other evaluations of status among one's fellows that Yoruba discern (Bascom 1951a). A man may be a "rich man," a "gentleman," or a "man of renown," or alternatively a "poor man," a "miser," or an "unlucky person.'' All of them are unrelated to the job that a man holds, though some cannot be achieved without high income.

This relative detachment of occupation and social status has several important consequences for society. As we have seen, it predisposes Ijebu, at least, toward jobs close to home where they may begin to behave as an aspiring ẹnia pataki should. Second, it permits (or produces) a great deal of career-switching. Instead of aiming for a particular occupation and status, achieving or missing it, and settling down to enjoy the associated status, for Yoruba the pursuit of prestige is a career in its own right. Bọla Ọnadele has been a photographer, repairman, gravel dealer, and builder; Saliu Wahabi, Abel Ogunkọya, and Victor Falujọ (see Chapters VII, IX and X) have also changed occupations as they aimed for more income and more status.

It the working style of one's job and the durability of one's job tenure are thus subordinated to the quest for status and prestige, so is the importance of one's day-to-day work load. Bọla gave up hour after hour and day after day to arguments and anxieties over his personal reputation among neighbors and acquaintances. In the single long quarrel with Ma Lara he ''lost'' at least five working days. But ''lost working days'' is an improper phrase. Days are not defined as ''working days'' which can be ''lost.'' Bọla simply devoted the time he found it necessary to devote to pursuing a variety of important personal goals. For urban Yoruba like him, work is but one activity among many which may lead to those goals.

Footnotes

[1]Ogun, the Yoruba god of iron and of war, patron of hunters, warriors, blacksmiths, and recently of automobile and truck drivers, may be sworn to using any iron object.

CHAPTER VII

Getting Up: The Wahabi Family

New Buildings

The newer sections of housing in the predominantly migrant quarters of Ibadan seem at once both more and less ''urban'' than the older areas. Like small towns and villages, they present a basic quietness which voices, radios, or vehicles pierce only individually, not with the hubbub of busier areas. There is as well more interaction among neighbors in different houses, both because there are fewer people in each house and because the many empty building lots and grid-patterned streets tend to separate clusters of houses. The inhabitants thus share a sense of place — a sense of being cast together in a way more common to villagers than to the urbanites of the densely-settled central areas of the city. On the other hand, there are far fewer goats and chickens foraging about than in either villages or the center of town, and the costlier houses reflect the greater affluence of their tenants. All within the same municipal boundaries, the city grades, by degrees, into suburban fringe.

One such area lies south of Liberty Stadium. Many of the streets are paved, though narrow. Nearly all the houses are two-storied and are made of faced cement blocks. The most impressive of them are painted in bright hues, have louvered glass windows, a bit of lawn or garden, and sometimes a wall built all around: these belong to wealthy traders and senior civil servants, even to kings of other cities. Most are much less elaborate, and are the homes of middle-level civil servants, private business officers and professionals. About one in five is uncompleted, with only one story so far built, or unpainted, or with yard and kitchen and bathroom stalls still to be finished. Since the second floor is a layer of concrete which will not weather, the flat-topped, single-story house is perfectly liveable until its owner can raise enough money to get on with the job.

One of these undecorated dwellings is that of *Sáliù Wahábì,* a senior records officer in the Western Nigeria Housing Corporation and a younger son of a pious Muslim family in Ijebu Ode. Only thirty-three when he moved into his own house in 1963, and already the father of six children, he is prospering well by dint of his own early efforts and energy. The study of his family stretched over Christmas, New Year's, and Muslim Ramadan, and afforded a view of his own celebrations of his urban success.

A Busy Season

At three o'clock the children are eating their lunch in the passage through the house. Four of them, two older girls and two younger boys, are eating eba with a sauce of ewedu leaf. A fifth, a boy who looks weak or sick, is being fed rice by his mother. Mama *Olóbì,* Saliu's elderly mother, comes in from the back yard carrying an old green dress she is cutting up to make into some other piece of clothing. The sixth child, a baby boy, crawls up to the four who are sitting together but is pulled away to the front porch by his mother, Saliu's second wife. When the radio in the tenant's room booms out an advertisement, this wife, Ma *Èbùn,* chimes in with it, "There's protein in Tomapep!"

Mama *Yínká,* the senior wife, returns to her table in front of the house, where she earns money primarily by hairdressing but also by selling small amounts of salt and peppers, tomatoes, and palm and peanut oil for cooking. When her sick boy, Wọle, asks for some gari and water to drink with a piece of *mọyín-mọyín,* [1] she asks her oldest, Yinka, to get it for him. Yinka, who at nearly eight is both a bright and obedient girl, does so at once. Yinka, Wọle (who just turned four), and *Dayọ̀* (a twenty-month-old boy), are the senior wife's children. In the same order by sex but somewhat younger are the junior wife's children, Ẹbun (a girl, six), *Ráfíu* (at 3 3/4 called "Manager" because he used to cry from morning till night for no obvious reason and was nicknamed by his parents *"Ijágbọn* Manager" ["Manager (i.e. boss) of Trouble-makers]), and *Dọyin,* a boy of fifteen months. Soon all the children are running around in the passage shouting, pulling each other down, and laughing loudly. When the noise gets so great that the women on the front verandah cannot hear one another, Mama Yinka yells at them to stop.

Ma Ẹbun is telling about the time she bought a block of ice at one of the Levantine trading companies to sell in smaller pieces. She had been surprised to see how much she got for her three shillings (42¢). She brought it home and proceeded to sell it as she had seen other women doing, insulating it with a heavy blanket of sawdust and chipping off small pieces to sell to curious children at a penny each. The next day she found she had made five shillings already and had about a third of the block left. She ran out of curiosity-seekers, though, and the rest melted before she could sell it!

At about four-thirty Saliu himself returns from the office. He works regular government hours, from eight to three without a scheduled break. He says hello to everyone briefly, then goes into the parlor to turn on his large radio. A few minutes later he calls for Dọyin, his youngest child, and Ma Ẹbun carries him in. Soon Mama Yinka goes in, too, to welcome him home properly — a quick nod at the door, in Yoruba culture, ordinarily signifies not simply preoccupation with some other thought but hostility or anger. Ma Ẹbun shows her husband some clothes, made from the same material, that she has just finished sewing for her two elder children. Saliu remarks that it is a nice Christmas present,[2] and Ẹbun herself, after putting on the new dress, dances the new "kpalongo" step to the radio tunes in joy and appreciation. Because of a long series of arguments, Ma Ẹbun no longer lives in Saliu's house, but her two older children do, and Dọyin will probably join them in a year or so when he is weaned and toilet-trained. Ẹbun and Rafiu get no deliberate second-class treatment from Mama Yinka, who serves as mother to all five children who live in the house, but they nevertheless feel a bit lonely. Ẹbun's dance expresses her happiness at getting this special treatment.

A man with a small goatee walks in. Ma Ẹbun kneels to greet him, while Saliu shakes his hand. The man is an Alhaji (a Muslim who has made the holy pilgrimage to Mecca), who is from the same quarter of Ijebu Ode as Saliu and also works at the Government offices in Ibadan. "Alhaji" remarks that Ẹbun dances well, and says that he is on his way to visit the site where his own home is being built. Saliu, who is known as "Number One" to his friends because he always got the best grades in his primary school class, decides to go with him.

After the music stops, the children start playing again. Little Dayọ climbs up on his half-sister Ẹbun's lap and she tosses him up and down with her belly. Accidentally he pokes her eye with his finger. Ẹbun shouts to Yinka, "Come and get *your* brother off me!" The distinction between the sets of full siblings is accented in the breach.

Soon Saliu returns, chases the children from the parlor, takes his goatskin from its nail on the wall, and kneels briefly to pray. Though he offers a drink, he himself takes no food or drink at all during this month of Ramadan from sunrise to sunset.

Later on, returning from a brief errand, Saliu starts talking about employment. He says there are not enough jobs, and that the government should create more agricultural projects and other jobs to absorb the rising population. He observes broadly that if there are any economists in the government they must not be doing their jobs well, because they should see to it that such projects are started, not just sit around and watch people helping themselves to public funds.

At that another visitor enters. He, too, is from *Igboro* quarter in Ijebu Ode, and is a builder. His brother built Saliu's house, but he himself is going to put up the second story since his brother is now too busy. Several more visitors enter and leave — a woman to thank Saliu for settling a quarrel between herself and her brother, another man simply to say hello, and a third woman who speaks privately to Saliu. Finally it is seven o'clock and dark enough out to break the day-long fast. Mama Yinka brings in a plate of àmàlà (made from yam flour) and ewedu sauce with two large pieces of meat. Saliu finishes, and then prays again on his goatskin. Outside in the passage Mama Yinka and the children are eating their supper, too.

At seven-thirty Saliu leaves to go to the nearby mosque, taking his prayer mat with him. He avoids one street because, he says, there is a small mosque there and the people always ask him to pray with them. He prefers a larger mosque beyond that one. On the way he stops to greet a friend he calls "Oba" ("King") because his surname is the same as that of the King of Ijebu! At the mosque are perhaps a hundred people, many ritually washing their feet and faces or spreading their mats in preparation for the service, which is signalled by one man who rises and, in a booming voice, calls the faithful to prayer. Saliu hurries in to join the throng.

At home Mama Yinka is carrying the contents of her sales table inside for the night. The tenants of the room-and-parlor on the right, an Ijebu couple with no children, are sitting outside on the verandah talking and joking, but the house is otherwise quiet. Old Mama Olobi is already in her room, and Ebun is dozing in the passageway. Mama Yinka has already put the smaller children to bed in the last room on the left, and she wakes Ebun to send her in, too. Mama Yinka sleeps in the same room, on one of the two beds. A few minutes later she decides to retire as well. At nine Saliu returns with two friends. They listen to the news quietly, commenting only that "we're still one country yet" when it is stated that a man who stole a car in Lagos and drove it to Onitsha in the disaffected Eastern Region has been returned to Lagos for trial. After the news, his guests departed, Saliu himself goes into his bedroom, behind the parlor, where he sleeps alone.

A Woman's Work

On Friday afternoon the electric current, suffering one of its frequent breakdowns, comes back on just in time for the call in Arabic to Friday prayers, the most important of the week. Mama Olobi rises from the verandah to go inside to listen. The postman comes to the house with an infrequent letter, which turns out to be a calendar for the new year sent by Mama Yinka's brother-in-law from Lagos. Mama Yinka is plaiting the hair of a woman in a standard style, called "rattlesnake's tail" after the way each plait is woven. She calls Yinka to take little Dayo away from her feet. The girl carries him into the passage where the middle boys, Wole (who is now better) and "Manager," are sitting on a board set onto two empty milk cans and rolling forward or back until one end of the board falls off. Dayọ cries and starts to toddle back to his mother, but Ẹbun picks him up and soothes him until he is willing to get down and play.

Outside a boy who looks Ibo or Urhobo asks to buy a bottle of palm oil. Mama Yinka tells him the price has gone up. He says he has to go back and tell the woman who sent him.

Fifteen minutes or so later, Dayọ starts to cry again. His mother guesses that he is hungry, and gives him some ẹ̀kọ, a steamed paste made from cornstarch. But he is not satisfied; since Ẹbun and Yinka have gone out, Mama Yinka runs across the street herself to buy a penny's worth of candy to pacify Dayọ. Such interruptions are expected by women having their hair done, but they are frustrating to Mama Yinka, who has several customers now waiting. Yinka returns a few minutes later and her mother asks her to light the fire to heat up the sauce. The girl cannot find the matches and her mother has to interrupt her own work. When she finds them just where she said they probably were, she throws them at her daughter and yells insults at her. Even at the age of seven, Yoruba children have responsibilities that they cannot take lightly.

Mama Yinka spends between one hour and three combing out, blackening, arranging and tying the plaits of each customer, for which she receives, depending on the time the whole job takes, between one shilling (14¢) and two and sixpence (35¢). It is because of the holidays that she is as busy as she is today; often she has only two or three customers in a day.

A few minutes later, a finely-dressed woman whom Mama Yinka must know turns the corner and heads down the street. Mama Yinka calls Yinka to go and carry her obviously heavy satchel. Wọle wants to follow, but his mother calls him back saying, "Adéwọlé! Adewọle! If you go, you're in trouble!"

Wọle doesn't turn back. Ten minutes later both youngsters return, each carrying an orange. Reciprocity has been quick and full. As brother and sister sit down to peel their fruit, Ẹbun and Manager march up and down the verandah chanting a nonsense verse that includes Mama Yinka's empty threat:

Ram kills Ram
You won't escape today.
If you go today
You'll not repeat it soon!

Outside the women are talking about the increase in the price of palm oil (which is the staple cooking oil and sauce base). Mama Yinka says that, as usual, people think it's the petty traders like her who just want more money and refuse to believe that the wholesale price has risen. An orange hawker who has paused on her rounds agrees, but adds that the worst part of such rising prices is that husbands don't want to increase the "chop-money" (household allowance) they give to their wives. Though it is not obviously apropos, she tells of her friend's husband, who stays in the office until nine at night and then complains that, even though he didn't eat at home, there was never any money in the house. At last he came home drunk one night and his wife realized that he was drinking his money away in beer and that she was not to blame at all.

Yinka is next set to cleaning the rice that is to be cooked for supper — she has many more chores in this large household than does Ẹbun, who is less closely supervised since her own mother is absent. Yinka goes slowly through the bowl of rice for bad grains, washes it once, and then "pans" it carefully to take out the last pebbles and bits of dirt. This last operation is difficult for her. At that moment a pregnant neighbor has come across the street to borrow a few of the large leaves used for steaming food from Mama Yinka. In return, she asks the neighbor to do the rice since she is so busy with her customers. The woman agrees, if she can have a few more of the leaves.

"OK, take them," says Mama Yinka. "But just do that rice for me. I don't want my husband to grind pebbles with his teeth along with his rice tonight. After a whole day with no food you wouldn't like that too much — or aren't you fasting?"

Evoking a laugh from all the women, the neighbor replies, "No, my own God is not so hard to please that I have to go so many hours without food for Him." She refastens her wrapper under her arms and tackles the rice while Yinka watches. By six o'clock Saliu is still not home from work, and Mama Yinka puts supper on the firepot in the backyard for the children.

Holiday Court

January 2 is a holiday from work, since the first was on a Sunday. "Number One" has locked himself inside the parlor, where he is reading a book of law for the layman that he enjoys. His attempt at privacy is futile, though, for visitors start coming by midmorning. First it is the builder, who wants only to take some tools he has been storing in an unused kitchen stall in Saliu's yard.

Next comes Ma Ẹbun, with Ẹbun carrying her handbag. When Yinka sees her she kneels respectfully in welcome. Ma Ẹbun calls all the children, then gives Yinka a packet of cookies to distribute to "all of you and to Ẹbun's as well", meaning the two sibling groups separately. Then she enters the parlor.

She barely gets started talking to Saliu when a woman enters with a thick black sweater on under her blouse, her head tie covering her ears, and a baby on her back. In January the cold harmattan winds blow south from the desert, and the mornings in Ibadan may reach a chilly fifty degrees. She greets Saliu in a thick Ijebu accent, then sits down to relate her problem.

It is her junior wife, she says. The junior wife gets more favors from their husband. Not that she minds that by itself, but now the woman won't do any cooking.

At this point a second woman who is not Ijebu comes in, greets everyone, and takes a seat, while the first woman goes on.

Last night, she says, the junior wife would not prepare food for the kids, though it was her turn to do so. Their husband demands that the kids always be fed before seven thirty. He knew that it was the junior wife's turn to cook, so he didn't say anything. But when he saw her — the senior wife telling the story — eating ẹba and meat, he started raging.

Again she is interrupted, this time by a man whose cap is pulled down over his ears, too. Saliu talks to him in the passage for a few moments, then comes back in, only to have another man, with facial marks indicating he is from Ibadan, step in. Saliu greets him and then dresses the younger man down for going off with the change from a one-pound note (bill) nearly two weeks ago. The man has contrived a story about how he was called home before he could bring the change, but it convinces no one even though he repeats it three times. Saliu lets him go, giving his other guests a knowing smile as the man sheepishly departs.

The woman starts up again. Her husband yelled at her, saying she shouldn't eat if the children have not and thus blaming her for what is happening. She explains that she wasn't even eating, really, since she never eats ẹba — she was just nibbling at it from hunger. She says she knows the second wife is not willing to be the junior — that she was married before and was used to ordering people around, not obeying orders as a junior wife should.

Before Saliu can respond, yet a third woman, also Ijebu and perhaps five months pregnant, comes in, and starts telling her story to the growing assembly.

Her husband won't give her the money to go to the prenatal clinic at the hospital. The first time he gave her enough money, but now he says he will give only ten shillings, though it will cost almost twice that. She notes that she explained where every penny went the first time, but that her husband just told her to get the rest herself if she needs more. Now she is determined not to go to the hospital at all, in the hope that he will get angry and complain to other people about her, so she in turn can tell everyone how mean he is.

Saliu settles her problem quickly. He says that you do not have to pay again for your registration fee and card at the hospital, so it will cost her less than the ten shillings her husband gave her. She doesn't believe this, so Saliu says that if she does spend more, she should come and tell him, and he'll give her the extra cost and retrieve it himself from her husband.

The second woman who came in has other advice, of a sort. She says the next time her husband wants to "do it" she should shut her thighs tight. Then she won't have any problem with hospital fees. Saliu laughs and agrees that that would be the best solution.

All three women rise to go. Saliu promises the first one that he will speak to her husband. The third says she will return to tell him what happens. After they go, he says that all three are the wives of Ijebu acquaintances of his who have built houses not far away. In the days following he attends to each problem as he finds the time and energy for discussions with the offending husbands.

It is briefly quiet, and Saliu talks about his own family. He wants his children early, he says, so he can take care of their educational expenses before he stops working. Now that he has six, he plans to stop having children — though if he has a seventh, he hopes it will be a daughter. Meanwhile, he adds, he wants to divorce his second wife. She is "too troublesome," and were it not for the baby still with her, he would stop her from coming there at all.

Breaking the Ramadan Fast

The first day of the new month in the Muslim calendar, signalling the end of the daily fast, is Id-el-Fitri, second only to the Muslim New Year (Id-el-Kabir) in importance. Again government offices close. By eight in the morning Saliu has left for the vast open praying ground outside the city, where scores of thousands of faithful Muslims will gather to offer their thanks to God. The four older children have accompanied him. Mama Yinka is dressing to go out, too. She has no new clothes for this holiday, but takes out a well-ironed "bottom-boxi," a suit of fine clothes that lies at the "bottom of the box" for wearing only on special occasions. This set is a matching light green cotton wrapper, blouse, and high head-tie, to which she adds earrings, arm bangles, necklace, and a well-cleaned pair of sandals. Dayọ's outfit is of similarly-colored material.

Later, when everyone returns, general preparations for a modest feast begin. A huge pot of rice is set to boiling, and a sauce is made with perhaps four pounds of beef in it. An Ibadan man and his wife who are planning to build a house on the vacant lot next door come to visit, and stay for the meal after greeting some people in neighboring houses as well. "Ọba" stops by and is persuaded to stay, too. When the rice is done, the tenant's wife begins to dish it out. Mama Yinka is at the sauce pot and serves the meat. The girls distribute the dishes on trays according to Mama Yinka's directions, starting with several of the families next door and across the street. Mama Yinka serves her husband herself, bowing slightly to mark the exceptionality of this final fast-breaking meal. While everyone is eating Ma Ẹbun arrives, and she is also given a large plate of food.

When all the men go out briefly an hour later, Saliu's two wives, with the arbitration of the Ibadan woman guest, settle an argument between them over whether Ma Ẹbun should have arrived earlier to help cook, and whether she should also have contributed some money toward the expenses of the meal. Ma Ẹbun's ambiguous status in the household is really at issue: if she wants reconciliation, which seems to underlie her frequent visits, from Mama Yinka's point of view she is not behaving in an especially exemplary way to get back in. On the other hand, Mama Yinka herself has mixed feelings about wanting her junior wife back: she would enjoy relief from her double duties as mother to five children, but has had serious differences with Ma Ebun before that make her not extremely unhappy that the current fight, which is between Ma Ebun and Saliu, may end in final divorce. In any case, the guest, in good Yoruba style, finds fault with both of them in the current tiff. Later in the afternoon the women's talk turns to religion, to the conversion in school of one of Mama Yinka's sisters to Catholicism, and to her own conviction that trees and other objects may really be inhabited by spirits.

More Visitors

On Saturday afternoon Saliu is again holding informal "court" in his parlor. The woman whose husband would not pay for the clinic is back again to complain, and a second woman, herself from Ibadan, but the senior of three wives of an Ijebu friend of Saliu's, is there at Saliu's behest because of the quarreling in that household.

Mama Yinka is outside, plaiting hair. When two motorcycles pull up from opposite directions at almost the same instant, everyone laughs loudly at the coincidence. One is the "contributions man" to collect from Mama Yinka. She saves two shillings a day in this modified esusu, and on the first of the month, gets back two less than the total number of shillings she puts in. For that fee she saves a good deal of money she would otherwise spend in bits and pieces. Since she knows the contributions man "right down to his parents' house in Ijebu Ode," she has complete confidence in him.

The other young man, dressed in a European-style suit, wants the "landlord." He turns out to be a life insurance salesman. He has a fast and high-pressured pitch, assuring Saliu that all the people who take out policies today are to be awarded prizes. He ends with a flattering, "I don't think I need to tell you the benefits of owning an insurance policy, do I? You already know . . ."

He loses. Saliu says he does not intend to take out insurance now — perhaps next month. After he escorts the man out, he comments that he has too many things to do with his money already, and that his house is a form of insurance anyway. When the second story is put up, he explains, he will move his family upstairs and rent out all the rooms on the ground floor. That should pay for most of his children's school fees. If he should die prematurely, he will have his family move back to Ijebu Ode, and the income from the upper floor, too, can go to support the children. He does not think he will be able to afford university education, but he does want all of his children to finish secondary school. These calculations also enter into his decision not to have as many children as he otherwise might.

Monday is the first day of the new school year, and Yinka and Ebun are gone most of the day. Yinka loves school and has been anxious to get back; Ebun is not so sure, having only attended private pre-school classes before.

In the afternoon Mama Yinka is doing the hair of the new tenant in the second room on the right, who moved in on the weekend. She gets a routine style, similar to the one Yinka usually has, with twelve divisions of the hair and thus twelve long plaits. A firewood seller comes down the road from the direction of the bush outside of town with a huge load of branches on her head. Mama Yinka calls her, and says she hasn't much wood left. The woman wants one and six (20¢) for the whole load. Mama Yinka offers one and three. When the woman at last agrees, Mama Yinka offers one and two instead. After a briefer argument the woman gives in, and with some effort takes the wood down from its perch. As is usual in dealing with hawkers, Mama Yinka then hands her even less — a shilling. The woman, not anxious to have the wood reloaded, nonetheless says she cannot take only a shilling. A penny is added, and she accepts, somewhat coolly. After she goes, the women congratulate Mama Yinka on getting such a load so cheaply, and she smiles proudly.

Two new customers come for Mama Yinka, and then another. It is getting toward nightfall, so she breaks off to put a pot of beans on for supper while Yinka does dishes. The smaller children are back in the parlor riding around on each other as horses. It is not until well after dark, nearly eight o'clock, that Mama Yinka finishes her last customer of the day and sits down, fatigued, to eat. The harmattan is breaking now, and the evenings are warmer and more humid. The whole family and the tenants sit together on the verandah chatting until late into the night.

Biography: Saliu Wahabi

Number One's grandfather was a slave dealer who turned to the quieter pursuits of farming and religion at the end of the last century. His trade ties with the Islamic city of Ilorin influenced him to be among the first Muslims in Ijebu Ode, and Saliu's close relatives include the present *imam* of his quarter of the town. Saliu's father was a farmer but was an excellent student of the Koran in Arabic as well; the first school that he sent Saliu to was a Koranic school. It was Saliu's mother (Mama Olobi, who lives with him now) who saw advantages to Western education, being herself a trader in fish (and later *obì* or kola nuts) along the Ijebu coast with relatives in the colonial capital, Lagos. She was the second of four wives, and had only one other child (a girl much older than Saliu), so his conservative father, who had had ''many'' children, said that the boy could attend Western school only if his mother would be responsible. It was she, therefore, who paid all the fees for his primary schooling. With a late start, Saliu finished Standard VI in 1949 at the age of nineteen.

For the next few months he worked as an attendant in a shop in Ijebu Ode owned by a kinsman of his mother. A man a few doors away owned a typewriter, and Saliu bought a typing book and practiced an hour every day after work until he knew how to type. Then he got a job with the local government as a clerk-typist for £6 ($16.80) a month. Four years later a shuffling of local administration left Saliu in what he considered a dead-end position, so he applied for and won a post at the Housing Corporation in Ibadan, where he has been for the twelve years since.

He started in 1955 as a typist at £10 ($28) a month, but moved fairly steadily upward to his present position of senior records officer at £33. 10s. 0d. ($93.80) a month. The only serious threat to his position came in 1965, when political victimization of Ijebus was underway after the Regional government changed hands in 1963. Some Ijebus in his division of the Corporation were removed, but Saliu's own immediate superior, though not an Ijebu, protected him. Saliu does not know how far he might rise before he retires, but thinks he could become department head unless the turnover in the senior positions is very slow.

One of the facilities available to him at work is the Cooperative Thrift and Loan Society, from which he borrowed money to build his house. Repayment of that loan takes £9. 10s. 0d. ($26.60) from his current monthly pay packet. Income tax takes £1. 15s. 0d. ($4.90, about 5 per cent of his income). A savings plan, from which he withdraws to distribute gifts on trips home to Ijebu Ode, takes £4 ($11.20) more. From the remaining £18 ($50.40), he gives Mama Yinka £10 ($28.00) ''chop money,'' Ma Ẹbun £2 ($5.60) for support of Dọyin, and Mama Olobi perhaps ten shillings ($1.40) for pocket money. With the remaining £5. 10s. 0d. Saliu pays his own minor food expenses and for transportation to work; he gives extra money to Mama Yinka when her allowance invariably runs out before the end of the month; he pays dues to two associations he is in, one of young Muslims from his quarter of Ijebu Ode and the other of Muslims interested in modern education; and he provides for the entertainment of his guests. He never goes to movies, plays, or night clubs, nor does he drink, smoke, or play the betting pools: all of this, he says, is forbidden by his religion. Finally, though he could get a government loan to buy a car, he could not now afford to run it; and when he is finished paying back the loan for his house, he will have larger educational expenses to meet.

Biographies: Wives, Children, and Mother

Saliu's main expenditures, thus, are on his own household. Originally he did not mean it to be so large. He married Mama Yinka in 1955, just before they came to Ibadan to live. She was also a Muslim, but her father worked for the local public works department and saw the value of western education even for his daughters. Though he had had three wives, the only children surviving are six of the nine (eight of whom were in four sets of twins!) born to Mama Yinka's mother — three of hers and all of the other wives' children died in infancy or childhood. Mama Yinka went through Standard VI and graduated in 1953. After two years as a shopkeeper's assistant at home in Ijebu Ode, she finally consented to Saliu's frequent proposals, and they married with full Muslim rites and a large reception.

When they came to Ibadan they rented a room near the heart of the city, in the oldest migrant area. The house was owned by an Ijebu hardware wholesaler from Epe and his wife, who sold provisions. Ma Ebun is their daughter. She was then in secondary modern school. "I got attracted to him — despite the fact that he brought his wife then. I never cared about boys in school. But here is someone quiet and gentle, admired by everyone in the house . . . I felt it wouldn't make any difference if I married him and became his second wife. That was, of course, if he took my notice — and he did. By the time I was taking my final exams in 1957, I was already pregnant for him. It was a blow to my parents. They thought I would grow up and further my education some more before settling down and marrying. And the cheek of it all, that I had laid myself down for a tenant! Anyway they didn't have any choice but to let me marry him. I did, and we moved on to Foko. I gave birth to a baby boy early in 1958.''

Ma Ebun had this boy before Mama Yinka had given birth to any children. Sometimes, in fact, Saliu says that he only married Ma Ebun because he thought that Mama Yinka might be permanently childless. In any case Ma Ebun says that trouble began immediately. She firmly refrains from accusing Mama Yinka of jealousy or anything worse, but says only that the baby died when he was eight months old, "miraculously." Soon thereafter, Mama Yinka also had a boy, but he died in 1960. Yoruba believe deeply in the power of personal forces in human affairs, and seek explanations of death in terms of human enemies and motivations.[3] Each woman had lost one child, and though Mama

Yinka says that the two deaths were simply "fate," a basic distrust between the two wives grew.

As they each began to have children who survived infancy, however, there ensued between them an accommodation which allows them to continue to be friendly if not intimate with one another. Mama Yinka bore Yinka in 1959, going home to Ijebu Ode to have her post-natal recuperation in the bosom of her family. In 1960 Ma Ebun had Ebun. In 1961 Ma Yinka had twins who died the same year, and in 1962 Wole was born. Ma Ebun had "Manager" in 1963. Finally Ma Yinka had Dayo and Ma Ebun had Doyin in 1965. All of the children after Yinka were born in Ibadan hospitals, and all had large "naming" ceremonies, at which Muslim religious leaders officiated, a week after their births. And except for Yinka, who was once treated by "native doctors"[4] in Ijebu Ode for a severe fever, all the remaining children have been notably healthy.

Ma Ebun confirms Mama Yinka's statement that the separation of Saliu and Ma Ebun is their own quarrel. She says that Saliu began criticizing her as soon as Ebun was born, and that his accusation that she was behaving too warmly toward his friends led to a particularly bitter fight. Ma Ebun's parents never liked her marriage very much, and have allowed her to come home to live without making very great efforts to help solve the problems. Meanwhile she is vague about her means of support — she sells some stockfish, but hints have been passed that she may also be earning money less honorably.

Mama Olobi, who has her own room, completes the household. Until two years ago she lived in Ijebu Ode, but Saliu says that he used to spend £3 or more for transport and gifts to other relatives every time he went to see her, which was sometimes twice a month. After he moved into his house, therefore, he brought her to live with him. She would rather be living at home, but is dependent upon Saliu. Her only other child, who, she reports, is "old enough to be Ba Yinka's mother," lives with her husband and grown children in Lagos. Mama Olobi is thankful that she had even those two children, for she thought she was going to be barren altogether. Though she is nearly 70 and physically feeble, she gets satisfaction from thinking that she is helping raise her grandchildren. In fact she does not do much at all in the house, moving from seat to seat as a quiet presence.

The New House

Saliu, his wife, five of his children, and his mother occupy four of the six rooms of his house. Another room was Ma Ebun's, but has lately been rented to a recently-married couple. A man who works as a night watchman and his wife have lived in the last room since Saliu moved in. Though the wife of the new tenant is at home in Ijebu, about to have a baby, and there are frequent overnight guests in the house (a daughter of Saliu's full sister visited for about a week), the usual population is twelve. The density of two people per room is the lowest we have seen so far. Rent from the two tenants covers both the electricity and the water bills for the whole house, and since there are no real estate taxes or other fixed costs, Saliu's expenses on the house are therefore only those of the original investment and further improvement.

Indeed, much remains to be done on the house. Though the construction blocks have been faced with cement, the building is unpainted inside or out. A stairway from the back yard leads up to the flat cement roof, which is, of course, to be the floor of the upper story when Saliu can afford to complete it. Two sets of kitchen, bathroom and latrine stalls also stand in the rear, but so far Saliu has not put in the flush toilets he intends to. Odd scraps of building materials lean against the sides of the house and lie in the yard, a pile of gravel lies at one front corner of the house, and of the few feet of earth between the street and the house, some is paved by reason of having been the spot where cement was mixed. It has taken five years to get the house to its present state of completion, and may take many more before it can be called finished.

The rooms, too, are spare. The three rooms used as bedrooms have only beds and a few clothing boxes in them; they are meant as sleeping-rooms, not as places of privacy or as assertions of individuality. The three areas that are heavily used are the back yard, the passage and verandah, and the parlor. The yard is ringed with a variety of receptacles — two large drums of water stored against the possibility of a break in the supply from the tap, a large earthen pot for cooling and storing drinking water, two smaller drums of palm oil, and large cans used as washing basins and rubbish containers. The passage and verandah are bare except for two wooden folding chairs and a narrow bench.

The parlor is easily the most decorated and comfortable place in the house. Yet much of the time when Saliu is not at home it is locked, especially so that the children will not disturb it. Inside are five cushioned chairs, a large combination radio-phonograph set, and two tables for eating, studying, ironing and writing. A large piece of linoleum covers most of the floor, and green printed curtains hang on the windows and doors of the room. Besides Saliu's prayer skin, a number of large calendars, almanacs, and two pictures decorate the otherwise gray cement walls. On the tables, window sills, and radio cabinet are books, mosquito coils, alarm clock, magazines, tumblers and other eating utensils, phonograph records and cans and packages of food and medicines. The "radiogram" is the proudest of the family's possessions: Saliu's fascination with the news reports and the women's frequent furtive dance steps to whatever music is on — even European classical — make it a center of enjoyment for everyone.

Summary

In the Wahabi family have merged the spartanism of the Victorian Christianity of Nigerian civil service life, of Islam and its many specific prohibitions, and of Ijebu ascetic values as well. Saliu's major goals concern the care of his family and the education of his children, and he is meeting those obligations comfortably. Nearly all of Saliu's and Mama Yinka's recreation takes the form of mutual visiting and discussion with friends and acquaintances. Some of their social contacts are from their home town, some are from work and some are from business contacts; neither Saliu nor his senior wife has any other kinsmen in Ibadan that they recognize. The devotion to people — it is far more than simple "gregariousness" or "sociability" — that characterizes Saliu has a return in the form of the respect and honor so many people show him by bringing their problems to him, asking him to join their associations, and listening to his advice. With a successful social career in progress, at the young age of thirty-seven he is already treated like an elder.

Discussion: Modern Muslims, Husband and Wives, and Domestic Conflict

Modern Yoruba Muslims. In literature on modern West Africa the impression is often given that the "educated elite" are nearly *all* Christians and that Muslims make up the poorer and more conservative sectors of the population. There was indeed heavier European impact among West African coastal societies, more intense Christianization and the growth of Western educational institutions there, and greater development of coastal natural resources. Conversely there was less intense European impact and development in the inland areas where Islam, having spread around and across the Sahara, was strongest. Nonetheless, the forces of Islam and of Christianity met in Yorubaland (among other places) and almost half of the people now adhere to each of the two world religious traditions. Only in northern Yoruba areas did Muslim governmental and legal institutions get established. Elsewhere Islam, like Christianity, is a personal religion.

Yoruba Muslims have all along been active participants in modern life, and not backward or passive. In fact, in the early colonial period in Lagos, there were more mosques and Koranic schools than there were churches or Western schools. Many of the richest of the African merchants and moneylenders were Muslims (Hopkins 1964). And it is generally agreed that the commercial wealth of Ijebu Ode, one of the most affluent of Yoruba provincial capitals, was built by its Muslims (Lloyd 1962).

Colonial institutions had, of course, a Christian and British cast. Since the mission schools pressured their pupils to become Christians, some dedicated Muslims forbade their children from attending altogether. Other Muslims realized the opportunities that opened through western education, and finally resolved to build schools in which the secular aspects of western education would be taught in an Islamic moral and religious environment. In Ijebu the first Muslim primary school for boys opened in 1930, in Ijebu Ode, and added a girls' section after World War II and a secondary school in 1950. Both Saliu and Mama Yinka went to this school. More recently many other Muslim schools in Ijebu (as elsewhere in Yorubaland) have been established.

Some of the encouragement of these modern educational developments has come from the Ansar-ud-Deen Movement, an association founded in 1923 in Lagos to promote the secular education of Muslims. Though originally Ansar-ud-Deen membership bore no implications within religious life proper, later on the members in various chapters began to pray by themselves even on Friday. It is their mosque that Saliu attends, and he considers himself an active member of the Movement.

In such men as Saliu Wahabi and his friends, therefore, Nigeria has a set of modernist Muslims, integrated into its public institutions but proud of their own religion as well. They contrast with other Muslims who incline away from European life styles and towards a more orthodox Islamic value system. Since there is no legally established doctrine in the Yoruba Muslim community in the sense that individual Middle Eastern societies are historically associated with one or another tradition, modernist and orthodox Muslims are competing now in building the foundations of Yoruba Islam. For example, Nigerian newspapers have carried arguments as to whether Yorubas should practice purdah (the veiling and seclusion of women), with some seeing it as a vital element of true Islam and others suggesting that it is antiquated and unnecessary. There are few vested Yoruba Muslim interests on either side, and the outcome of such debates is therefore open. In such a situation, educated and secularly-oriented people like Saliu are bound to play an enormous role.

Husband and Wives. One major difference between educated Christians and educated Muslims lies in their attitudes toward polygyny. There are, of course, African Christian churches which accept polygyny, finding Biblical support in the Old Testament. Most sects, however, only "tolerate" polygynists. They use such legal fictions as a distinction between the "ring" wife (the one married with a church ceremony including a ring) and other wives to create monogamists for purposes of maintaining church respectability. Whatever the church position, though, and whatever the individual behavior of Christians actually is (it is an open secret, for example, that not a few highly-educated men have monogamous homes but maintain "outside wives" as well), Yoruba Christians in general know that their European counterparts are much more strictly bound to one wife at a time, and they tend to believe that monogamy is at least a "higher" form of marriage. Yoruba Muslims of whatever educational status are under no such constraints, although, like their Christian friends, they may realize that it is costly to raise and educate children, and may choose to have fewer wives so that in turn they will have less offspring.

Is polygyny inconsistent with contemporary urban life? Saliu Wahabi does not think so. In passing he once remarked that when work slackens, talk at the office frequently turns to problems with women. Some of the men with one wife, he said, have more marital trouble than others might have with six! Besides, he added, women have only one husband, but have as many complaints as men with one or with several wives.

The problems of the polygynous household are, in substantive ways, different from those of the monogamous one. The "cases" that Saliu listened to included ones involving a husband's favoritism among co-wives, and squabbles over the relative contributions of co-wives to household management (most polygynists realize that attempts to share cooking chores are fraught with conflict, and that each wife should have her own cookpot). The deaths of two infants produced strong reactions of fear and hostility between his own two wives. A monogamous wife may feel more threatened than a polygynous one by the possibility that "outside" wives or children will one day challenge her privileges, or, if she feels that men are "naturally" polygynous, she may fear that her own hold on her husband's attention is fragile, and then turn these fears into jealousies and suspicion. A wide range of problems, of course, may arise irrespective of the number of wives a man has — a husband's stinginess with money, a wife's sterility, a man's mistrust of his wife's loyalty or either parent's lack of attention to a child are examples we have seen. In sheer arithmetical probabilities the household with three or more adults in it (whether related as multiple wives, mother-in-law or in some other way) will undoubtedly have more frequent problems than the one with only two.

Whatever the marital arrangements, husband and wife or wives maintain largely separate worlds. This segregation is even represented physically, by the separate beds or bedrooms of the spouses and, in Saliu's home because he can afford the space, in the sense of the parlor being his preserve in which others must tread with care. Socially, the friends and acquaintances with whom Saliu prays, eats, or exchanges visits and discussion are by and large his own, as are those of each wife. While a husband and wife (wives only rarely) sometimes visit a friend together, such occasions — as on holidays — are more formal, and less comfortable, than the everyday patterns by which each spouse comes and goes by himself/herself, without necessarily even telling the other one where (s)he is going (but wives are expected to announce their intentions more than husbands). There is not a strict segregation of men from their children, or from women and children, as there is in some other cultures, but rather an easy independence which persists in the most "Westernized" of families (Lloyd 1967c:173-181).

Polygyny is not the statistically dominant marriage pattern for modern Yorubas — it probably never was, even in traditional villages. Under missionary influence, open polygyny is practiced these days by progressively fewer people the higher their educational attainments. But there is little evidence that it is inherently maladapted to urban life. The European names and clothing styles that colonial life once urged upon Africans have fallen away under the surge of nationalist rediscovery. Just as they debated not long ago whether only Western (but no less "tribal") names of Teutons, Celts, or Latins could be legitimately Christian, church conferences held in Africa have in recent years been asked to discuss the more serious question of polygyny. What the future holds in attitudes, in law, or in behavior remains open. Models of romantic love and individual choice, and the present conduct of the most highly-educated, are before the mass of urban Ijebu, but so are models of prestige and status, and the conduct of the most wealthy and powerful, many of whom are polygynous.

Domestic Conflict and Its Resolution. Yorubas deepen conflict by direct and indirect insult and resolve it by involving outsiders. The casual observer of the simplest type of altercation notices at least three distinct phases.

In the first, the use of insult and indirect abuse are distinct skills for manifesting hostility. Tade Oyebanji's older brother brought to a head his growing dissatisfaction with his first job as chauffeur for an executive's pompous wife when a girl carrying the same kind of rustic earthen pot that his mistress' mother made happened to dash across the road in front of the car. "You daughter of an earthen pot seller. . ." he began to yell, with his mistress in the back seat. The ensuing diatribe, not very subtly, included her as well as the girl. Ma Ebun retold a case in which one co-wife repeatedly insulted the other, whose ears stuck out, by loudly mocking the large ears of any dog, goat, or person who walked by. More serious conflict can be generated by imprecation and curse. Since many events are seen to be functions of human will, such statements as "May you have an accident!" shouted after a speeding car, or "The food will make you sick!" said in anger to a husband bear the logical possibility that such outcomes will in fact transpire.

In the second phase of expatiation and the gathering of support, outsiders of all sorts enter the conflict. Marshalling one's own friends or permanent allies does little good alone, since it only ranges larger groups against one another. With or without help from friends, an approach to a neutral party, or better still a friend of one's opponent, is the only route open toward redress. The case will move into the process of resolution if such people can be persuaded of the plausibility of one's argument. This is so not only because the neutral party has the obligation of reciprocity for having been consulted or the desirable end to be gained of peace in a friend's family or a neighboring office or shop, but also because he has a reputation to preserve and augment as a person of wisdom and discretion.

The resultant flow of information about people's personal difficulties is enormous, and contributes to the quality in Yoruba life, which we remarked in discussing the Odusanya family, of living in the public view. Even the consultations are not held in private — the presence of yet other outsiders, such as the woman who sat through the cases presented to Saliu one day, may later be useful to testify to the lack of partisanship of the arbiter, or to the extent of his promises of aid. Other Nigerians, it may be added parenthetically, find all this indirectness of Yorubas extremely irritating.

Finally, the resolution phase of interpersonal conflict quite generally involves the apportionment of responsibility to each side. Yorubas call this one of the signs of a valid judgment. Decisions are palatable in part because one is at least partially vindicated. The neutrality and prestige of the arbiter are reinforced, and the particular conflict, if not the underlying cause, abates.

His position in the flow of information and his qualities of fairness and persuasiveness make arbiters like Saliu Wahabi influential persons. Thus neighbors, the wives of friends, and co-religionist fellow townsmen of Saliu's all seek out and listen to his advice. Despite the problems in his own family, his prestige in the community is high indeed.

Footnotes

[1]Mọyin-mọyin is made from ground beans, to which small amounts of red pepper, salt, palm oil, fish and onion are usually added. The mixture is molded into lumps and steamed in leaves.

[2]The prevailing culture in Western Nigeria is Christian, and few Yorubas are in any case very exclusive about religious boundaries. In small towns, for example, both Christians and Muslims may contribute to the building of a new house of worship, whatever its affiliation. Here Saliu, a Muslim, notes simply that the gifts have come closest to Christmas-time.

[3]Among many others, one celebrated case occurred in 1957, when *Adégòkè Adélabú,* a powerful Ibadan politician and outspoken opponent of the Ijebu migrants, was killed in a one-car automobile accident while driving through Ijebu Province. Few could believe that Ijebus had not had some hand in his death (for details, see Sklar 1963:303-305). For a case in Tivland, see Bowen (1954).

[4]This is the English phrase that Yoruba use to include a range of traditional specialists from purely mundane herbalists to purely supernatural healers.

Saliu Wahabi's senior wife at work plaiting hair and selling ingredients (Chapter 9)

A corner of Bola Onadele's sitting room, the children's sleeping mat on the floor (Chapter 6)

Hausa "Kayas" outside Mama Bankole's provisions stall (Chapter 8)

CHAPTER VIII

Self-Reliance: Madam Bankọle

Dugbẹ Market

The city of Ibadan has two centers. One is the heart of indigenous Ibadan, and lies between the hills on which the first inhabitants settled. It is a vast and open marketplace, serving the hundreds of thousands of descendants of those nineteenth-century settlers, whose homes now cover the hillsides and fill the gullies and fluvial plains below. The second is nearly two miles to the west, at the Iddo gate where the railroad station was built. Along with warehouses and European stores, there grew nearby a new market, called *Dùgbè,* to serve the new immigrants to the city.

Dugbẹ market, more compact and closely supervised than the markets of old Ibadan, lies on the side of a gentle slope. Long sheds, divided into hundreds of individual stalls, run across the hill, broken by two major lanes running up and down. At the top, along one road, is a taxi and bus lot, and at the bottom a small footbridge across a stream leads to a road adjoining the foreign business area.

Each line of stalls is given to a different commodity. The plate, pot and cup sellers have one aisle, piled high with crockery and bright aluminum. The meat sellers have another, their wares on open tables covered with leaves for protection from the sun and from flies. The *ògùn* (Yoruba medicine) sellers have yet another, filled with the skulls and skins of animals, pieces of bright ore and semi-precious stone, dried leaves and bones. As well, there are dealers in hardware, European vegetables, cloth, fruit, chickens and ducks, Yoruba grains and tubers, manufactured clothing, palm wine, bedding, jewelry, and dozens of other lines of goods. The sound of a hundred bargains being struck at once, the sight of the latest fashions bedecking the shoppers, the tastes and smells of natural and cooking food unneutralized by sterile packaging, the odor of open drains and refuse too infrequently removed, the jostling of a half dozen languages and peoples competing to buy or to sell the products of fifty lands — twelve acres in all serve the needs of half a city.

Along the main lanes into and through the market are the "provisions" sellers, women who deal in manufactured goods from canned meat to candles and from hair cream to powdered milk. It takes, in relative terms, a lot of capital to venture into the "provisions" trade; in contrast a girl may begin her career with only a half-crown's worth (35 cents) of peppers and tomatoes from her father's farm. At the bottom of the market, near the footbridge, is the eight-foot-wide stall of Madam Alice *Apàrà Bánkólé,* a heavy-set woman nearly sixty years old who is in some ways the very model of the intrepid, proud and acuitous Yoruba trading woman. Both the formal "Madam" and the informal "Mama," which is used by her customers and neighbors, indicate the general respect that she has achieved.

Customers and Trade

At two o'clock she is attending to a customer, a young man who must be someone's houseboy, because he is carrying a long list of things to buy. Right after he goes, another, older man comes. Both are on familiar terms with Mama, and the second one asks to leave his heavy bag at her stall while he goes to get something that is sold farther "inside" the market.

Then an old Ijebu man comes, wanting six of the cheap cigarettes that cost half a penny each. He is sloppily dressed and apparently drunk. He says he will pay for his cigarettes "tomorrow," but Mama will not let him. So he grabs a passing woman by the arm, pulls her over, and tells Mama that this is the one who will pay for his cigarettes. The poor woman is afraid that she has fallen into the clutches of a madman, and does not want to risk a fistfight, so she simply pays the threepence and hurries away.

A small girl with a large calabash of palm wine on her head[1] pauses briefly to say, "One 'heavy' please, later."

Mama explains that a 'heavy' is a carton of sugar, used by the palm wine sellers to sweeten its flavor. A 'small' is a bottle of saccharin, used for the same purpose. Artificially "enriched" either way, it is lamented by urbanites who cannot get the "real" thing from the farm.

A woman comes to buy two jars of skin cream. She is to pay 4s. 6d., but she hands Mama two five-shilling notes. Mama returns one, saying, ". . . or do you want to dash [tip, or give] me that extra one?"

The woman thanks her. Mama tells a story about one boy who forgot his whole month's salary, fifteen pounds ($42), at her stall once. He got all the way home, remembered, and came back in fear that she might say it was not there.

"But I didn't have any cause to keep it, because he had bought something from me. He was so grateful he took out five shillings and offered it to me. I told him that was senseless, that what he bought was worth more than five shillings, and that in fact the whole fifteen pounds was a paltry sum for me."

She continues with a story of a woman who accidentally switched boxes with her, leaving behind a box of old clothes and taking powdered milk worth nine pounds ($25.20). Mama told the traders around her that if the same God that she worshipped was the one who watches the whole world, then the woman would bring back her milk. And, to be sure, she did.

By this time the woman with the five shillings is getting bored. She thanks Mama again and goes.

Around four o'clock a woman, mid-Western or Ibo by her looks and clothing, brings a table out from inside the market and begins to sell her iced fish right in the center of the busy lane. A tomato seller, and then a meat seller (the meat sellers are all men, as are those who sell hardware, European vegetables, and a few other items) up the lane, do the same thing. Soon they are pouring from everywhere — meat, fruit, fish and vegetable dealers fill the road, leaving only narrow passages at the side for shoppers. These are the sellers of the perishables, trying to make their sales before the market slows and closes by nightfall. They begin to advertise their wares ever more loudly, and soon everyone has to shout to make himself heard while bargaining. It is difficult to walk without being accosted by them or shoved by others impatient to get past.

While this part of the market is at its busiest, Mama is packing her goods back inside her stall. She is closing early today in order to say hello to a friend, who will be passing through Ibadan on the train, bound for Kano in the North. Back behind her shelves she changes her blouse, then lowers the door of her shed which doubles as an awning when propped up for the day. Two strong padlocks bolt either side of the door. Later, at the railway station platform, Mama is disappointed since the friend is not in fact on the train. Instead of returning to Dugbe, Mama heads home.

She lives in an old compound only a few blocks north of Dugbe, in Eko Tedo ("founded by Lagos"), the first migrant settlement in Ibadan. There is a six-room, single-story house in front, and a long row of rooms down each of the two side walls of the courtyard in the back. The yard is cemented, and clotheslines are strung from side to side so that one has to duck and twist to get to the kitchen and bathroom stalls at the far end. Mama's room, with a small ante-room divided from it, is one of those along the right wall.

Mama greets her co-tenants, walking all around the yard before entering her own room. There she stops just long enough to fetch her glasses and prayer book, for she is going to evening service at the Anglican cathedral at Oke Bola. Only about fifty people are there, but they are kept busy rising and kneeling for over an hour of devout attention.

Back at home, she hears the day's gossip, eats a light meal of roasted plantain with salted peanut oil, and, by nine o'clock, is beginning to get ready for bed.

Panic in the Market

The next day is an eventful one at the market, though it starts routinely. Mama arrives early, for her, at about eight thirty. Usually she stays at home until nearly nine, having a good meal because she does not eat much at the market. She is also well enough off, and old enough, not to push herself to long hours. As soon as she raises her door, customers start to come, so that it takes her nearly an hour to get her things properly arranged on the tables she takes from in back to place under the overhanging door.

Some people bargain very hard to get a last penny off the price of an item — a box of detergent, a tube of toothpaste, or a can of evaporated milk. Mama is always easy on them — she seems not to want to start high and argue penny by penny down to the normal selling price. Instead she just calls out the regular "final" price, though she may allow an extra penny off just to satisfy a customer. She says she is more interested in having her customers come back than in exacting a high price on every sale. The goods she sells do not fluctuate in value very much anyway, and she knows that people would find similar prices at every provisions stall.

It is a busy morning, without much talk. At one point three boys, each with a long list, are standing in front of the stall waiting their turn. Meanwhile other buyers and traders call out greetings as they pass. These include a number of Hausa *kayas*, the men who work pushing loaded wagons from warehouse to market or carry heavy purchases from Dugbe to a shop or market where further selling may be done. Mama traded for three years in Northern Nigeria herself, and her knowledge of Hausa makes her a favorite of the Hausas at Dugbe. One, in fact, is saving his money with her until he is ready to go home at the beginning of planting season there.

Mama has barely finished arranging her wares for the day when suddenly people start running out of the center of the market. No one knows what is wrong at first, but there is an obvious panic. Five minutes later people are still coming. Someone shouts that a Hausa madman is loose and is attacking people at the platesellers' area. Mama suggests that perhaps it is a gang of thieves creating a situation in which people will leave their stalls untended. She begins to put her own things inside. The corn and gari sellers' aisle behind her stall is already nearly empty.

While people continue to flee, one woman ventures back to lock her stall. She is trembling so much she cannot close her door properly. A man nearby uselessly directs the crowd — "You go through there . . . . it is coming from down here. . . ." Meanwhile two of the Hausa kayas have quietly come to sit in front of Mama's stall, offering their protection.

Only a few minutes later about fifty riot policemen, a front line with tear gas guns, the remainder with long truncheons and shields, march up the main pathway toward the trouble. An onlooker standing near Mama's describes how a Hausa man seized a cutlass from a cutlass seller's stall and attacked an Ibo second-hand clothing seller in the hope that he would flee so that the Hausa and his friends could grab the Ibo's money. Others report that the Hausa ringleader was struck by a Yoruba taxi driver and overpowered. Mama remarks that, whatever happened, sales would be finished for the day since no one would come to Dugbe for fear of further trouble. Riot police are now swarming everywhere, and soon people from nearby offices come out to see "how people's heads have been cut off at Dugbe!"

Now there are more sirens, and the Military Governor's car arrives together with a contingent of soldiers with machine guns at the ready. People begin to cheer, and the Governor, seeing that there is no continuing difficulty, brightens and waves back. Nevertheless, for the next two hours the whole of Dugbe looks like a military camp, with policemen and soldiers marching back and forth.

Mama says that she will go home, as she is sure that the market has been "spoiled" for the day. By about two she has packed up and departed.[2]

The Sales Routine

The following day is busy, but undisturbed. At noon Mama is rearranging cans on her shelves and tables. She explains why her stall is in such apparent disarray.

There is a young inspector who has been coming around from the City Health Office. He would ask the women, "who are twice the age of his mother," to sweep the path in front of their stalls. Mama thought the Health Office itself should hire cleaners for the market. Once he demanded money from the fish sellers, threatening that he would condemn their fish if they refused. They paid, but complained to Mama, as one of the most respected older women in the immediate area. When the man heard that, he was furious, and reported one of the fish sellers to the local police on a charge of selling unhealthy food. The policemen also saw a chance for a bit of hush money, so they threatened to take the woman to court. Ultimately, though, a police officer of higher rank intervened and stopped the whole affair.

The health inspector was still angry, for he had received no vindication at all. Last Friday he came to Mama's stall. Mama expected him to apologize, but instead he asked in a loud voice to buy a certain brand of cigarette not available in Nigeria except by smuggling. Mama said, of course, that she did not have it. But suddenly a policeman appeared (obviously by prearrangement with the boy), saying that contraband cigarettes were alleged to be available in Mama's stall and that he was going to search. Search he did, turning her stall inside out so thoroughly that now, five days later, she is still putting things back where they should be.

She relates this story between sales, which are brisk. A man wants a disinfectant for some sore he describes to Mama. She recommends a petroleum jelly instead, though she has none in stock. Then a young boy returns with a bottle of hydrogen peroxide he bought an hour or so ago. He says his mother didn't want that kind. Mama is about to put it back into the carton when she notices that the bottle is a little less than full. She calls the boy back, returns the bottle to him, and says to tell his mother that she will not take it back.

By this time the sellers of meat, fish and other perishables are as usual filling the roadway. Suddenly a small girl picks up her tray of tomatoes and yells for everyone to get out of the way. A city refuse truck is coming down the hill toward the dumping area. One fish woman does not move quite fast enough, and one of her pans of fish is crushed by the huge truck's wheel. As soon as the truck passes, all the traders resume their quarreling for the best locations and their loud proclaiming of their wares.

As Mama is once again putting all her things away, this time to close up early in order to go to church, the boy who brought back the peroxide returns with a bigger lad. His arguments as to whether the level in the bottle had dropped are weak, and Mama sends them both off with neither exchange nor refund. It is not unusual for sellers themselves to adulterate their goods, or for buyers to use a little of some item (a couple of aspirins from a bottle, or a half cup of bleach) and to try to return the rest as untouched.

The next morning Mama arrives at the market at her usual time, around nine. A swelling on the back of her right hand between her thumb and forefinger is growing, and is hurting, so it takes her a long time to get her stall set up.

Soon a girl about eleven comes up and asks for a large can of powdered milk. Mama says it costs ten shillings ($1.40). The girl offers nine and six ($1.33). Mama says, *"Kò gbà!"* ("It does not accept.")

As she starts to go, Mama calls her back, and says, "If you go to other places and find the price the same, will you come and buy it here? Please, it's just so you can start the day for me — I think that if you do, I'll sell a lot today."

The girl nods and leaves. Mama smiles, saying that she won't find the milk for less than ten and three ($1.43) anywhere else. "She'll come back!"

And she does. The girl buys many other things, too — sugar, soap, toothpaste, and so on, for a total of £2. 10s. 0d. ($7.00). Mama is delighted.

"It's the way you treat the customers that brings them back," she beams. "I get that milk powder for nine and nine per tin. Threepence profit is enough for me. The people who say they don't sell enough — how can they at the prices they want."

She points to a disheveled-looking Hausa man going up the road. "See that man?" she says. "One day he started the day for me, and I had a great day. He only bought a penny razor blade, but after him came people with long lists. I sold £20 ($56) worth of goods that day."

Having opened the subject herself, Mama goes on to relate that at holiday times her gross daily sales may reach £35 or £40 ($98-$112), but on ordinary days her sales total about £10 or £12 ($28-$33.60). She keeps no written records, and uses no bank. She pays the wholesalers for her stock, and uses the rest herself. As a result, she has no ready idea of her profit during a period of, say, a month nor of the exact total value of her stock (it may be about $300 or $350). Moreover, while she keeps her money as well as her stock locked in her stall overnight, she has no fire, theft, or any other insurance.

"It's God that watches over everything. Even last year, when people said that Dugbẹ might be burned down,[3] I didn't pack my things away like many people were doing. I just left everything to the protection of God."

Mama's hand is hurting more, and she sits down to rub some liniment on it. Another provisions trader who has noticed the hand swelling sends her small daughter to help Mama with errands and lifting. Later Mama applies another liquid to her hand, this time from a small bottle containing, Mama says, palm oil, rock salt (believed to absorb germs), ground beans and shea butter.

Sales go on, too. Soap, cigarettes, cocoa mix, tinned sardines, tea, razor blades, matches, coffee, detergent, starch, aspirins, sugar, Ovaltine, blueing, pens, hair cream, writing pad, envelopes, and many other items sell one or two at a time. Often the sale totals only a few pence or a few shillings, but sometimes someone comes with a whole list of items he needs. Mama, bothered by her hand, is quiet now, except for a story about her grandson *Bíodún*.

One day, she remembers, some people came to "interview" her about what she thought was the best food for babies. She named a certain brand of enriched milk powder. They asked why she thought it was good, and she replied that it was because it had made her own grandson quite healthy. She explained how, when she was taking care of her grandson while her daughter was at university, she fed the baby first this milk, then corn flakes and rolled oats, and later canned chicken. The interviewers asked why she used all these foreign foods. She answered that it was not that they were foreign but that they were prepared cleanly and were easy to use. At any rate, it turned out that the questioners were from the Nigerian Broadcasting Corporation. They thanked her for her cooperation and gave her a pound ($2.80) for her help. A few days later, at home, she heard her own tape-recorded voice over the national radio station on the *"Ìyá Ni Wúrà"* ("Mother is a Gem" [literally, gold]) program.

An Illness Stops Work

By the following day Mama's hand is hurting so much that she decides not to go to the market at all. The hand gets worse, and it is finally almost two weeks before she returns. She calls her discharging swelling a whitlow, but she will not go to the hospital to get it diagnosed and treated, because she will not tolerate the disrespect that she feels the young nurses and doctors show. Over the twelve days many people visit her at home, expressing their sympathies and offering suggestions. She tries leaf concoctions, an injection from an off-duty nurse she knows, and various European and Nigerian patent medicines. At its peak it is quite painful, and her neighbor in the compound has to cook for her and help her bathe. Of course she has no income when she does not work.

Mama passes the time getting a great deal of sleep, chatting with her neighbors and friends, and taking care of a few errands. There is no end of gossip, either of homely quarrels and troubles — a street hawker fired for laziness or a girl unmarried but pregnant — or of events on the national political scene.

One day Mama's third ex-husband comes to visit her from Lagos, not knowing of her indisposition. Mama recounts the day the Hausas attacked the Ibos at Dugbẹ, and tells another story she heard about some young Ibo traders at Dugbẹ who sold rice, beans, and other foodstuffs imported from Northern Nigeria, until one day during the political riots and killings of late 1966 their junior partner in the North disappeared. One of the Ibadan partners went by passenger truck up to find him, and he, too, disappeared, presumably killed by local thugs. Now there is some fear that the Northerners will attack Yorubas, too. Mama's ex-husband says that if that happens, the country will be completely shattered, with the Hausa quarters of every large Yoruba town put to the torch in the process.

It is very important in Yoruba custom to offer one's sympathy to a sick person. Just as failing to greet someone you know every time you see him may be interpreted as an expression of malice, so may failure to visit an ill person be held to implicate you in wishing and/or causing his illness. Many of Mama's visitors are other traders from Dugbẹ. One morning a meat seller comes to commiserate with her. He, too, has advice on a good remedy to use, but he quickly changes the subject to talk about a young kinswoman of his who is staying in his house. He will not allow her to have "boy friends" unless she is seriously thinking of marrying one of them. He is afraid she will go to bed with them, and cannot bear that thought. He asks Mama's advice on what to do. Mama has little to offer, both because she is tired and because her own daughter had her child long before the father agreed to marry her. Mama sleeps a bit more after the meat seller departs.

In short order three other women come, and then the daughter of an earlier visitor bringing some leaves which her mother said should be boiled and spread on the hand. Mama has the girl help her start her fire just outside her door in the courtyard. An obese woman who lives across the yard helps her with her cooking, while a wrinkled old washerman who lives two rooms away brings some firewood. Mama has had a room in this compound for twenty-one years (although she was not living here for nine of them), and has become the "old mother" of the whole place both by longevity and by her calm and helpful spirit. It is at times like this that she benefits from the security she knows she has here, and which confirms her feeling that the compound has become "sort of a big family — if there's anything wrong with anyone, we all talk about it and deal with it as if we were one family."

Her best friend in the compound is a "yellow" (light-skinned) woman whose husband is an Ibo man who is now in Eastern Nigeria. The evening's chatter is again about events in the country. Each of the neighbors has a story about incidents in Ibadan or in Northern Nigeria involving Ibos. Mama says that the trouble is affecting them more than anyone else, and that it looks to her as though God is angry with them. Mama calls the "yellow" woman's oldest daughter.

"Chizorba," she says mock-seriously to the half-Ibo child, "Pa Ojukwu [the Eastern Military Governor, soon to be leader of secessionist Biafra] has sent me a message for you . . . says you should come now, that your own guns and sticks are ready . . . and the message is signed by your father. Njikoka Transport Company [owned by Ibos and operating throughout the country] is waiting for you and whatever luggage you have."

It is clear by this time that most people expect the Ibos to take some revenge for what has happened over the last few months. Chizorba is silent.

As Mama feels stronger she attends to a letter she has received from her daughter *Ayò* at the University of California. Ayọ is homesick for some vegetables that she cannot find in Los Angeles. Mama gets the four things together and seals them in a large can. Though she can write slowly both in Yoruba and in English, she has a son of one of her neighbors write out a letter she dictates to send along with the parcel. Finally she takes everything to the post office, where one of the clerks packages it properly for her in his slow moments, for a few shillings. In all it costs over £5 ($14), and many hours, to get ingredients for perhaps four meals mailed off to the U.S.; Mama is happy to be able to afford this bit of indulgence for her only child.

Back to Work

Days later, Mama finally returns to the market. The price of a powdered baby formula has been raised by the distributor, reports another trader across the road, who envies the fact that Mama still has some left that was bought at the old price which she can sell at the new markup. Many people stop to ask where Mama has been, or to apologize for not coming to her house to see her. It is the end of the month, and business is brisk.

A girl about ten comes with a carton of canned milk that her mother wholesales. Mama remarks that the carton itself is in a condition too bad to sell, and that the girl should have brought a better one. The youngster replies that she cannot carry the heavy carton all the way back, and leaves it. Mama determines not to use it but rather to speak to the wholesaler herself the next day. With profit margins in halfpennies Mama is unwilling to forego the two pennies she can get for the cardboard box.

Early in the afternoon there is a sudden shower. Mama scurries for some large plastic sheets that she keeps in her stall, and a girl from the corn seller's stall behind Mama's helps her to get all her things covered.

Later it clears off, and it is still sunny after the perishables' dealers crowd into the road. Mama stays late, until the market slows down towards seven o'clock.

On the next day, Saturday, sales are quick and constant. Mama has little time to chat with customers, except for one old and kindly-looking man with whom Mama jokes.

"Pa, today is Saturday. Shall I come? Or it doesn't rise any more? If so you better get some tablets. I want a nice Saturday night!"

"Pa" says "it" is on a permanent holiday.

"Why should it be?" continued Mama. "You are not dead yet, are you? Why should you let a part of your body be dead?"

Pa points down at his trousers, shrugging. He repeats — it is on a permanent vacation.

Several wholesalers also stop by. The man with Maggi bouillon cubes cannot sell Mama any, nor can a woman carrying toothpaste. There is a new brand of tomato paste mixed with red pepper, and Mama, having heard that people like it, takes two dozen cans from yet another woman.

Across from Ma's stall, at the head of a sparsely-patronized aisle of charcoal dealers, a blind and lame Hausa man sits begging all through the morning heat.

"*T'órí Ọlọ́'un!* T'ori Ọlọ'un!" ["For the sake of God! For the sake of God!"] he wails, in accented Yoruba, throwing his arm up and his head down in wild gesticulations of some private horror — or of some dramatic expertise! Passing shoppers drop pennies into his tin bowl.

A girl comes, sent by a rich wholesaler with whom Mama is well-acquainted, to ask if Mama wants to buy a large case of toilet tissue for £3 ($8.40). If so, the girl goes on, she is to send her money along now, as the people selling it will not wait to get paid later. Mama agrees, since the price is good, and sends her money.

The day wears on. A man comes looking for an ointment that Mama does not carry, so she directs him to an Urhobo woman three stalls away who does have it. She buys some water leaf, a green vegetable, from a girl hawking it through the market. The old woman who draws drinking water for the busy trading women brings a pailful to Mama, who pays a penny for it. More customers come, raising sales today so far to nearly £10.

The day is cooling down when a boy brings the toilet tissue that Mama paid for, but to her surprise there is only half a box, not a full one. Mama says she won't accept it.

"That woman!" she cries. "I lent her £40 last week to celebrate the anniversary of the death of some relative of hers. She's only paid back £25 so far. You'd think she'd buy this stuff and ask for the money later. But no! I put more money on top of the money of mine she already has, and now she sends me only half a carton! What happened to the other half? If she needs my money let her come and see me. Meantime take this tissue back and bring me my money."

At the end of the day neither the woman nor either of the children has returned with the three pounds.

Biography: Alice Bankọle

Born in 1909 in Ijebu Ode, Alice Bankọle is from one of the Ijebu families that opened to Western influences very quickly after the British conquest in 1892. Her father, though he had two wives, was an early and staunch Anglican, and was among the first tailors in the town to use a sewing machine. Her mother, the senior wife, traded in foodstuffs, buying products like fish and kola nuts from specialized rural areas and selling them in the capital. She became a Christian at her marriage, and both parents learned to read the Bible in Yoruba. Mama had two older full brothers, one of whom died in childhood and the other of whom, a farmer who still lives in Ijebu Ode, she rarely sees. Nor is she friendly with her only half-sibling, the son of her father's junior wife.

Mama herself was an *àbíkú,* as a woman's children will be called if a series of two or three of them die in infancy. As a result she got both a special name, Apara, meaning "one who comes and goes" (the belief being that one malevolent spirit is repeatedly incarnating and leaving simply to torment a woman), and the indulgence and spoiling that go with the attempt to induce the abiku to stay. Few girls went to school in those days, but her father wanted her to go, and she finished Standard VI in 1926 at the age of seventeen. She learned how to sew in Ijebu Ode but when her father refused to buy her a machine of her own, she ran off to Lagos to a cousin of her mother's and worked at his machine as a seamstress for three years.

It was there that she met her husband, a teacher from Abẹokuta. For several years she had no child, and her husband meanwhile took two more wives. When one gave birth, Mama bought the baby some pretty cloth, and on the day it was named she was dancing around with him in her arms. Mr. Bankọle had grown bitter towards Mama by this time, and snatched the baby away saying, "If you love children so much, why don't you get your own?" Mama, feeling all too painfully her childlessness, was distraught, and only the calming words of her father-in-law made her stay with her husband then.

By 1939 he was barely paying any attention to her. One night he came home drunk and upset, and demanded that she go to a doctor immediately to find out what was wrong with her. The only thing preventing her getting pregnant, it turned out, was that he was not sleeping with her! The doctor talked at length to Mr. Bankọle, and for a while he "came to me" more often. Soon, however, he again stopped, and, declaring that he did not want to keep a wife in Lagos, he sent her home to his father's house. Astonishingly, though she did not know it when she went, she was pregnant! Her daughter Ayọ was born in 1940.

Mr. Bankọle had not let his junior wife keep the cloth that Mama had wanted to give to her baby two years before. Mama found it, and resolved to use it for her own daughter now. Her husband interpreted this action as spiteful or provocative, and demanded that Ma take the new dress off Ayọ at once. Another huge fight developed, and so, when Ayọ was four months old, Mama left her husband for good.

A year and a half later she married an old suitor from Ijebu Ode who had gone on to become a very successful produce buyer. He put up the money for her divorce, brought her to Ibadan to his house there, and gave her money to buy a sewing machine and start trading. She got a stall in Dugbẹ market where she sold cloth and also made dresses. The year was 1942.

For four years things went well, but then her new husband had a child by the teen-aged relative of a tenant in the house. She hated Mama, and persuaded their husband to throw Mama out. It was in 1946, thus, that she moved into the house where she still lives.

In 1949 she married a third man, another Ijebu man who was a supervisor in the telegraph office and had recently been widowed. He was transferred frequently from place to place, and she went with him, changing her trade each time. From Warri in the western Niger delta she transported palm oil to Ibadan and re-sold it there to retailers. Then from Jos and Kano she sent rice and beans to a woman to whom she sublet her Dugbẹ stall, and received crockery in return that she sold in the North. She also cooked and sold food in the migrant quarters of those towns. From 1949 to 1962 she moved around with him, but she hung on to her room and her stall license in Ibadan, both because she was still visiting occasionally and as a hedge against the insecurities of marriage that by now she knew well. In 1962 her husband, Mr. *Kòyí,* retired and wanted to go to Lagos where his children were living. Mama thought trade would be better at Ibadan — there was a boom going on — and also needed to attend to Ayọ, who was then having problems of her own. She has lived alone since then, her economic independence allowing her to dispense with the bothers of late middle-aged housewifery. At Dugbẹ she switched to the provisions trade only because the city government had decided that the line of stalls she was in should be a provisions line. Rather than lose her good location she made the change.

Biography: Mama's Daughter Ayọ

The core of Mama Bankọle's life is her involvement with her daughter. That relationship has been intense. When Ayọ was only one year old, she became very sick. Mama had not yet moved to Ibadan. Everyone thought Ayọ would die. Someone advised Mama to take her to the shrine of some worshippers of *Òsun,* an important Yoruba deity who inhabits a river of the same name. She went, accompanied by two other women. Ayọ was given some of the river water to drink, and almost immediately started to feel better. Mama was inside praying, and was beginning to shout and behave like someone possessed. Ayọ was outside playing, but started drifting away in a boat she was in. But suddenly she started coming back by herself, making paddling motions with her little fingers, which were barely touching the water. It was the most wonderful thing that Mama had ever seen — a one-year-old child rowing a boat. They all agreed it was the work of Osun, and Mama sacrificed many things in gratitude.

She took Ayọ twice more to this remote village, once when she had a large boil on her back, and again when she had acute neck pains that no one in Ibadan could diagnose. Later, when Ayọ got pregnant and was very ill, Mama went back to the village while Ayọ herself was in the university hospital in Ibadan. She gave the Ọsun worshippers many gifts, and they said that in fact as soon as she had thought of them her daughter had begun to recover. Sure enough, when Mama got back home Ayọ was up and around. They asked Mama to bring the baby to show them when it arrived, but Mama and Ayọ thought it not a good idea. Shortly — and, Mama feels, *consequently* — her grandson began to pass blood in his stool and became very weak. So Mama set out once more for the shrine, and returned to find Biọdun virtually all better.

Ayọ finished primary school, second in her class, in 1956, and passed an admissions exam for a prestigious girls' secondary school in Lagos. Against many of her friends' advice that she should have Ayọ learn a trade, Mama was persuaded by Ayọ's own commitment to send her on. She paid all Ayọ's fees for three years, but then Ayọ dropped out to finish her high school work by correspondence. In 1960 she began a job at the government offices in Ibadan.

A year later she was pregnant. Mama was not too hard on her — at least she had not done so while still in school. But the father, a university graduate in engineering working for the government as well, was reluctant to marry her. It was to this situation that Mama returned from the North in 1962.

Soon Biọdun was born, at Eastertime. It was not until two years later that his father finally agreed to marry Ayọ, just before he was to go off to the United States for graduate study. Meanwhile Ayọ herself had passed another admissions test, this time to the University of Nigeria at Nsukka in Eastern Nigeria. Mama had many doubts: the cost would be over £200 ($560) per year for three years; she herself would have to take care of Biọdun; Ayọ's marriage was still not settled. But once again Ayọ begged and pleaded. When Mama went to Lagos to see her first husband, Ayọ's father, to ask if he would help, he laughed and said that Mama was crazy, that even rich men found their budgets bursting with a child at university. That was enough to convince Mama to go ahead!

By borrowing a large sum of money from old friends and adding her own savings, Mama made it possible for Ayọ to go. Mama kept Biọdun, who went to a nearby nursery school and was then picked up and cared for by Mama's compound-mates until she returned, earlier than usual, from the market. After her first year at Nsukka Ayọ's marriage went through. And upon her graduation, her husband, Mr. *Fágbèmí,* sent for her and Biọdun to come to Los Angeles while he finished his studies. There they will stay until next year.

If it were not for the debt that Mama has incurred for Ayọ's education, she would join the *Ẹgbẹ́ Ọmọ Ìjẹbu Òde,* the "association of children of Ijebu Ode." Certainly her present feeling, given the way her life and her daughter's have worked out, is that she has earned a great deal of respect and admiration from her peers. She is esteemed by her neighbors, by her fellow traders at Dugbẹ, and by the Market Women's Association of Ibadan, which embraces most of the traders in the migrant areas of the city, and which has made her the "advisor" to the provisions sellers. Certainly if her health and her trade keep up, she will be able to begin enjoying the stature that she has won.

The Compound and the Room

As is evident in several ways from Mama's story and from her own explicit statement, the isolation from both relatives and former husbands that she might feel is mitigated by the warmth and cooperation within her urban compound. Fifty-eight people live in sixteen fairly small rooms here (four rooms are used only as shops and one is vacant). Only one household occupies two rooms. Whether there is any self-selection in the matter is unknown, but it is interesting to note that of the fifteen households (including Mama's), seven are headed by women temporarily or permanently separated from their husbands, while an eighth is a man (the old washerman) whose wife has left him. Their geographical backgrounds are diverse, but all except five of the residents are Yoruba, and about half are Ijebu.

The structure of the compound itself encourages communal life within it. The rooms which stretch down the sides of the long narrow yard have no outside windows, and the stuffiness that results from the lack of ventilation encourages the residents to live outside their doors. The fact that the only doors to the outside are at the front of the compound, and that the water tap, latrine (there is only one), and bathing stalls are at the back means that there is a lot of passing to and fro. And since cooking, clothes-hanging, scolding, wood-cutting, food-preparation and many other activities are carried on outside, interaction is necessarily intense among neighbors. Only one family that lives in the front house of the compound, by doing its household tasks in front of the building, manages to avoid systematic contact with the others.

Mama's own room costs her £1 ($2.80) per month (in 1948 it was only 7s. 6d. [$1.05]). When she returned from the North she spent £13 ($36.50) repainting and furnishing it. It is a fairly cluttered establishment. In the larger room in the rear, which is perhaps ten feet deep by thirteen wide, are Mama's large bed and a variety of cartons, boxes, suitcases, and odd other items belonging to Ayọ and her husband, stored there temporarily. A table in the left corner contains boxes of items from the market, especially extra stock of things that don't sell very quickly like toothpaste and mosquito coils. A large wardrobe on the left wall contains most of Mama's clothing.

The ante-room is only about six feet deep. The end away from the door is filled by a single bed that Ayọ and Biọdun formerly used. It is now covered with old clothing, though visitors often use it to sit on as well. Beside the bed and against the wall is a new pedal sewing machine that Ayọ bought for her mother the year she was working. To the right of the door is a table covered with cups, bottles, pans, a tea pot and a few packages of food. Most of the food, though, and the pots and charcoal to cook it with, are in a small cupboard behind the open door. A mirror on the wall with a shelf at its bottom is Mama's make-up area, containing shampoo, face and hair cream, and bits of other cosmetics. Filling the remaining corners and underneath the table and the one chair are more small boxes, a few low stools, and more clothing. The decoration is provided by several photographs of Mama, Ayọ, Biọdun, and Ayọ's husband

Gbọlá, and three calendars with large pictures on them. The landlord has not seen fit to run electricity wires into the house, so the only light is provided by the residents' own small oil lamps. In fact Mama has no watch, radio, or any other appliance.

Summary

Against this meager background, Mama Bankọle's accomplishments stand out all the more. When she returned from Kano in 1962, she had £48 ($134.40), a room with a few sticks of furniture in it, a license for a Dugbẹ market stall, a daughter, and some old friends. Thirty years after a first promising marriage to a well-educated man, that was little for anyone to show. But by the most careful application of all the resources she had or could call upon, by skilful trading to enlarge those resources, and by heavy investment — involving a great deal of personal sacrifice — in her own daughter, she has been able to push back the boundaries of her isolation and find a new sense of honor and destiny.[4]

Discussion: Yoruba Traders, and the "Position of Women"

Women in Trade. The homes, the streets, and the markets of Yorubaland are alive with women trading. In part this is a response to the cultural injunction that each wife be responsible for her own and her children's daily food and sundry needs. Nearly every Yoruba woman buys and sells something, and Ijebu women are reputed the sharpest of a generally formidable breed. In the physical insecurities of the war-filled nineteenth century, women were probably restricted in their entrepreneurial pursuits to the farms and markets of their own home towns. There they might sell the produce of their husbands' farms after processing it one or two steps toward readiness for consumption, by grinding or drying or shelling or cooking it. Or they might buy goods imported from other regions or abroad from passing caravans of armed traders for resale to local farms and nearby small markets. Of course wherever roads and markets were secure women traded over larger distances and in greater scale: the wealthy Madam Tinubu was a major political figure in Lagos and Abẹokuta from 1840 to 1870, and Mama Bankọle's own mother bought and sold farm produce and fish from town to town in the Ijebu kingdom before the turn of the century. After 1900 the peace enforced by the British allowed women to move rapidly into all levels and types of trading relationships.

Trading careers usually begin modestly. A girl may learn to haggle by hawking with, and later for, her own mother. She may be given a few tomatoes and peppers or a gourd of palm wine, and if her family is poor she may begin by collecting firewood or chewing sticks in the forest for sale in town. Alternatively, as a young woman she may be given trading capital — a sewing ·machine or special training as well as money — by her mother and/or father to get her established (Mama ran away when her father could not do so). Finally, whether or not she has started trading before, her husband-to-be is expected to provide her with capital at the time of their marriage.

If a young woman trades successfully, she is likely to switch to more and more heavily capitalized trade. Many women never get beyond "petty trading," a term signifying a fairly standard variety of goods — cigarettes, needles and thread, biscuits and snack foods, bits of common cosmetics — that can in total be head-loaded and sold from house to house, on a curb, or outside one's own door. Some, like Mama, go on to provisions, large quantities of foodstuffs, pots and pans and the like, or even further into the wholesaling of soft drinks, cloth, or manufactured furniture. Sites change, too, from door or curb to market stall to shop or store. It is probable that there are standard "routes" or progressions from one commodity to another involving similar knowledge and skills (sewing to cloth-selling, or palm-wine to proprietorship of a palm-wine bar or full night club are two examples). Women work toward calculated long-range goals, and they accord great prestige to women who have built and can maintain large-scale trading enterprises with little outside aid. When one very "rich" trader in Ibadan was found to have large debts outstanding, Mama reports, her prestige plummeted.

There are women traders at virtually every level of commerce in and beyond Yorubaland. Nigeria's modern economy is commercial rather than industrial, and a small number of importing and exporting firms, nearly all foreign-owned, still control the flow of goods in and out of the country. From their warehouses, though, indigenous traders take over. Wealthy women have lines of credit with the large trading houses which permit them to wholesale in some cases thousands of pounds or dollars worth of merchandise to smaller-scale traders. In fact differences between "wholesalers" and "retailers" are extremely blurred. When Mama sells a carton of cigarettes or even a packet of needles or candles, her customer may either intend to consume them or to sell them in yet smaller amounts to other buyers. The woman with whom Mama agreed to buy toilet tissue buys directly from the warehouse of a French importing firm, but has a retail shop of her own. Only when the smallest unit of merchandise — a single cigarette, a few sheets of paper, one small tomato — is sold by a "petty trader" in a rural market far away from town can it be reasonably certain that it will be consumed rather than resold.

Why this profusion of traders at so many levels? Is it not somehow "inefficient" or "wasteful" for nearly every woman to be so engaged in trade?

The economist P.T. Bauer attributes the "multiplicity of traders" to the poverty of capital and technical skills in the distributive process as a whole (1954: 22-34). Briefly, he indicates that by making commodities available in ever smaller quantities, the many intermediaries make it possible for traders and consumers with little capital to have goods that would otherwise be beyond their reach. With the great scarcity of telephones, transport, supervisory skills, wide knowledge of the market, and other resources, individuals step in with their own labor and knowledge to find customers, carry goods, service at their doorsteps consumers with few storage facilities, and make their own small profits at the same time. Their labor (and that of children and other dependents as we have seen in this chapter and others) is contributed extremely cheaply: if Mama Bankọle, for example, counted the "cost" of her labor at even three and six (fifty cents) an hour, her "net profit" as a businesswoman would probably be zero. Of course she does not so calculate. But the abundance of labor willing to work for tiny profits keeps the overall cost of goods much lower than it would be if high transport, supervisory, advertising costs and employees' wages were added. Since so many women are ready to supply their labor so cheaply, the present labor-intensive distributional system will likely prevail until other, more rewarding, pursuits occupy women instead. Already schooling withdraws large numbers of children from the labor force — the alternative "rewards" need not be immediate or monetary. On the other hand, is it a mark of "efficiency" that most Western women are housewives? Why exchange time in the market for time at home? In the last analysis, only if it can be clearly shown that working in the kitchen is more "rewarding" than working in the market will Yoruba "traders" turn into Yoruba "housewives."

The fine-grained network of Yoruba trading women that results from all this activity has spread from western Nigeria eastward to Zaire and west to Senegal, three thousand miles across the monetary and customs systems of a score of countries, across boundaries not only of local languages but of trade and official languages as well, and across diverse economic regions.[5] Mama Bankọle has learned Hausa and English, and smatterings of other languages, to trade as she has moved up and down Nigeria. In Ghana and in the Ivory Coast the large size of the Yoruba trading community has made it the victim of official and unofficial hostility. There are Yoruba men, and men and women of many other ethnic origins, involved in trade, too, but Yoruba women give a flair and good humor at least to Nigerian markets that make them the centers of public life.

It is easy to see that Yoruba women's involvement in the marketplace goes far beyond the sheer societal demand that they feed and clothe themselves and their children. Success in trading and control of her own income gives a Yoruba woman economic independence that few Western women have. It gives her a place to stand in domestic discord, for example. It has allowed Mama, and allows other Yoruba women, a choice as to whether or not she will spend her middle and old age with her (or any) husband. And it gives her real political power in the community, where market women, individually or in groups, have held key roles of all types in political parties, factional disputes, and ritual affairs. In the political riots of late 1965 in Yorubaland it was not infrequent that groups of women set out from markets or other rallying-places to set fire and club to an opposition politician's house or car.

In short, trading provides a major avenue for the Yoruba woman's ingenuity and self-expression, and the freedom it gives her pervades other activities and roles as well. Being in the market is gratifying in its own right. Long past the sheer need to make a living, Mama and many other traders will keep their market stall licenses, if only to visit them occasionally for gossip and stimulation. Asked whether she sees an end to her trading days, Mama snaps back "I am not yet an *arúgbó*," a doddering old woman.

The "Position of Women." Madam Bankole has had three marriages, of which at least one was purely by mutual consent. She has raised and educated a daughter virtually by herself, with no particular stigma attached to her or her child. She has chosen to live her later years by herself, not having the need to depend upon a man's income. She has become skilled and self-fulfilled as a small businesswoman, thinking deeply about turnover, location, supply and demand, "loss leaders," and other retailing concepts, and, in common with other Yoruba women, is hardly a mindless drudge weeding cornfields or cooking dinners for a husband at work or at leisure. Further, Mama's daughter has had a child out of wedlock, again suffering no social sanction except for pressure that she marry. Do these facts and the generalities they may illustrate mean that contemporary Yoruba women are "liberated"?

Anthropologists have spent a great deal of time discussing "the position of women" in African society. Extensive debate on the division of labor, on matriliny, on polygyny, on childrearing, on divorce, on law, and on ritual, demonstrate that older attempts to sum up the position of women in Africa in a phrase or a sentence are misleading at best.

At least three questions, concerned with equality, freedom, and creativity, lie at the roots of the debate about the emancipation of women. First, are all the roles (political, occupational, educational and so on) in the society open to women, and open with equal reward, or are there disabilities in law or in fact to their achieving statuses equal to those of men? Second, are women free to deviate from norms and expectations in whatever direction to the same degree as men, or do "double standards" and sheer power keep women within narrower latitudes of individual behavior? And third, are women encouraged to the same degree as men to develop their individual intellectual, creative, and other talents? While these questions may overlap, they do not necessarily do so.

Women may be urged to create for instance, but in their own "place," a kitchen or a kitchen garden. Or their roles in society may be said to be "vital," but they may be barred from other "vital" or non-vital roles. Or they may, in a society based on a strict division of labor by sex, suffer the double disability of not being allowed the same range of innovation *or* individuation in their spheres that men are allowed in theirs. The case of Madam Bankọle illustrates a number of these matters at least as they affect contemporary urban Ijebu women: again our discussion can only point to more detailed studies (Little 1973).

To take the third question — about the encouragement of creativity — first, the preceding section showed that trading allows a woman great freedom to develop her skills and talents, a freedom which carries over as well into domestic and political roles. There are, to be sure, certain restrictions upon this freedom. Certain trades and crafts are reserved to men (and some to women). A woman is more likely to follow her husband to a new job location than vice versa. As well, she arranges her trading career around her children — curtailing it when they are small and expanding or re-expanding it later — much more than her husband does. Nonetheless, the possibility to make arrangements like those for Mama's grandson Biọdun while his mother attended university permits women an independence that many other societies do not grant.

On the other hand, women certainly do not have the second kind of freedom — to deviate from expectations about roles and role performances — to the degree that men do. For example, men's individual dispositions have much greater possibility of fulfillment given the larger number of adult roles open to them, and the probability that training for them will more readily be given by parents. Again, in the polygynous system of the Yoruba, men are freer than women to find new companions or sexual partners without immediately risking old ones — Mama's first and second marriages encountered strain on this account. And while there is much greater sexual freedom for women, especially before marriage, than there once was, society's demand that women bear children is so strong that Mama suffered from both her first husband's harassment and her own self-torment because of her early childlessness. In fact, as Aidan Southall has said of urban Ugandans, "the vast majority of women, as well as men, want children fervently, even out of wedlock, and they do not therefore sterilize their pleasures [i.e., use contraceptives] as Western women do" (1960: 215). Men can almost universally expect to become fathers, even if only socially through raising other men's biological children.[6] But a woman who has no children and does not succeed in the market has neither a means of support in old age or other need (especially if she has had few relations with her father's compound over a long period) nor the immortality that descendants provide. So, activities and attitudes that she uses to cope with the possibility of sterility start much earlier. Thus the creativity and independence of a woman in the marketplace rarely replace, and nearly always come second to, success as a mother, and deviance from this pattern is costly. These considerations shed additional light on Mama Bankole's devotion to her daughter.

Finally, the most important question about the emancipation of women remains that of equality, their distribution through the entire role and reward structure of society. The answer is ambiguous, and shifting. Traditionally women did have access to some political offices, to ritual specializations, and to economically rewarding positions other than in trade (as the owner of and profiter from slave labor, for example). It is true that some of these places were *reserved* for women, but the result was in any case that women played extremely active roles in community life. A hundred miles away the Dahomeans had war regiments of women, and while that institution was not replicated by the Yoruba, there are women's names in dynastic lists, in legends of trading fortunes, and among the principal deities. On the other hand women were excluded from many of the central political and religio-political associations and suffered legal and social disabilities in most of Yorubaland.

For all the deficiencies of the traditional order, however, it is not clear that the one now developing is any less discriminatory. It is true that as a doctor or a teacher a Yoruba woman may gain the same kind of economic and domestic freedom that her sister in the market has. But the modern Western-derived educational and political systems include as few Yoruba women at their top levels as do their prototypes in Europe or America. Yoruba Islam, like Islam elsewhere, grants prestige to a man who can afford to keep his wives secluded, and a few Yorubas have managed to convince their wives to don veils. In another sphere the costs of modern education are high enough to require the cooperation of both parents, and thereby to lessen the independence of each. The same costs, measured against the assumption that a girl is less likely to finish a given unit of education or may not put it to profitable use, produce a reluctance to invest in girls' educations to the same degree as boys'. Mama Bankole challenged both of these last tendencies to put her daughter Ayo through university, but there are not many women who could afford to do so.

There is not space enough to discuss here the frequency of divorces, recent changes in inheritance patterns, or other specific institutional changes. For some of these patterns we know too little, especially relative to urbanites. For others, we have statistical material, but we know much less about attitudes and consequences (a high divorce rate, for example, may indicate *either* emancipation or subordination). Rather, we have sought to raise some questions that underlie such institutions in any case, and that the life of Mama Bankole poses for Nigerian urban society. As Nigeria changes, Yoruba women have their own history of freedom as a point of departure for engagement with both male-dominated Islam and male-dominated Western industrialism.

Footnotes

[1]Calabashes are large gourds, dried and hollowed for carrying non-oily liquids; palm wine is the slightly fermented sap of the oil palm or the raphia palm, drunk in many of the same situations as beer is in other cultures; and, here as in many other places in the world, the normal and comfortable way to carry anything — from a school notebook to a load of firewood or a pail of water — is on the head.

[2]This incident was one of only a few interethnic conflicts between civilians in Western Nigeria in the months preceding the Nigerian civil war. Eastern Nigerians, especially Ibos, took this episode as a sign of the deterioration of their security in the West, even if it was not as serious as the massacres of 1966 in Northern Nigeria; many fled or sent their families home as a direct response. Nevertheless, Yorubas in general were furious that, in their eyes, one set of "guests" in their land should have attacked another, and calls were soon heard to drive Northerners out of the West. Later, during the war, Biafran Easterners took Yoruba inaction after the incident as evidence that the West was in fact "occupied" and immobilized by Northern troops, but by that time Yoruba public sympathy had swung away from the Easterners.

[3]During the Western Region political violence of late 1965 and early 1966 the migrant population of Ibadan was especially embattled. As a central public institution of the migrant sectors of the city, Dugbẹ market was the subject of all sorts of rumors and threats. Most of the property destruction, however, was of individuals' houses and cars.

[4]There is an old Ijebu legend about a wealthy but barren trading woman named *Sùngbọ́*, who, to achieve immortality, had an earthen wall built around the whole kingdom to protect it.

[5]In mid-1967, for example, the author counted at least a hundred Yoruba women, perhaps ten per cent of all the sellers, in the central market at Treichville in Abidjan, Ivory Coast.

[6]Men's private anxieties about impotence, however, are noted in LeVine (1966b), and Leighton, Lambo *et als*. (1963).

Chief Ogunkoya's sons play soccer in the street (Chapter 9)

The meat seller discusses his wares with a tenant of Chief Ogunkoya (Chapter 9)

CHAPTER IX

The Strains of Success: Chief Ogunkọya's Family

Keeping a Large Household Running

Early on the same holiday morning that Saliu Wahabi is busily preparing to go to the praying ground for Id-el-Fitri, a compound much closer to the heart of the newer migrant area is only awakening. Three buildings, one a two-storied house, one a large shop, and one a small house with only four rooms, form three corners of a large but cluttered yard. Two small craftsmen's stalls and a long row of latrines, shower stalls, and "kitchens" line much of the rest of the wall which runs between the buildings and around the remainder of the paved compound. This is the residence of Chief Abel Ògúnkòyà, one of six compounds the rents from which provide his income. Most of this one, however, is occupied by his immediate family and other relatives.

Ten-year-old Banji is sweeping the room upstairs where several of the older children sleep. He is the second of his mother's five children, and the tenth of his father's seventeen.[1] Yétúndé, a niece of the Chief who is looking for a job in Ibadan and staying with them, starts a fire to warm the sauce left over from the night before for her uncle's breakfast. The Chief is still in bed. Bisi, at seventeen the oldest girl still at home and therefore the substitute mother for the four boys whose mothers are no longer living with the Chief, buys some ẹko from a passing hawker to have with the sauce. Fẹmi, fifteen and about to go to an excellent residential secondary school across town, sweeps the parlor upstairs until Bisi asks him to come down and wash dishes in the yard. Mama Àgbà ("Old Mother"), the Chief's childless first wife, steps out of her room downstairs dressed to go out, and leaves after brief greetings by the children.

Only a couple of minutes later Papa calls down sharply to Délé, who is eight, to ask why he has not swept his portion of the house. Dele grumbles under his breath that he is eating, but gets up to get the broom anyway. Papa washes and calls Bisi to bring up his food.

After breakfast Papa asks *Kẹhìndé,* who is returning to his secondary school in Lagos[2] in two days, to bring his school bill for first term. He calls in Bisi and Fẹmi, the other two children now in secondary schools, and they all discuss their respective needs for tuition, boarding, books and uniforms, and spending money.

Soon Mama Agba returns, and Kẹhinde runs to the street corner when he sees her to help carry the things she has bought at the market. After she changes clothes she remarks how few people there are in the market today because of the Muslim holiday. One of the two women tenants in the main house, whose room is opposite Mama Agba's downstairs in front, comments that the Muslims are having trouble, since two separate orders (with differing calculations of the lunar calendar) have disagreed on the correct date for the festival. Mama Agba says they always disagree, and she takes this as a sign that God must not approve of the Muslims. The Christians, she affirms, never disagree on the dates of their holidays.

This tenant, an Ifẹ Yoruba woman whose husband is a typist, is Mama Agba's best friend in the house, and helps her to put her wares out in the little stall she keeps just outside the front door. Like Saliu Wahabi's wife Mama Agba sells basic items for cooking, but in slightly greater quantities. Palm oil, peanut oil, gari, and coal are the major items she stocks. The only other co-wife now living here uses the large shop that is a separate building next to the house. Her main items of trade are beer and soft drinks, much of which she sells to small night clubs in the neighborhood. Both her capital and turn-over are much larger than Mama Agba's. In consequence, she has hired both a girl and a boy, who help her in the shop and with her cooking, and who sleep in the shop to protect it from thieves. Though the two co-wives' own rooms are but two doors apart, they keep aloof from one another, exchanging only a few pleasantries in the course of the day.

Late in the morning Kẹhinde, carrying a bottle of beer from his mother's shop to someone in the next house who has yelled over for it, remarks to Mama Agba that no one sells beer in their small home town, *Òkè-gan,* in western Ijebu. Mama Agba says of course not, that in Oke-gan all they do is make gari, nothing more. Kẹhinde adds that in fact they eat gari there morning, afternoon and evening. They both laugh at what they take to be the signs of an unrefined palate and a generally unenlightened people.[3]

At that moment Banji chases Dele out the front door, catches him and starts to hit him. Papa, who has been napping upstairs in a chair, comes out onto the balcony and calls them in to explain why they are fighting. Banji is so angry that he has a hard time talking. Papa tells him to calm down, and he finally states his case. Dele has lost a pen of his, and offers no defence. Papa punishes him by telling him to stand against the wall with his arms raised — a common punishment that, for example, "Manager" Wahabi frequently got. A while later he is released with a stern warning.

Near one o'clock Papa asks Femi why he has not started the fire for the children's lunch. The boy responds that he too was sleeping when Papa was, but that he is arranging the firewood now. Papa asks whether, then, he has bought the tea bag and sugar that he wants to have with his own lunch, and Femi says no. Exasperated, Papa calls Mama Agba upstairs and asks her to make sure that at least *his* lunch is ready. Bisi, Banji and Dele grind pepper, get water and help with other tasks. Papa himself comes down to supervise Bisi, who is cooking for the children. He tells her to heat the palm oil first before adding the meat. Finally he takes over, putting in the meat himself and stirring the pot. Mama Agba comes over from her cooking as if to say something, but then hesitates and goes back. When their eba and sauce is ready, Bisi divides it nearly in two, keeping the smaller portion for herself and Dele, her full brother. She gives the larger part to Femi (the only one now at home of the four children of his mother, the Chief's fourth wife) and his younger half-brothers Banji and *Modúpẹ́*, whose own mother, the fifth wife, only recently left the Chief, taking her three other children with her to her parents' home in Lagos. Mama *Níkẹ́*, the third wife, cooks for her own children Kehinde, *Kólá, Walé,* and Debọla separately. Papa eats upstairs, alone as usual, and afterwards he again dozes.

Strained Relationships

Two days later the Chief and Mama Agba are both away. Papa has gone to the funeral of an eminent Christian pastor in a village near Ijebu Ode, while his senior wife has gone with a friend of hers to the funeral of the friend's relative in Oke-gan, their home town. After lunch Bisi and Femi are reading their father's *Daily Times,* Nigeria's largest-selling newspaper, in the parlor. If the Chief were home, they would neither use the parlor nor open his paper until he was finished with it. In fact all the children seem freer. Five of the middle boys, Kehinde (17), Banji (10), Kọla (14), Dele (8), and Wale (8), are kicking a soccer ball back and forth in the dusty street. The two youngest ones, Modupẹ (who is 5) and Debọla (3), are down the block in a field playing with some other children. Papa always keeps the children close to home and busy at household chores, so they make the most of this chance to burn up some energy.

A gleaming Peugeot breaks up the soccer game momentarily as a prominent lawyer/politician in Lagos who also comes from Oke-gan pulls up in front. He is disappointed not to find the Chief at home, but accepts Mama Nike's invitation to have a cold drink upstairs after his hundred-mile drive. She goes up with him as Bisi and Femi scamper down the stairs nodding respectful welcomes as they pass.

Soon voices grow louder upstairs. Mama Nike complains bitterly to Lawyer Ìdòwú that the Chief is not giving her any household money at all, and that she is very upset. The lawyer tells her that she should not worry herself, and should certainly not leave. He argues that her first care should be for her children, that there is no comparison between money and children who are raised well. Calming a bit, she grumbles that her sisters are doing well in their husbands' houses, and that she deserves more help than she is getting. She notes that her youngest co-wife has just run to Lagos because of the Chief's refusal to help her support the younger children. Lawyer Idowu is reluctant to get mired in details, since he will not be there to speak to Papa anyway. He insists instead that her obligation is to her children, and that she knows what is best for them. He finishes his beer and leaves.

Towards evening Banji shouts to Bisi that Kola has a "love letter" of hers and is reading it. She drops the pan she is washing to run and get it, but he has finished it by the time she snatches it away. She comes back out to the yard, telling Femi cryptically that she had an "arrangement" with somebody for something, but it has fallen through. She has to find out from the boy who sent the note why he refuses — to do what, she will not say. Another boy enters the house and talks quietly to Bisi for a few minutes in the passageway. She breaks away, though, scolding him not to bother her any more.

Shortly before dark Papa returns. He says he did not stay overnight in Ijebu because he is afraid of thieves in Ibadan; it is just as likely that there was simply no adequate place for him to stay in a small town having a large funeral ceremony.

Bisi has gone out with a friend, so Femi and Kehinde look for food for Papa. Kehinde finds some eba in his mother's shop, and Femi warms some sauce. While he is eating, Bisi returns, fearing that Papa will be angry that she was not there when he returned. She goes up in trepidation to greet him, and finds him not annoyed.

By eight o'clock Modupe has fallen asleep on a stool at Mama Nike's shop. Papa tells Bisi to take him up to the room where all the boys but the youngest sleep. Nike, the Chief's oldest child, who is a high school teacher, has herself returned today from Lagos where she went to sit for advanced exams which could gain her university admission. She goes to talk with her father for a short time. He is tired from his trip, however, and by half past eight he is ready for bed. He calls Femi to fetch him a pail of water so that he can wash. He asks Femi where Bisi is now. Around the corner, seeing her friend off, replies the lad. Papa tells him to get her at once, and when she comes in he yells at her for

leaving the house after dark. Then he retires to his room. By nine only Bisi and
Femi remain outside in the yard, talking about school.

A Chief's Problems

Chief Ogunkoya's investments in housing in the expansive 1950's provide an
income that he needs to do little to get except to collect rents and occasionally
see to it that a tenant who is in arrears vacates his rooms. Other money is loaned
out to traders as capital, on which he earns interest as well as social
indebtedness, but what part of his total income such money-lending plays
remains unclear. In any case he passes his days in a sedentary way, entertaining
visitors, supervising his family, or solving quarrels in the compound. He rises
early but naps once, often twice, during the day. He moves up and down the
stairs, but only every two days or so does he even leave the compound on an
errand or a visit. The researcher is, in this situation, a captive audience for the
Chief's own complaints and ideas, and he often adds commentary on his
problems as he directs the activity going on below from his solitary redoubt
upstairs.

Two days before Femi is to leave for school, Bisi and Femi are washing his
clothes in the yard. Papa descends to ask Femi to go to the garage behind Mama
Nike's shop and clean the car, which he has had to store for about a year now
because he is financially unable to keep up its maintenance and registration. On
the way back upstairs he begins to talk angrily about the condition of the
compound. He says that if he complains, the tenants, many of whom in the
small house at the far corner of the yard are distant kinsmen from Oke-gan, will
spread bad stories about him at home. So what can he do? This is why, he says,
he lives alone upstairs. It is the women who make the compound dirty, he
thinks. If one has just one wife it is better, but with many wives there is hardly
anything one can do.

He only married more than once, he continues, because Mama Agba's
mother began to say that he was responsible for her not having any children. She
got pregnant once, but miscarried and was then badly treated by native doctors
in some way that he thinks ''disorganized'' her womb. If it had happened
nowadays, proper medical treatment would have been available and he might
have had only that one wife. Anyway, after his mother-in-law began to say that
the infertility might be his fault, he got annoyed and resolved to take another
wife. It was ten years after he had married Mama Agba. His second wife was an
illiterate townswoman, and then he decided to marry an educated co-worker of
his as well. Soon he was up to five.

If only one can free oneself from the temptations of women, he feels, one will retain the forcefulness and discipline for success. He points to a famous Nigerian politician as an example, repeating a story that he has not slept with his wife in many years out of a belief in the enervating capabilities of women. As for himself, he must remain calm. When things in general are not going well for a man, people will be quick to backbite if he lets his temper get the better of him.

"That is why," he concludes, "I usually sit silently in the house. This is not the time for much company. All I pray for is my daily bread and some money to train the children."

Even at that moment the children will not grant him the solitude he seeks. They are banging pans and shouting in the yard. With a sigh he goes down to reprimand them and demand that they keep quiet. He speaks gravely to them, and asks the women working in the yard to see to it that the children do not make so much noise. As mothers they should try to spare him, he pleads, from having to come down and scold the children himself. He asks the children to "name" their parents (that is, to signify who is responsible for them). But as some do so, the son of one of the tenants hits another on the head with a stick, and the inquiry stops to attend to the crying child. Papa gives up his lecture, warning the parents that they should make sure their children are not the cause of any trouble. Although it is before lunch, he calls his own younger boys upstairs to their common room, spreads a mat for them and demands that they nap for a while.

A Better Day

Friday is a busy day. By eleven o'clock Papa is ready to take Femi to Regional High School. He says he will stay around until Femi gets assigned to his dormitory. The school requires that the boys appear by six o'clock, but Papa figures that the earlier they arrive the better choice Femi will have in the dorm. Femi has his few belongings packed in a small suitcase which he carries on his head. He is wearing khaki shorts and a white jersey, while the Chief wears a flowing agbada of pale orange. They walk toward the main road two blocks away to hail a taxi, and Bisi runs after them to go along, too.

Mama Agba is sitting outside by her stand chatting with her tenant friend, Ma *Toyin*. A third woman, who goes in and out of the bedrooms as if she is no stranger, now joins them. She turns out to be Femi's mother and the Chief's fourth wife, and has also come today to see her son off to school. Mama Agba is telling the others that a woman collapsed and died right in the open market where she was shopping yesterday. Everybody ran out of the market, and she herself was frightened, too. This is the second time that she has seen it happen in the same market. There must, she thinks, be some spirit in the place which causes this kind of thing.

A meat seller passes, his wares spread on a table perched on his head and shielded from the noonday sun only by leaves covering them. The tenant calls to him, but he ignores her, indicating that he has no patience for the miserly offers she makes.

A bit later a visitor is dropped off by a green Hillman. Mama Agba takes him upstairs, then tells him that Papa has gone out. The man, an old friend and townsman of the Chief's from Lagos, is sorry not to find him in, for he is not sure he can wait long enough to see him. Mama Agba quickly heats some soup and sends one of the boys for two pieces of ẹko. She puts it all in a plate and offers it to the guest, kneeling in respect. She begs him not to be upset by the quality or quantity of the food, because she had no idea that he was coming. The man says not to worry.

His wife and son left him off here, he says, to do some shopping, but they intend to double back to Oke-gan and sleep there before returning to Lagos the next day. The mention of Oke-gan cues a complaint from Mama Agba. She reports that she had a severe argument with a relative of her husband's at Oke-gan. She speaks with bitterness, although she is quick to say that her husband supported her. Nonetheless, she cannot understand why the relative wanted to provoke her (and thus to force Papa to choose between the loyalties he owed each). The relative knows that she has no children, she says, and that her position in her husband's house (here meaning his family) is insecure. She was prepared for the worst that day, because she was so furious she would have fought the woman physically except that other people prevailed upon her not to. Why should people provoke her to behave badly, she asks, when everyone can see "my position." God sees that she is not wicked, that she envies no one. . . .

She talks on, angrily, until the man interrupts her to say that he is doubly sorry that Papa is in, since he would have known what to say to him on her behalf. He tells her to be patient, in fact to try to forget what happened, because every event in life is God's work. Finally he goes downstairs because his wife and son have come back to pick him up.

Within only about fifteen minutes Chief Ogunkọya arrives home. The school was not going to assign rooms until two o'clock, and the Chief needs to eat and rest before getting ready for his Lodge meeting late in the afternoon. He left Bisi with Fẹmi. He remarks that he is sure Fẹmi will do well, because he reads all the time. He is happy that he won admission to so good a school. Mama Agba tells him of the visitor he has missed.

At half past two Bisi returns, reporting that Fẹmi has been assigned a bed and been given his bedding. Papa asks her what she would like to eat. She says ẹba. He tells her to go down and start a fire quickly; a bit later he goes down to help her cook. He complains about the ẹba, though, saying that only poverty forces them to eat it so much, and that other foods are much richer-tasting.

After Papa naps, another visitor turns up. He says he came before but was told that Papa was sleeping. What he wants to talk about is the wife who ran away to Lagos a few weeks ago. He asks if any attempts have been made to settle their differences. Papa says no, he thinks her parents must have decided that he is guilty and should come to them, but that is the last thing he would do. They should at least be the ones to ask him to come discuss the problems. The visitor responds that since there are no children involved, the husband should seek reconciliation. Papa does not think so.

At this impasse the discussion turns to politics. The visitor says that now that the military government has decided to accord state funerals to the officers killed when it took power the previous July, perhaps everyone may learn to forget the past. The Chief, however, maintains that there are many other disagreements remaining, and now the East has withdrawn from the National Provident Fund (a social security instrumentality for employed workers). He still fears that the East might retaliate for last year's massacres. Recounting how the Ibos rose from obscurity to surpass the Yorubas within thirty years,[4] he says he thinks that they will have to do something now to regain their position. Closer to home, he hopes that the Western Regional Government will make sure that all the money and property which was gained corruptly by the politicians of the former civilian government will be confiscated and returned. Papa's visitor agrees.

After he sees the man off, Papa asks Bisi to spread his agbada in the sun. Then he gets his shoes out to be cleaned and gives them to Bisi, too. He sees little Modupẹ sleeping in the yard near the tailor's shed, and scolds Bisi for not having carried him inside. Bisi replies that she told him to go inside, but he refused. The Chief remarks that Bisi is full of back talk, but that she works hard if you ask her to.

For the Lodge meeting Papa wears a special trousers, blouse, and agbada of heavy aṣọ oke. Draped over one shoulder is his chief's insignia, a piece of handwoven cloth with a special fringed overweave made only in Ijebu Ode. A few minutes before five a friend comes to call for him, wearing a sparkling white agbada but no chief's cloth. Papa locks the door to his room and the two men walk down the street to get a taxi.

Another Week and Its Difficulties

The activities of Friday and a weekend of visitors and churchgoing have obviously cheered Papa up, for on Monday he is in a lighter mood. When two visitors arrive in a blue Opel, he rushes from Bisi's room (she uses the room of the wife who is in Lagos, her own mother's having been let out to tenants) to greet them joyfully. He asks them to come upstairs, and says on the way that he was sorry that they were not in when he stopped by last time he visited Lagos. He calls over to Mama Nikẹ's shop assistant to bring over a large bottle of beer and one of stout, reaching into his pocket to pay for them when the girl brings them up. They, too, plan to spend the night in Oke-gan and return to Lagos in the morning, so they apologize for having to cut short the brief conversation they are having over their beer.

On the way out, one of them, receiving Mama Agba's greeting warmly, jokes that she is looking very old. Is it our friend, he asks, who is wearing you out? She answers with the indirectness and feigned shock appropriate to the joke, that she is very surprised by his question, and had better ask his friend the Chief, since he will know what he's been doing. The visitor responds that she should try not to let him make her get old, and then speaks some of the words said during the marriage ceremony:

"Hè! Mi ni lọ, yìn mi nù!" ("I won't go, leave me alone!")

Everyone including the Chief laughs, while Papa notes that it has been thirty-three years since that happened. The visitor nods knowingly. He says that now his children are doing what they used to do when they were young. He sometimes tells his wife that they should not reproach the children so much, since they are merely repeating behavior they have somehow acquired from their parents. Then the visitors drive off.

Moments later Mama Agba's cousin comes to announce that his wife had a baby last night at the Catholic hospital. Papa says that the Catholics run the best hospital in Ibadan. They charge more, but they give better service. Mama Agba's cousin agrees, saying also that every government hospital in the country is short of drugs. With their fees the mission-run hospitals get the right drugs for the patients and have them on hand. After the cousin leaves, Papa takes little Debọla by the hand and goes upstairs, where they both nap before lunch.

On Wednesday morning Mama Agba is carrying her stock outside to her stand as Chief Ogunkọya returns from an errand at one of his other houses up the hill. Mama Agba reports to him that the boys were playing on the street, and would not come in when she told them to. Papa asks Bisi to buy some *ògì* (cornstarch) for him from a passing hawker to make a late morning snack. Mama Agba gets some, too. As she adds it to hot water to make some ẹkọ for herself, she tells her friend Ma Tọyin about her trip home to Oke-gan yesterday afternoon for a funeral. In Yoruba practice, the more age and children and wealth and honor a person accumulates during his life, the larger and happier is the celebration of his passing. With this yardstick a young person's death is thus a tragic blow, but a respected elder's is a time for thanksgiving. In each case it is the variable quality of the life that was led which is marked, not the simple and universal fact of death. At the ceremony in Oke-gan there was plenty of food, drink, and music, Mama Agba reports, and people stayed up all night without sleeping. She reflects sadly that people with children have money spent on them when they die, but if you have no child, no one will "hear about" your passing. She prays that God will give everyone children.

Mama Nike, meanwhile, brings her three-year-old Debola over to Papa, saying he is being too mischievous and ought to be punished. Papa drags him upstairs, threatening to beat him, but Debola is howling so much by the time they get there that Papa cannot bring himself to hit him. Downstairs a boy from across the street chases Modupe into the house. Mama Agba, at the front door, stops them. The boy says Modupe has broken a toy of his. Mama, determining that this is not sufficient cause for a fight, tells him to go home.

The children must be restless today. Next Kola comes into the passage from the yard with a short whip in his hand, running after Banji. Mama Agba tells him to go put it away, but he refuses. When she rushes toward him, though, he dashes out the back door. A few minutes later Mama Nike's shop assistant has to go and drag a struggling Debola out of the street where he is playing with two friends while cars try to pass.

Annoyed at Bisi's slow preparation of lunch, Papa calls her wicked and stupid. Upstairs, he laments again how difficult it is to cope with all these children, especially because their mothers are not around. His one aim is to see that they all get a high level of education. One major reason why he always urges his oldest daughter Nike to get a university education if she can, he says, is that if she has a degree, she will surely find a husband who will treat her with respect. In turn she will have a stable household, and avoid the troubles he himself is having. He is sure that Femi and Kehinde will do well, but Bisi is having trouble in secondary school, and that, combined with her stubbornness, makes him sometimes want to withdraw her. It is Kola, the next one, who is the real problem, however. He has sickle cell anemia, and has been in and out of the hospital for the last two years. His absence and the disease have caused him not to do well in school. Sometimes Papa is fed up with him altogether but the mother continues to buy him the special foods and medicines he needs. Papa says he does not know whether to have him learn a trade or send him to secondary school, if he succeeds in gaining acceptance. After all, he sighs, even if the children do finish secondary school they may not find any work to do. Papa hears that now university graduates often wait several months before finding anything to do. And he does not see how the situation will improve in the future.

The future, he goes on, holds little hope. Perhaps the young men in the universities will bring about a new way of doing things. Even that is doubtful, he notes, given that those running the country now are university graduates. Most of the ones he has seen active in politics were just trying to get better conditions for themselves, although they are already earning more than £2000 ($5600) a year.

Sunday: No Respite

As usual, on Sunday morning Papa opens the dining room and invites the six children who are living at home now (there are in fact seven, but Debola is with his mother who is ill) to come up for breakfast together. Bisi has prepared boiled yam, fried eggs, and tea. When they finish, Bisi and Banji clear away the dishes, the smaller boys run outside to play, and Papa dresses to go to the Seventh-day Adventist Church, of which he is a prominent member. Mama Agba is also dressed up, but she is not going to church.

After Papa leaves, Nike comes out of her ill mother's room. She asks Bisi to make her some eba. Bisi says that she is too busy, but Nike begs her to do it. They make a fire in the pot at Mama Nike's shop. For a while they talk about the high school that Bisi goes to, which was Nike's school as well. But then Nike takes advantage of the privacy they have to confide to Bisi the fact that she is pregnant. Together they discuss how that news may be broken to their father. It will not be easy.

Biography: Abel Ogunkoya

The Ogunkoyas of Oke-gan are a large and important family there, whose head bears a chieftaincy title and a place in the traditional government of the town. The present Chief Ogunkoya was chosen head of the entire family in 1954, in recognition of the place he had won for himself outside the town and of the contributions he was making to his relatives at home. His own father had not been the family head, though he was a wealthy enough farmer, supporting five wives and twenty-five or more children. He became a Christian, as did most of the men in town (there are few Muslims to this day), but was conservative in his daily life. Most of his sons obeyed his desire that they "follow him to the farm," but young Abel saw that they all worked very hard for very little return. Since his father would not send him to school beyond the "infant" classes where you learned only enough to read the Bible in Yoruba, he ran away at the age of fourteen to Lagos, to the house of his mother's cousin, a tailor whom he had previously visited. He exchanged housework and tutoring for school fees at first, until his father conceded, after witnessing Abel's determination. By 1932 he completed most of a secondary education. Finding work first as an electrician with the Public Works Department (he had somehow learned the trade while he was in school), he quit two years later because, he says, so many electrical workers were dying in accidents. His uncle got him a job as a clerk in the Ijebu Ode Native Authority (the colonial institution of indirect provincial rule), and four years later he became a sales clerk for a higher salary in a foreign-owned store.

In 1943 he got caught up in the excitement of nationalism which was spreading throughout southern Nigeria. Transferred by his company to their Ibadan outlet, he began to be active in local politics, at first by writing newspaper articles. By 1946 he had enough money saved and enough contacts made in Lagos and Ibadan to begin trading on his own, at first as a wholesaler of general provisions. Advised against the high risks of the transport business (both motor accidents and crop losses could ruin truckers), he turned his profits instead to land speculation. It was an opportune time to do so, because constitutional and social developments in the country were making Ibadan a more and more important center of migration and trade. To remove a major obstacle to land dealing Papa and other migrants (most of whom were Ijebu) created a Taxpayers' Association, which successfully challenged the City's restriction against selling lots in the new lay-outs it was developing to non-indigenous city residents.

The four-room house at the rear of his present compound was the Chief's first building in Ibadan. He moved in in 1954 as one of the first settlers in the whole area. As profits allowed, he built one house at a time and added more building lots for future growth. Along the way he helped many friends and acquaintances to secure their own lots, and he aided his church in finding land for a new school. The deep involvement he has thus had in the growth of the new migrant residential district makes him, he says, feel that he is no "stranger" in Ibadan. Though Oke-gan is still "home," Chief Ogunkoya is also proud of his own part in the development of Ibadan.

Out of his profits he has also built a house at home. He opened it in 1955, a year after he was granted the chieftaincy of his family. His involvement in Oke-gan reaches far beyond his own family, though. For twelve years he was a member of the Town Council and had to go home every week to meetings. Not only did he receive less stipend per sitting of the Council than it cost him to do all this commuting, but he usually found himself giving small sums of his own money to relatives and friends besides. Since he went off Council in 1964, he says he has saved a great deal of money.

Helping townsmen who come to Ibadan, however, has continued. He keeps the four-room house in back as a way station for Oke-gan families, many of which have stayed there, rent-free, until they get established in Ibadan. He has arranged jobs, lodging, political favors, and even hospital beds for Oke-gan people. And, in concert with many other influential "sons of Oke-gan" living in Ibadan, he has helped to secure the many amenities — piped water, electricity, paved roads, maternity/dispensary — that make Oke-gan one of the most highly "developed" small towns in Nigeria.

Chief Ogunkoya's interests have stretched to regional politics as well. From the old Taxpayers' Association many men went on to lead Western Regional politics, and the Chief served them in various capacities, perhaps the highest of which was as Secretary of the Youth Wing of the *Ẹgbẹ́ Ọmọ Odùduwà* (Society of the Descendants of Oduduwa), the Yoruba "cultural" association which focussed the nationalism of the Yorubas and in turn gave rise to the Action Group (political party), which led the Western Region in the 1950's and early 1960's. Chief Ogunkoya's stature at home, in Ibadan, and in the community at large is symbolized, in part, by his membership both in the Reformed Ogboni Fraternity, which includes many of the leading Yoruba in Nigeria (the Chief Justice of the country is its current head), and in the Masons. Abel Ogunkoya has tasted success, but in recent years he has seen his ability to maintain his status waning.

Biographical Notes: Wives and Children

With his first wife, Mama Agba, he maintains a warm and trusting relationship. Mama Agba's father was a tailor in Lagos (and a friend of the tailor Papa lived with when he ran away from home), and a member of the same Christian denomination as the Ogunkoyas. He had three wives and a dozen children, of whom Miriam (Mama Agba) was the oldest. Because her mother needed household help (and because education for girls at that time was rare), Miriam left school after only a year. Later she and Abel Ogunkoya agreed to marry, and after gaining their parents' consent were wed "according to native law," that is, in a ceremony that was a Christianized version of the Yoruba marriage ritual, but was outside the British marital law that some people chose to follow. Since her mother had not objected to having junior co-wives, neither did she, and for a long time the *menage* worked fairly well. Papa gave each wife her own "chop-money," as is customary; the most junior wife cooked for him. It has only been since his money has been so scanty that there has been all this domestic trouble, Mama says. Since she has only herself to feed, she manages on what she earns from her small trade.

The second wife, the mother of Bisi and Dele, comes from Ijebu Ode, where Papa was still working at the time they were married. When she left Papa, she went to stay with her oldest daughter, Yetunde, who is a nurse there. Since then, however, she has in fact remarried.

Ma Nike, the third wife, is also the most well-off, with a turnover in her trade of perhaps £10 ($28) a day. With five children, the two oldest of whom have gone far scholastically, she is in a secure position. Her complaints about Papa's treatment have led her to a brooding isolation recently, and her mood in turn influenced her to decline being interviewed during our study.

The fourth wife went home to a town near Oke-gan two years ago, taking her two youngest, who are girls, with her. With Femi now in secondary school and *Adédáyò,* her oldest daughter, working as an accounts clerk in Lagos, she, too, is happy to be independent. While she and the Chief have patched up their quarrel, she continues to live on her own.

Finally, the fifth wife is presently in Lagos. As we noted, mediation of the argument between her and the Chief is beginning. She took her oldest, *Túí,* with her to help take care of her two youngest, a boy of three and a girl just one, whom she also took. Banji and Modupe have remained in Ibadan, and stand to lose the most if the argument is not settled, since they have no elder full sibling to supervise them closely. Modupè is bright and mischievous already, and being without a mother (or a mother substitute) for long may get him into real conflict later with his father.

In all, Papa, two wives, and seven children remain at home. The three oldest children have jobs and live elsewhere, two are away at school, and five live with the three wives who have moved out. Of the seven children at home four do not have their mother there. Since Mama Agba is not expected to substitute and does not, Papa must superintend the cooking, cure fevers, settle the bickering and do all the other activities primarily attendant upon a mother's role. Together with the financial difficulties he has in providing for all his children, the disharmony at home saps his energy and sours his outlook on life in general.

The Compound

Even the house itself reflects some of the disarray into which the Chief has slid. The main house has six rooms downstairs, three on each side of the passage. Mama Agba and Mama Nike occupy their own rooms, and Ma Toyin, her husband and their four children have been renting their room for six years now. The fourth wife's room is empty, while Bisi is sleeping in the fifth wife's room. Bisi's mother's room has been let out to the Ibadan carpenter (and his wife and two children) whose shed is in the yard. From the back part of the passage leads the stairway up. The passage is dark, and under the stairs trash collects, to be removed only when the Chief finally yells at someone to do so.

Upstairs it is lighter and airier. The space of what would be the passage and two rooms downstairs form a large sitting room above. The Chief's own bedroom, his storeroom and the dining room (in which there is a small electric refrigerator) adjoin one side of this parlor, while the common room where the boys sleep on mats is in the back corner near the top of the stairs. A dozen soft chairs, couches, a study table, and the Chief's desk line the walls of the parlor. There is linoleum on the floor, a large (and rarely used) electric fan on the ceiling, and a number of calendars, photographs of the family and of the Chief in various regalia, a clock, a mirror, old greeting cards, and long fluorescent lights on the light blue walls. Despite the decoration, the good quality of the various items, and the half dozen windows, the overall impression is one of mustiness; the floor and furniture are rarely swept or dusted, spills are not well cleaned from the chair arms or floor, and papers are left lying around for many days in various parts of the room. None of the wives or children finds either time or motivation to take care of this preserve of Papa's and it is only as clean as it is because Papa often locks the door to the stairway when he goes out, keeping the children downstairs.

Although "only" twenty people live in the eleven-room main house, a total of nearly fifty in the whole compound use the yard in back. The carpenter and tailor have shops and apprentices who spill out into the open area. Several cookpots stand in odd corners between the buildings, and four goats and a larger number of chickens share the yard as well. Clotheslines hang from garage to house and from house to shop. The side of the yard containing the latrines and bathrooms reeks: for some unexplained reason the latrines are stalls without even buckets, so that people must carry pieces of newspaper in when they defecate. Some of the children do not even bother, and excrement lies on the floor until it is washed out a hole through the base of the wall that leads outside the yard. This wholly atypical slovenliness is but further evidence of the disintegration of authority within the compound.

Summary

Chief Ogunkoya has been close to the wielders of power in Western Nigeria. Once he lamented the fact that, with the politicians replaced by military rulers, he could no longer get favors done for people he knew. Perhaps this lack of brokerage possibilities — of his former ability to secure and dispense the concrete evidences of power — has been partially responsible for his decline in stature and even in self-esteem. He sees only the most self-seeking of the politicians maintaining their wealth, and many people have turned out to be only fair-weather friends. Finding it hard to match expenditures with some of his former acquaintances, he restricts his visiting now to those closest to him. Within two years three more of his children will be ready for secondary school, so he does not see an early end to the domestic demands on his finances. Achievement in modern Nigeria can be lost as well as won. Chief Ogunkoya, whether his setback is temporary or more permanent, has been severely buffeted by the unfolding of the very social relationships — several wives, many children, intense involvement with townsmen and fellow community leaders — which are the proof of his earlier success.

Discussion: Success — At'ọmọ, At'owo, At'alafia Ni . . .

"Success" for Modern Ijebu: Values and Methods. The reflections on women in the discussion of Madam Bankọle make explicit some of the methods by which wives and mothers hope to consolidate their present positions, achieve long-term security, and gain prestige and honor among their kinsmen and friends. It is important as well to abstract some of the strategies and goals that men pursue, that is, to define "success" and review the strategies by which men achieve it.

Perhaps one good way to define success as Ijebus would is to cite a Yoruba proverb that concerns ultimate values: *"àt'ọmọ, àt'owó, àt'àláfià . . . mo fẹ́ bẹ́ẹ̀!"* is a not uncommon adage painted on the back or side of passenger trucks ("mammy wagons"). "Children, and money, and alafia . . . I want (it) thus!" Examining each term of this formula will illuminate the general goals of most modern Ijebu like the individuals we have met so far.

At'ọmọ . . . ([and] children . . .). In primarily horticultural societies like the Yoruba, in which productivity can be increased principally by the addition of manpower (rather than by tools or the acquisition of especially rich but scarce land, for example), men tend to use their surplus income to increase their labor force. Indeed, such societies have a high frequency of polygyny (Clignet 1970:22-23). In former times investment in slaves was also a means toward increased productivity, and wealth. Obviously a family unit benefited not only from the actual agricultural labor of such "recruits" to its ranks, but also from the capacity of wives and female slaves (most of whom were taken into individual domestic units) to bear children, and hence new laborers. Put more simplistically, Yoruba (and other) horticulturalists valued wives and children highly, in part because of their productive worth.

Certainly such an explanation must not be overinterpreted. Family relationships were built on far more than mutual economic productivity, and it is doubtful that very many people were so calculating in their actions as might seem implied by such correlations. Further, the independence of the value on wives and children from sheer questions of productivity is amply demonstrated by the vitality of the same values in the new context of urban family life, where productivity is much more minor an issue. Most (but not all) Ijebus, even if they consider themselves good Christians, say they would take a second wife if their first did not have any children. Michael Odusanya was advised to make sure his wife-to-be was fertile before he married. Chief Ogunkoya took more wives because his first had no child. Tade Oyebanji says he would do the same thing. Mama Bankole reveals the intense emotional involvement between Yoruba mothers and their children.

The reasons for valuing children so highly are thus extremely complicated. Miriam Ogunkoya, "Mama Agba," was expressing a widely-shared hope for immortality when she commented that if you are childless no one "hears about it" (or you) after you die. The Ijebu legend of Sungbo, noted in the discussion of Madam Bankole, contains the same idea. For men, the creation and management of a large family is counted an integral part of what a successful life should include, and doing it well is a source of pride and respect.

Even the few very highly Westernized and monogamous élite families have five or six children. Knowing that families of their economic status in Europe or America have perhaps only three, they sometimes blame pressure from their old parents for the fact that they have more. Nevertheless, birth control information and technology is readily available to such people, though not easy for others to come by. So it must be assumed that the value of children remains high among all segments of the Yoruba population.

At'owo . . . (and money . . .). Money is seen by other Nigerians to be a fundamental value in Ijebu life. So deep is this stereotype that a counterfeiting ring operating in Ijebu in the 1920's left a permanent mark — far beyond Nigeria, to this day, counterfeit coins are called "Ijebu money," or even more damningly, simply "Ijebus!"

Ijebu, as almost any Nigerian will go on with the stereotype, are notoriously materialistic. When the author mentioned to anyone who knew their reputation that his research was among the Ijebu, an almost invariable response was, "Ah, so you've probably discovered how stingy they are!" Non-Ijebu mean by this remark that, according to the yardsticks by which they measure peoples, Ijebu do not redistribute enough of their income or profit socially, but rather hoard it for themselves. Whatever their relative position in this regard (and it would take comparative research to measure it), it is certainly true that Ijebu do make and execute plans for the personal accumulation and use of goods and property. The Odusanyas want a radio-phonograph; Tade Oyebanji is saving to purchase a taxi; Saliu Wahabi has built most of a house; Alice Bankole paid for a decade of high-cost education; Abel Ogunkoya has seven houses, a car, and other expensive items. Furthermore, Ijebu do not simply invest for productive purposes: like Western materialists they spend in part simply to show that they are wealthy, and to enjoy the wealth they can gather.

Patterns of investment vary. Of course, many strategies to get rich involve whole careers. As is true for women, there are several "typical" career lines that men follow. A craftsman seeks first to purchase additional tools with which he can set journeymen or apprentices to work; later he may begin naturally enough to buy and sell the materials he works — cloth for a tailor, wood for a carpenter, cement blocks or gravel or sand for a builder. In earlier days many men who had some capital to begin with fanned into the countryside to buy marketable produce, especially cocoa and other export crops, from farmers for resale to still larger-scale middlemen. If profits allowed, they purchased a truck and continued to buy produce to haul in it, or even later became solely "transporters." Many an Ijebu fortune was built this way, and many lost through the vagaries of accidents at critical moments or drivers who learned to swindle their employers. More recently, employees of government or private enterprise like Michael Odusanya and Abel Ogunkọya have used both savings and knowledge gained on the job to begin businesses of their own.

Reinvesting in one's overall career provides a basic thrust toward success. The major material demonstration that one is achieving it, though, is the building of a house. Until the 1950's most people considered building a house in their home town as that tangible proof of success. There was nothing new in this attitude, for the initiation of a social grouping around oneself had always been the mark of eminence and a guarantee of immortality. This is the house, or compound, or lineage, of so-and-so, people would have to say. What was new was, first, the degree of ostentation shown in the construction and furnishing of the largest of these houses. Some few cost up to £35,000 ($100,000), (for examples, see Mabogunje 1962), but even when they were not so expensive, in many towns and villages the three- or four-story plastered and painted houses of a handful of successful men dominate the modest dwellings around them. A second new aspect of house-building was the number left vacant, against the date of eventual retirement and homecoming of their builders. (If both these new features seemed wasteful, it is probably true that the vast majority of new homes built by successful men, whether migrant or still resident at home, were modest and were occupied [rent-free by relatives] from the outset.)

In recent years, however, men (and some women, too) have built their first houses in the cities where they work, where rents provide an additional income with few risks, and where enough space for one's own family is thus available. Chief Ogunkọya saw the profits to be made in rental housing very early; Saliu Wahabi articulated his purposes in building his house most clearly. For this generation of Ijebus in Ibadan, income from a first house in the city can help build a later house at home.

Automobiles, television sets, refrigerators, air conditioners, and many other major consumer items are also available in Ibadan, and people buy them in increasing numbers. None, nor all of them together, is as important however, as either the first element of the Yoruba proverb we have cited, or the last.

At' alafia . . . Alafia is a complex and important concept in Yoruba that has no exact English equivalent. It signifies good physical health, peace and harmonious interpersonal relationships, and prosperity in a material sense. When a Yoruba asks, in a common greeting, *"Ṣe àláfià ni?"* — "is it alafia (with you)?" or simply "are you well?" — he implies all these dimensions of well-being.

The meaning of alafia does not simply lie at the intersection of the English glosses by which it may be approached. In Yoruba conceptions of the social order, physical health, prosperity, and social harmony are intimately interconnected. The hostility between Saliu Wahabi's wives, and the incident of Mama Bankọle's infected hand, led to comments on the theory of personal causation of illness and accident that Yorubas hold. The most common solutions to problems presented to the *Ifá* diviner involve the restoration of harmonious relationships with other people, living or dead. Similarly Yorubas consider themselves unable to enjoy their personal possessions, their tenure of farms or houses, or their work if they feel that the social relationships surrounding them are strained or ruptured. Since living under public scrutiny as much as Yorubas do produces frequent possibilities for personal strife, alafia is a scarce and treasured quality.

A man in modest circumstances can have alafia, if he is having reasonable good health and luck in his work, lives in a spirit of cooperation with his kinsmen and neighbors, and has personal peace of mind. A man with a large family may not have alafia, as Chief Ogunkọya evidences so clearly. The rich man will only have alafia if he uses his wealth in ways that gain the approval of others. Conceiving that one's physical health and continued material well-being cannot be separated from such approbation provides a powerful constraint upon one's activities. Chief Ogunkọya would not even criticize the tenants from his home town for dirtying the compound from fear of the chain reaction he might set off.

In addition to the belief structure, moreover, there are considerable rewards to be gained in the cultivation of one's fellows. Making oneself the center of a network of information and obligation provides a variety of possibilities for early profit advantage and for favorably-priced services and goods. To help ensure alafia, therefore, a man on his way to success invests part of his wealth in other men.

Such social investment takes several forms. First, he redistributes part of his income to kinsmen, friends, and neighbors, by giving gifts, especially of money and of food. Second, he engages in a special kind of "conspicuous consumption" which involves other *people* more than things. Yorubas comment that someone giving a party is "declaring a surplus." In the continuous and reciprocal obligations of hosting associational meetings or even simple home visiting, in the joint purchase of identical clothing for a holiday or other occasion, in the impressive celebration of a birth, marriage, or death by entertaining dozens or hundreds of guests, and in the monetary gifts and entertainments accompanying the acquisition of a chieftaincy title, he secures the fellowship and good will of his companions while spending high proportions of his income or savings.

Third, and most important for rising above other men in power and prestige, he constructs a loose grouping of followers and partisans who have incurred obligations of variable weight to rally around him in times of personal conflict or for the purpose of political competition. He may secure followers by recruiting them from his home town with favors he can do for them. They may be tradesmen, such as the builder of his house or the steady mechanic of his car, whose help he can count upon out of gratitude for his patronage. Or they may be actual subalterns of his — ex-apprentices, juniors at the office, young relatives from home that he has sponsored in the city, or even men to whom he has loaned money. Though people in all these categories owe him debts of support, few are totally dependent upon him. At any given moment or on a given issue they may find their gratitude on the wane or their loyalty divided: they may even desert to another camp. Put to the test, a man's success will be measured by how many of them support him unequivocally in conflicts with comparable leaders. Functioning at its best, such a unit of leader and followers can be a virtual juggernaut in local politics. At worst the followers can even hold their patron to ransom: though the worst cases are when political "hangers-on" (or retained thugs) demand more and more money from their supporter, Chief Ogunkoya fears that his tenants, too, have become the masters of the situation.

An ambitious man, in short, must invest in people, but the judicious application of money is hardly enough to guarantee alafia. He can continue to lead them and gain security and strength from them only if he continually deepens his own management and political skills. Peter Lloyd has described *traditional* Yoruba society as one in which wealthy and powerful men did not stand apart as a separate class, but were at "the apices of groups consisting of kin and followers" (1966b:332). This principle of social organization is very much alive in the contemporary activities of Chief Ogunkoya and perhaps as many as two hundred other Ijebu urban "chiefs" in Ibadan like him. But standing at the apex of a pyramid of human emotions, individual interests, and complex loyalties and conflicts is no easy task, as the signs of erosion around Chief Ogunkoya demonstrate.

Success: the Life Style. Many Ijebus like Chief Ogunkoya exchange the financial security of paid employment for the greater risks of commercial activity, and then seek to direct assistants, managers, agents, and other dependents from home or nearby office rather than participate actively in their enterprises. If one is bound up in the European "Protestant Ethic," one may view the fact that Chief Ogunkoya is not "working" although he is capable of doing so as stupid, wasteful, or even immoral. That view, of course, is wholly ethnocentric. What is perhaps most remarkable about the amount of occupational shifting in mid-career, is that it is aimed toward virtually the same life-style as that enjoyed a century and more ago by the traditional chief.

That life style is characterized by leisure and sedentarism. The most extreme illustration of it was that thrust upon the king of Ijebu, who was in pre-colonial days forbidden to leave his house except on rare ritual occasions. More typical examples these days include the chiefs and kings of small Ijebu towns, who, like Chief Ogunkoya, keep to their houses or yards except when they have errands to run for which they cannot send juniors, or when they have official appearances to make at courts or government councils. Stable as well over the years are the public signs of success: leisure should be displayed by frequent visiting and entertaining, and sedentarism should be evidenced by growing majestically fat!

Of course retirement from active business does not imply indolence for a successful man. His position at the head of a large compound and a wide group of followers demands a great deal of attention if it is to be carried on well. If Chief Ogunkoya did not have to see to the wifely activities with which he is burdened, he would in better days be spending a great deal of time mediating the domestic discord of others (as Saliu Wahabi does), assisting in decisions concerning the business activities of men who look to him for guidance, and deciding how to further the interests of those under him. As it is, the many minor activities of loaning keys to a man who has lost his, of providing minor medicines and advice to visitors or children in the compound who need them, or of turning on the electric fan when an important visitor comes, all continually demonstrate and reinforce the high status he still has.

In ordinary times, too, he would find more energy than he now does to accompany others of his status to the parlors and offices of those more powerful men who have patronage to hand out. Once the Chief noted that he was not one of those who visit such people to trade gossip, "tell lies," and "cringe" in subservience in order to get a few favors. Yet, were he in a mood of greater self-assurance, he might well view visiting and discussing politics with the leaders of the state in a far different light. Over much of Africa, and elsewhere, the leisure to participate in day-to-day politics has commonly been the preserve of successful elders, and Chief Ogunkoya is made in the same mold.

Footnotes

[1]For this, the largest family in this book, a modified genealogical chart may be of use:

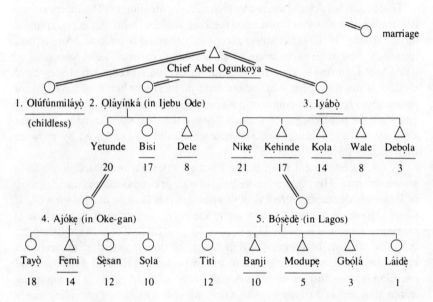

Note: Ages appear below names. Underlined names are of those resident in Ibadan for at least part of the study.

[2]Secondary schools in Nigeria are like universities in North America in charging fees, in being continually ranked in prestige and atmosphere, and in entailing stiff competition and successful application to enter.

[3]In fact, as most people realize, gari is cheaper than many other foods and so is the poor man's staple. In addition, in much of Ijebu Province yams, the staple starch of most Yoruba, does not grow well and cassava, from which gari is prepared, is the staple crop anyway.

[4]Yorubas say that no one ever "heard from" the Ibos until Nnamdi Azikiwe, later the first President of the Republic of Nigeria, returned home from the United States (and two years in the Gold Coast) in 1937. They date the rise of the Ibos from that event. While Azikiwe certainly gave quick expression to Ibo (and other non-Lagosians') political consciousness, Ibo achievement in Nigeria is of course not so dependent upon a single man.

Houses in various stages of completion in a newer residential area, where rooms are let one or two at a time

Political violence attends the struggle toward prosperity...

. . .while the Yoruba combine cultural strengths with social change

CHAPTER X

Elite Reserve: The Falujọ Family

A Different Style

On the northern outskirts of Ibadan, behind the hill overlooking the city on which the official regional government residences lie, is a quiet new housing estate. In its spacious single-family houses, surrounded by well-trimmed half-acres of lawn and garden, live some of the members of Ibadan's cosmopolitan technocratic elite. They are lawyers and town planners, professors and engineers, doctors and publishers, consular personnel and commercial executives. About half are foreigners, from a score of countries. The other half are Nigerian, mostly Yoruba from Western Nigeria itself but from other ethnic groups and other regions as well. The physical atmosphere of *Wásimi* Layout, and of the other estates at the city's periphery, is tranquil, and almost modest in its refinement. The social atmosphere, with so many of the managers of Western Nigerian society on hand, is one of unrushed professional concern muted by an obvious enjoyment of present privilege.

The *Fálujò* house comes to life in the middle of the afternoon, when the two oldest children return from school, and Dr. and Mrs. Falujọ get home from work. Benjamin, the houseboy, has finished preparations for lunch by then. As soon as Mrs. Falujọ comes downstairs after changing her clothes, he asks if it is all right for him to go for his "afternoon break."

"Madam, I'll be going, ma. I'll come back by half past five."

"Yes, of course . . . usual time," assents Mrs. Falujọ.

Little *Gbéngá,* who is two, starts shouting again as another car comes up the driveway. It is *Bándélé* and *Ọmọtọlá,* his brother and sister, home from school. Mrs. Falujọ tells them to change quickly and come to eat.

Tọla, who is eight, comes down first, and goes to her mother in the kitchen. "Mummy," she says, "my friend Elizabeth is not well. She wasn't in school today. I want to go and play with her this evening — her father asked me to come."

"Where did her father see you?" asks "Mummy" in English.

"He came to pick her brother up," answers Tọla, switching to English herself.

Mrs. Falujọ says she can go at four o'clock, and they sit down to eat. There are five places set at the dining room table, for Mrs. Falujọ, the three children (Gbenga has a high chair), and Mrs. Falujọ's elderly sister, who lives with them. Mrs. Falujọ serves herself first, then passes the bowls of rice and dòdò (fried ripe plantain) on to her sister. As in the other families, children get served after adults.

"Where's Daddy?" Tọla asks in English.[1]

"He had to go to Ijebu Ode today," Mrs. Falujọ replies. Mr. Falujọ is an economist in the Regional Ministry of Planning and Development, and often has to go out of town to evaluate development sites or meet with local officials. Mrs. Falujọ asks Tọla to say Grace.

"Bless this food, O Lord, for Christ's sake," intones Tọla, and the rest reverently echo her "Amen!" Then they all begin to eat, the old "Mama" (only she is so called) and Gbenga using spoons but the rest with forks and knives. There is little conversation.

Right after lunch the older children go into the study to start their homework, while Mrs. Falujọ and Mama do the dishes. At about four Mr. Falujọ drives up in his Peugeot, yells hello and regards from friends in Ijebu as he goes up to change, and comes down to eat. He has rice, but with tinned peas instead of dodo, and milk rather than water. He has two bananas for dessert. Then he tells everyone that it is time to go upstairs to rest.

It is quiet for about five minutes. First Tọla tiptoes down in a fresh dress and sandals, ready to go to her friend's house. She leaves by the kitchen door. Next Gbenga, who has stayed downstairs with Mama, starts running around with a small airplane he pulls out of the toy box under the stairs. He jumps on and off the chairs, and Mama cannot control him. Finally, half an hour later, the doorbell rings and a visitor for Mr. Falujọ enters, followed a few minutes later by another. Mrs. Falujọ, too, comes down to welcome them.

The first man is a clergyman. Mr. Falujọ notes on introducing him that he has been the Bishop of the Independent African Church in Ijebu since 1929, ". . . when I was in Standard II (second grade). I remember it well, because I failed the year-end exam that year, and he saw to it that I was readmitted to repeat the class."

The old pastor remarks that soon he is due for retirement, but Mr. Falujọ objects. "No, no, that wouldn't be good at all. We still need you at Ijebu."

Mr. Falujọ offers his visitors a drink. The bishop takes whisky and soda. Mr. Adélẹ̀yẹ, the other guest, declines the "hot" drink (liquor) but accepts some cake that Mrs. Falujọ had made the day before. After he finishes, the Bishop leaves.

Mr. Adeleye has come to put the finishing touches on a speech they have been preparing for the Military Governor to make tomorrow when he officially opens the new offices of the "International Exchange Corps," in which Mr. Falujo is active. The I.E.C. coordinates brief visits of families to one another's homes in various countries, and Victor Falujo has been interested in this sort of program since he stayed with a family in Michigan when he first arrived in the United States to study. The Secretary to the Military Governor has asked them to bring a copy of the speech to him at four o'clock today.

Mrs. Falujo (*Şadé* is her first name) expresses her surprise. She never knew, she says, that people making speeches always have it prepared for them like this. Her husband explains that the Governor's office will go over it and change anything they want to, but that this way they have basic information. He goes upstairs to telephone a third man that they are on their way to pick him up so they can all deliver the speech.

After they go Mrs. Falujo goes back up to rest a bit more. At 5:30, just as Benjamin comes back in from his quarters behind the house, she calls Bandele from the study to go for Ṭọla. When they return they are sent upstairs for their evening bath. At six Ṭọla comes down again in a pink nightgown, and Bandele in a loose Yoruba shirt and trousers which serve him as pyjamas. Benjamin goes to get the television set, which is kept upstairs during the night where thieves are less likely to enter. He puts it on a low table in the parlor. Bandele says joyfully that tonight the *Ògúndé* Theatre Party — a popular folk opera troupe — will be on, but that is much later.

For supper there is amala (cooked yam flour) with ewedu sauce. "Mummy" asks Bandele to set for only four people, as she and "Daddy" will eat later by themselves. The food is served on plates directly from the kitchen. Mummy feeds Gbenga on her lap.

Afterwards, Benjamin clears the table and cleans up. While the children watch TV, Mrs. Falujo reads the newspapers (two dailies are delivered to the house).

At seven-thirty Victor returns. He and Şade go right out again in order to make a quick visit to the University Hospital, where their third child, Akin, has been a patient for four months with a difficult liver disease. He has been responding well to the drugs, and is in good spirits despite his long confinement. At least one of the Falujos goes every day to see him. Tonight they return in half an hour. Meanwhile Mama has bathed Gbenga and put him to bed.

As Victor sits down to eat, he calls over Bandele, who has not taken his eyes off the television since it came on for the evening at 6:30. "Dele, did you show your homework to Mummy? No? Why? Didn't you do it? Go get it!"

Bandele goes to the study — and stays several minutes.

"Dele," his father calls again, "are you just doing it now?"

The boy yells no, and brings his exercise book out to his mother. She will look at it when she finishes eating, she says.

Over supper Victor tells Ṣade what happened at the Governor's office, but the children are laughing and yelling so loudly about the TV show that is on that their parents cannot sustain their conversation. As Victor finishes he learns from Bandele that Ogunde will be on in ten minutes. He reminds the children that they are supposed to be in bed at nine. They look downcast, anticipating enforcement of the rule.

"Well," smiles Victor, "let's see what happens. Perhaps he'll only be on for half an hour tonight." At that both he and Ṣade come to watch, too, leaving Benjamin to clean up the supper dishes.

Chores and Errands

Many weekdays pass like this first one. The menu changes, and includes many items and recipes rarely or never included by the other families — milk, fruit, eggs, toast, pies and cakes, sausages, and tinned European vegetables supplement the basic starches, meats, and oil-and-vegetable sauces of the Nigerian diet. Both the "siesta" and the early preparation for a regular bedtime are standard, as are the study hours (which the children frequently avoid) and television viewing for the children. From about five to six is often a play hour for the three youngsters at home, but they spend it with one another inside or in the yard, and do not have frequent playmates. At about the same hour visitors often come to see Mr. and Mrs. Falujọ, though sometimes one or both of them are out calling on someone else. Mr. Falujọ brings only a diary and appointment book home from the office with him, and Mrs. Falujọ as well rarely has work to do at home for the high school across town where she teaches mathematics.

On Saturday, however, the routine is different. Before breakfast Benjamin is busy washing the linoleum that covers the parlor floor. Breakfast is on the table, and Ṣade calls everyone to come. There is an additional girl present, the same size as Tọla, who is their cousin Àdùkẹ́. She is the daughter of Victor's older brother, who works as an inspector in the Ministry of Education and lives in Oke Ado. Adukẹ often sleeps over on the weekends.[2]

For breakfast, first there is corn flakes and milk. Then comes ewa with slices of bread. Ṣade pours large glasses of tomato juice after deciding that there will not be enough milk left if they all drink that. She says to Victor that she will be going to the market this morning, dropping Tọla off to have her hair done and doing her own shopping. First, though, she will go to the dispensary to pick up a fresh supply of anti-malaria pills. Victor, too, goes out in his car right after breakfast.

While their mother goes for the medicine, the children knock over the toy box and soon have the parlor filled with dolls, games, trucks and other things. Aduke sits on a chair in the corner, looking at a book about cats. Tola and Bandele sit on the floor throwing a ball to one another and scoring points when one does not throw it or catch it properly. Gbenga wants to go to sleep, so Tola puts him onto a large soft chair. Then Bandele goes out to get his bicycle from the small storeroom at the back of the house. He rides right around the house two or three times, then gives the bike to Tola. She rides around, too, and then comes straight at Bandele, yelling, "I'm going to run you down!" She tries again and again, but it is hard for her to turn on the grass and Bandele easily evades her.

Victor comes back, changes into a pale yellow agbada, and leaves again carrying a small package, saying that he is going to the wedding of a cousin of Professor *Akànbí,* an Ijebu historian who is his close personal friend. He adds, to the children, "Bandele, Tola, go in and study — dictate spelling to each other, and you, Dele, write an essay on . . . on the Ibadan Zoo. Hear me? Have it ready for when I come home." He gets into the car and charges down the driveway.

Tola goes back to the bicycle, but Bandele sits pensively at the table in the study. "In the Ibadan Zoo," he writes slowly, "there are many different kinds of animals. . . ." Then, after a few more minutes he gets up and again goes outside.

Sade returns to pick up the two older children for shopping. On the way toward town, Sade decides that she will first drop Tola off at Dugbe, next go to get some bread at one ot the large supermarkets, and finally return to Dugbe to do her own shopping there and pick Tola up again. The usual Saturday morning traffic jam in Gbagi (the commercial core of modern Ibadan, adjacent to Dugbe) slows down the whole process.

At Dugbe the hairdresser that Sade wants to use has a long line of customers waiting, so she takes Tola to another aisle of the market where a line of hairdressers have stalls. She picks one who says she will wait on Tola as soon as she finishes her current client. From there Sade heads to the Kingsway department store, passing on the way the large hall where the wedding is being held that Victor is attending. Its parking lot is full of cars and people. At Kingsway Sade buys a loaf of bread, a pair of children's socks, and two bars of chocolate candy.

Back at Dugbe Tola's hair is only half done. Sade tells Bandele to wait with Tola while she does some shopping. She gives them one of the chocolate bars to share.

First Sade buys fresh tomatoes and *èfó* leaf from a small girl. Then, because her own regular provisions seller's stall is a long walk, she stops at Madam Bankọle's stall to buy some floor polish. The price that Mama Bankọle wants is three pence higher than Ṣade expects, however, so she walks up to her "own" seller, an Ẹgba woman, after all. There she buys two dozen small cans of tinned milk, two small boxes of detergent, six cans of tomato paste and a large container of Ovaltine. She finds that the floor polish has gone up three pence everywhere, and so she returns to Madam Bankọle to buy it. From the produce sellers she buys yams, oranges, and grapefruit, and then puts everything into the car. When she gets back to the hairdresser's, Tọla is still not finished. It is already one thirty, and Ṣade is anxious to get home, but she sits down to wait another half hour for her daughter.

Visits and Visitors

Right after siesta on Wednesday Ṣade decides to visit Akin. She drives the mile or so to the hospital silently and parks in a space usually reserved for doctors, close to a stairway to the children's ward. About twenty-four beds line the two sides of the large, airy ward, which has windows on both walls. The high beds, white sheets, and roomy surroundings are in marked contrast to the homes from which most of its occupants come. At the far left end is Akin's bed, with a hospital table swung over it that is covered with bits of modeling clay, paper, and books. He does not look, or act, sick.

"How is Gbenga? And Daddy and Tọla and Bandele?" he greets his mother excitedly. "Did they get the books and the toy hammer I asked you to give them?"

Ṣade nods and gives him two sweet bananas that she has brought. In turn, he gives one of them to the boy in the next bed, who looks about ten. This boy is extremely thin and languid, and looks increasingly doleful as other mothers and visitors come in, but not for him. In a few minutes supper is brought by the attendants. Most of the patients get Nigerian dishes, but Akin is on a special diet that costs an extra ten shillings ($1.40) a day. This evening he has fish stew with mashed potatoes, and tinned pears for dessert. As he finishes up, Mr. Adelẹyẹ, Victor's friend from the I.E.C., comes in to say hello to Akin briefly.

After the meal, the children begin to fall asleep one by one. Many of the mothers stay to comfort their children, and depart after drawing the mosquito netting around the beds. By seven thirty the only visitors left are Ṣade and two other women, one of whom wants to take her child home then and there and is arguing with the nurses about it. As Ṣade gets ready to leave, Akin asks her if she will please empty his urine bottle and bring him the potty seat they use in this ward instead of bedpans. Ṣade laughs and says, "You just want to pester me because you haven't seen me for three days!"

Coincidentally, Ṣade and Victor arrive home again at the same moment, Victor with his brother in the car, too. As soon as they enter the house, there is a knock on the door behind them. It is their new next-door neighbor, who moved in only three days before. At that time Ṣade went over to welcome them only to discover that she knew the woman many years before, in high school. Now Mrs. Johnson curtsies a "good evening, sir" to Victor, and says that her husband is on his way over, too.

When she sees him, Ṣade exclaims, "Ah! I remember you . . . at King Edward's School, Lagos, when you used to come to our dances."

"I remember you, too," Mr. Johnson replies, in a booming bass voice and an almost-clipped English accent. "You were at Victoria College, weren't you?"

"Right, just like your wife. And I was in the same plane with her, going to Britain. She was the youngest passenger then."

"Oh yes," smiles Mrs. Johnson. "I was barely twenty-one — but I was feeling quite old then."

"I also remember one Hausa man on the plane," says Ṣade, "so crude and very, very uncivilized. He was the laughing-stock of the trip."

"Are you Yoruba?" Victor asks Mrs. Johnson.

"No, I am from Uromi in the Midwest," she answers.

"I didn't know that," says Ṣade. "You speak perfect Yoruba."

"Well, I came to the West when I was very young, and I went to school in Lagos, so. . . ."

"And got one of the famous 'King Edward School Twins' trapped!" Ṣade jokes.

"Right!" laughs Kehinde Johnson loudly. "Don't let us out now!" When he stops laughing he adds, "K.E. boys were so adventurous then, you know."

"Yes," says Ṣade, "and the Victoria girls were always keen on them. Maybe they still are." She goes on to observe, "Most K.E. boys are now lawyers and judges, like Justice Duke, Lawyer Ojike, and so on. I remember when Justice Duke was a student, not a very tall boy, always coming to our school, parading behind the barbed wire fence hours on end. . . ."

"Looking for girls, of course," Victor interjects.

Ṣade agrees. "Of course, that's how you got to know them. They would come and stand behind the fence as if they were planted there, and the girls would point at them and tell you their names. It was so funny in those days."

This whole conversation is in English, and Victor's brother is left out of it. After a few minutes he finds a chair and sits in front of the television set. Now the Johnsons are getting up to go, but their conversation takes a new turn, concerning the neighborhood, and they sit back down. At a quarter to ten the Falujos have still not had dinner.

The Homecoming

The following Saturday is a special one for the family. The doctors at University Hospital have said that Akin is well enough to try coming home for a weekend visit. Victor has a special meeting of economic advisors to go to at noon, so at eleven he hurries over to pick Akin up. The boy is obviously excited, and tells his father all that the doctors and nurses have said. He concludes, "Daddy, I'm never coming back here, am I?"

"Yes, you know you are," Victor replies matter-of-factly.

"No, I won't!" Akin bellows.

In fact Victor had questioned the advisability of letting Akin come home on the grounds that it might be difficult on everyone to make him go back. He stops packing up Akin's things and gives him a long lecture on how the hospital staff must watch over him so that he will get better more quickly. ". . . but if you won't come back then your illness won't disappear. You want to be as old as Bandele and still be sick?"

"No," says Akin sourly.

Victor finishes packing, in a rush to get home again. Akin has to remind him to get his medicine. At the end of the ward is an office where the doctor on duty works, and Victor goes to see him. As the doctor steps out, a large and well-built woman comes through the doors, followed by a sweating attendant pushing an X-ray machine. Both men stop what they are doing and watch her walk down the ward. Finally Victor looks up and says, "If you'll please. . . ."

"Oh, yes," replies the doctor, also waking up. He brings a bottle of medicine for Akin.

At home, Akin gets a hero's welcome. Everyone lines up outside when the car arrives, and Akin bursts into a huge and toothy smile. He runs the last few steps into his mother's arms, and Ṣade carries him to the big soft chair in the parlor. The other children crowd around him, asking questions all at once. Little Gbenga seems puzzled, until Ṣade asks him, "That's Akin! Don't you remember him? Shake hands now."

"Ah-Ah," smiles Gbenga in his own pronunciation of Akin, who stretches his hand to the toddler. And everyone cheers when Gbenga takes it and shakes hands with his brother.

Soon the children are all rolling model cars, balls, and other toys across the floor. Whenever Akin's goes under a chair, the others rush to have the honor of retrieving it for him. His smile never fades.

Half an hour later Ṣade comes to say that Akin should rest; he happily climbs back onto the chair with a book. A minute later he calls out, ''Mummy, I want some candy!'' Instead of saying no as she would to the other children; Ṣade climbs into her car and goes to the store for her usual Saturday loaf of bread, and two large bars of chocolate. The rest of Akin's visit home is almost as pampered as the first hour.

The Encyclopedia Salesman

On Tuesday Ṣade is home first from school. Ṭola is let off by Professor Akanbi's big Mercedes. At three o'clock they decide to eat without Bandele and Victor. Just as they finish the two men come in, and Gbenga jumps off the new tricycle he has hardly let go of in the two days he has had it to carry his father's diary upstairs. Victor changes his clothes and comes down to eat, apparently in a dark mood. When Gbenga acts up at the dinner table, Victor slaps his leg in anger.

Twenty minutes into rest hour a young man in a white shirt and tie, carrying a brief case, knocks at the door for Victor. He is an encyclopedia salesman, and says he met Victor at his office this afternoon and was told to come round to his home. The Falujos already have two encyclopedias in the study, but Victor says that Ṣade should buy this one, especially since an illustrated children's encyclopedia comes along with it (the others included a four-volume dictionary and a health encyclopedia). Ṣade agrees, and even volunteers to pay the hundred guineas cost ($294) in only a year instead of the two she can take if she wishes. The salesman, who is an Easterner, reflects that the trouble in the country is hurting his sales. He has just returned from a selling tour in the Cameroons, and now wants to stay in Lagos for a while. His own commission on his sales, he adds, is five per cent. The papers are signed with handshakes all around.

Later in the day Ṣade goes to visit Akin, Victor goes out, and the two older children do their homework. A supper of stew, fried potatoes, peas and bread, followed by the nightly television shows, concludes the day.

Conversations

There is little open discussion of politics in the Falujo household, a remarkable fact given that Victor Falujo once resigned from a former job on the basis of political principles, and that some of his good friends, like Professor Akanbi, are active in politics as advisors to political leaders or as lobbyists for particular interests or points of view. One Sunday afternoon, however, after church services and a lunch of rice and dodo, Victor and Ṣade sit down to read the newspapers.

" 'Nkrumah and Sekou Toure Feared Killed,' " Ṣade reads the headline aloud, obviously alarmed. She reads the whole story to herself, then summarizes it for the others. Some French nationals are alleged to have seized the President of Guinea and his guest, the deposed President of Ghana. She adds, "Why? But why? If Nkrumah is the criminal they call him, why does it have to be a foreign power that kidnaps him?"

"Well, a lot of people have old grudges against him," Victor says.

"So what?" Ṣade snaps. "Why don't they let the Ghanaians settle their own problems? I mean, I wouldn't mind so much if the people who have captured him were Africans — it would only give the OAU [Organization for African Unity] another punch in the jaw, but Frenchmen! Think of all that Nkrumah did for Ghana — all that development at Accra and so on. Maybe he wasted money, and he might be a megalomaniac, too, but I don't think his liabilities outrun his assets."

At this juncture Ṣade's older full brother, a clerk at the Ijebu Ode office of the Ministry of Education comes back in from outside, and, adding fuel to Ṣade's fire, remarks, "Nkrumah and Toure Killed? Fine!"

"Fine? Why?" says Ṣade.

"As long as he's alive, he's a threat to Ghana's security. And even if this story is untrue, Ghanaians won't stop until they do kill him."

"That's their own headache," Ṣade insists. "But who called on France for help? Our situation here in Nigeria could develop beyond control, and they could come again — plus the Chinese on one side or plus the Americans. And we would become another Vietnam! Anyhow, if anything is going to happen here let it happen once and for all. I hate to think so, but war is quite inevitable; it only seems we are postponing it."

Victor shies away from a discussion of recent events. "I've talked about it so much I'm tired of it. Anyway if we wait three days the leaders will give us something new to talk about."

At that Ṣade goes out to the kitchen. One of the girls at her school made such good jam tarts for her cookery exam that Ṣade has invited her over for dinner — on the condition that she would make them again. Ṣade prides herself on her own baking, and is learning the recipe from the girl, who is hard at work. Benjamin, too, is watching the process.

A few minutes later visitors arrive. It is *Olú Ajóṣé,* the director of the Management Research Centre, who like Victor is a Ph.D. in economics, and his wife. Mr. Ajose knows Ṣade's brother, too, and they exchange warm greetings as well. The Ajoses are just in time for the tarts. Mr. Ajose talks of the new assistant he is getting to represent him at meetings of the many national and international commissions of which he is an ex-officio member. "Right now," he says, "it's all so crowded together — a meeting in Lagos today, in Port Harcourt tomorrow . . . all that travelling tires a man out." After a few more minutes, though, they excuse themselves with the plea that they have a long round of visits to make.

Later in the afternoon Bandele and Tọla write to Akin, who has not come home this weekend from the hospital. Their uncle selects some of their old toys to take back to Ijebu Ode with him for his daughter Dupẹ. He says she'd like some coloring books, too, but Ṣade tells him that Akin is the "dealer in coloring books," and that they are all at the hospital.

Still later another couple visits, Mr. and Mrs. *Adélagun* from the University of Ifẹ, the second university in Ibadan. The Falujọs have run out of soft drinks and beer, so Victor offers milk instead.

"Milk?" questions Mrs. Adelagun. "I don't have dyspepsia or whatever they call it." But her husband says milk is all right with him. Victor calls for milk for everyone. The conversation moves from milk in schools, to the quality of schools, to high society, and soon to politics.

After a long discussion, Victor and the two older children excuse themselves to get ready to visit Akin at the hospital. On the way they drop Ṣade's brother at a convenient spot to find a taxi.

Biography: Victor Falujọ

Both Victor and Ṣade Falujọ have had to struggle to achieve their now full careers. Victor was born in Ijebu Ode in 1922, the son of a Christian farmer who had three wives. Of Victor's own mother's five children, three died young, leaving only Victor and the older brother who now lives in Oke Ado. His father's second wife had two children, both now deceased but with surviving children, and the third wife has one daughter who is herself married and also living in Ijebu Ode.

Upon his father's death when Victor was only three, his mother turned from farming to full-time cooked food selling, and sent Victor off to "infants' classes" at the Independent African Church school. He finished primary school in 1934 and, at the grand age of twelve, took a job as a teacher in the lower grades of a tiny rural school near Ijebu Ode, at a salary of 12s. 6d. ($3.00 then) a month. Two years later he passed an entrance exam to an excellent teacher training college, but he was refused admission on the grounds that he was not a member of its sponsors' denomination. In a show of contempt, his own primary school added him to its staff. From 1937 to 1941 he taught there, studying in his spare time and passing, along the way, two examinations ("Junior" and "Senior Cambridge") giving him the rough equivalent of what would now be a secondary school diploma. At that time he was offered the principalship of a remote rural lower secondary school, but he declined on the grounds that he wanted to seek further education.

Instead, he applied for jobs in government offices in Lagos, and was given one in the post office. Now twenty years old, his salary was £6 ($16.80) a month. He continued to take classes and to study on his own in Lagos, and in 1945 won admission to Durham University in England. But an uncle who had promised to sponsor him financially died two months later, and Victor had to abandon his plans. Meanwhile more Nigerian students were coming home from American universities, and he decided to try his luck with applications there. In 1948 Michigan State College offered him admission and a "work scholarship" that would pay his fees and living expenses.

At the age of twenty-six, with his own savings and help from family and friends towards transportation, and with twenty-five dollars in cash, he arrived in the States. Long before, as a teacher in the little rural school, he and a colleague there who is now a prominent university professor had decided that too few Nigerians were trained to plan the future of their own country. Later they both decided to study economics, one concentrating on agriculture and the other on industry. Victor studied hard, as he had at home, and graduated *magna cum laude*. He had no trouble winning graduate fellowships, and continued straight on to his M.A. in 1954 at Ohio and his Ph.D. in 1957 at Indiana University. His Ph.D. thesis was entitled, "An Evaluation of Methods for Predicting Demand for Local Manufactures in West Africa."

During his nine years in America Victor visited home only for one summer, in 1952. But that was enough to meet and plan to marry Ṣade Idowu, the younger sister of an old classmate and workmate of Victor's in Ijebu Ode and Lagos. He is "Pa Dupẹ," the education officer who took toys for his daughter from the Falujọs one Sunday.

Biography: Ṣade Falujọ

Ṣade Faith Idowu is eight years younger than her husband. Born in Isalẹ-omi village to a monogamous Anglican farmer and palm-kernel trader, she was the last of seven children. When their mother died soon after Ṣade's birth, the oldest girl took over care of the small ones. By the time Ṣade was ready for school her oldest brothers were primary school teachers, and she lived with two of them for the next few years. She did well in school and was admitted to Victoria College, a prestigious girls' secondary school, in 1943. Until she got a scholarship to board in, she lived at the home of a cousin.

After graduating from high school in 1949, she trained as a teacher in Ibadan for two years, and then taught for two more in Ijebu Ode. It was at this time that she met her husband-to-be. Two years later she, too, got the chance to go abroad, for a two-year advanced teacher training course in England. Finally, in 1956 she flew to the United States, where she and Victor were married. She returned home a year later, a few months ahead of Victor, to avoid the high costs of having her baby in the States.

Victor got a job as a Senior Research Fellow at the Management Research Institute when he returned, and held it until 1964, when he and three others resigned in protest over political interference in appointments, promotions, and the allocation of funds. His Ph.D. supervisor was at that moment helping to set up a Department of Economics in the University of East Africa, and invited Victor to join. Leaving his family behind, he taught there until the military coup in Nigeria in 1966 made it opportune for him to return. He returned home once more, got his present job as Senior Economic Advisor in the Ministry of Planning and Development, and moved into his present home in July of that year, only a few months before the present study.

Meanwhile Sade held on to the high school teaching post she had had since 1959. Because she was working, her eldest sister, who had ''mothered'' Sade herself more than thirty years before, came to stay and help with her children. ''Mama,'' whose own two children both died young, is the second of four wives of a market inspector at Ijebu Ode. When she is there, she trades in small amounts of provisions outside her door. She says she will soon return home, but is vague enough about an actual date to suggest that she is happy to remain with Victor and Sade.

Biographies: The Falujo Children

Bandele Falujo was born in July of 1957, and his naming ceremony, done in a traditional style, was really a welcome-home party for his parents as well. Bandele's name commemorates the double event: it means ''Follow me home.'' Bandele started school at the expensive and exclusive Senior Service School, but after the second grade Victor and Sade thought he needed more discipline than he was getting there. They transferred him to a local government public school where he has been doing so well since that they may have him try the Common Entrance Examination (for secondary school) after only four grades instead of the usual six.

Tola was born just seventeen months after Bandele, an unusually short interval for Yoruba families. Now in the third grade, she is, her mother says, much more mischievous than Bandele.

Akin was born just two weeks after Nigerian independence in 1960. Like the other children he was baptized at the Protestant chapel on the university campus. From their daily concern about his illness and from their feeling that he is the "genius" of the family — he is very quick both with his hands and his mind — both his parents appear to favor Akin to some degree.

Gbenga, the youngest, was born in the political crisis at the end of 1964. To show off this accomplishment in the face of his trouble, Victor *in absentia* gave the baby one name *(Adégbèsan)* which means "The crown gets revenge." Gbenga lacked a father's hand until recently, and is at a rebellious age anyway, but his temper and emotional experimentation with his parents are given more freedom than other Yoruba children often have.

The only other member of the household is Benjamin, the houseboy. With a primary school education he left Eastern Nigeria for the greater employment opportunities in the West in 1960. He has been working as a domestic, for a variety of English, Nigerian, Canadian, Israeli and American employers ever since. The Falujọs provide room and board and £4 ($11.20) a month. His duties include some cooking, most of the house cleaning, washing dishes, ironing, washing clothes, and occasional baby-sitting if all the adults go out. This is neither the lightest work nor the highest pay that he has received, but the family is a good-natured one, and he says he is happy to be here. The Falujọs, in turn, who have in the past had young relatives live in to do housework in return for schooling and general support, but who have not been very satisfied by such arrangements, find it comfortable to have a straightforward employee instead.

The House and the Budget

The imposing two-storied house into which the Falujọs moved when Victor returned home from East Africa came with his job. Two small trees will one day shade the parlor, and a few marigolds along the front wall are the only other landscaping that the family has had time to put in. Behind the house is a "boys' quarters" with a toilet, shower, and two bedrooms, only one of which is currently occupied.

Inside, downstairs are the L-shaped parlor and dining area, a large kitchen, and a study room with an adjoining half-bathroom. The furniture, supplied as well, is in standard styles, but newer and more diverse than that of the other families we have met. Wedding pictures of Victor and Ṣade dominate the parlor wall. Ceiling fan, several cushioned chairs, a couch, small serving or end tables, and a linoleum "carpet" are in the living room; two desks and bookshelves line the study; a large table and six chairs furnish the dining room. Upstairs are five bedrooms, two for the children, one for guests, one for Mama, and one for Victor and Ṣade (who is thus the only wife among the families we have met who shares her husband's bed rather than her children's). There is also a full bathroom (toilet, tub and sink) near the stairway.

Beds for the children, storage areas including chests of drawers and closets, the sheer spaciousness of the house (eleven rooms including the boys' quarters for eight people including Akin), and the modern kitchen with its gas stove, sink, hot water heater, and two refrigerators (one came with the house, one belonged to the Falujos earlier), provide a level of comfort for this family radically different from any of the others. Further, the television set, two radios, two cars, books, and other personal items mark a gap in material well-being which the other families can only dream of closing.

For the Falujos, however, this level of affluence is relatively easy to maintain. Victor's present annual salary is £2575 ($7,210, which is over six times Saliu Wahabi's), and Sade's is £725 ($2,030). Victor's pay check comes to £215 ($602) per month, but taxes and a civil servants' retirement scheme take the first £20 ($56). Rent for the government-owned house and its furnishings is pegged at only seven per cent of Victor's salary, or about £15 ($42) a month, and all the household expenses including rent, food, utilities, Benjamin's salary, and the like amount to perhaps £60 ($168). Car maintenance and insurance, and a small life insurance policy come to another £20 ($56).

Of the £115 ($322) left, as much as £30 ($84) may go to gifts and charity. Before he went to East Africa, Victor used to be active in family and church affairs in Ijebu Ode, and visited there as often as once a fortnight. If he were made, for instance, chairman of a church bazaar, he might spend fifty or sixty pounds ($140-$168) of his own money on the affair. Since his return he has been more modest in his involvements, going home only for an occasional wedding or funeral. In this way, at least £80 ($214), and sometimes as much as £115 ($322), of Victor's salary is available for savings and investment. Of Sade's £60 ($168) a month, much also goes into savings. Household incidentals and the maintenance of her own car may take £20 ($56). Sade gives spending money to Mama, and also bears the full financial responsibility for the schooling of her other sister's four children. But she saves at least £25 ($70) a month (less, of course, now that the encyclopedia payments are to be made).

By their own account, in short, the Falujos are able to save between thirty-five and fifty per cent of their combined salaries. In 1962 they invested in a house in Ibadan which they lease to a foreign firm for an additional £800 ($2,240) a year. Part of that income is being put toward a house for themselves in Ijebu Ode for which they recently bought the land. But the major additional investment, into which Victor and seven other professional friends of his (doctor, lawyer, engineer, transporter, two economists and a fisheries expert, all Ijebu except one) have each put £1500 ($4,200) so far, is a coordinated fishing industry that will eventually have its own boats, equipment, processing plant, and marketing arm. The group is working with the people of two villages on the Ijebu coast, hiring and training them to extend fishing skills they already have to a larger and more profitable scale of operation. Victor Falujọ and three other students first had an idea to do something like this fifteen years ago, as a means of increasing the supply of protein to the region-at-large. Though two of the original four could not participate when the opportunity arose, the group that has carried on still has that general goal in view.

Both Victor and Ṣade Falujọ complain about the number of relatives they have who are "always" asking for money. To those that helped them in the past they give moderately and gratefully, but to more distant kinsmen, who "beg just as hard," they give as little as they can. They say they gain nothing from such aid, but they feel preyed upon, and guess that such relatives must think their money is limitless.

Summary

In relative terms their wealth *is* unending. But the Falujọs have many ideas as to how to spend their money and leisure that do not involve their kinsmen, or people in general, to the same degree as the other families in our study. To some extent their attitude of reserve reflects the disruption they suffered when their initial expansive and gregarious period was struck down in the political crisis two years ago. It also reflects their concern over Akin's illness. But they also have permanent values on and interests in maintaining a style of life for themselves and their children that requires a large amount of resources. By attending church at the university, by sending their children to exclusive schools, by speaking at least as much English as Yoruba in their home, they distance themselves socially from other migrants and from Ijebu still at home, and try to insure their children's positions in the country's elite. They are concerned about the state of their nation, but do their best to keep the life that they came from behind them. The clashes between these conflicting interests and attitudes have not yet occurred with the intensity they may one day have.

Discussion: Wealth, Social Class, and Ethnicity

The major questions that the record of the Falujọ family poses have to do with how the similarities and dissimilarities between them and the other families we have met should be interpreted. Are the Falujọs like the other people in this book, except richer? Are they, and those like them, members of a distinct social class with interests different from those of the "masses," urban or rural? Are they, in fact, members of Western society, living in a different world with a different world-view from the overwhelming majority of Yorubas and

Nigerians in general, or are they as "Ijebu" as any others we have met? And is there any difference between their own perception of their position in society at large and an outsider's judgment? Answers to such questions must be complicated, always relative, and partial at best, but since they are at the core of much recent research on "modern" Africa, they must be attempted.

Wealth and Emulation. To suggest that the Falujos have only more of what all the others we have met want, but are otherwise not very different from them, is to suggest, with minimal connotation, only that they are members of the "elite." Social scientists (e.g., Lloyd 1966a: 50-55) use the term elite to signify the socially superior individuals in a relatively open society, individuals whose behavior influences others and is imitated by them. The elite need not be an interacting, cooperating, or self-conscious "group"; its boundaries may be arbitrarily drawn around the highest-ranking individuals in a variety of relevant social categories (for example, business, political, military leaders, etc.). The superiority attributed to such individuals should, however, be generalized; that is, they should not just be held to possess the most of some particular value (skill, success, wealth, for example), but their lives and their values should be considered worthy and admirable in a general way.

Certainly there is no disputing the economic superiority of the Falujos. With a combined income from all sources of around £4100 (nearly $11,500), they are *well* within the top one per cent of Nigerians, indeed of all black Africans. They spend probably twice as much on food alone as any family of comparable size in this study, and have large amounts of money for all sorts of other purposes. Moreover, they are among the most highly educated Nigerians, and both their jobs, in the civil service and a prestigious secondary school, are among the most senior positions in the country.

It is also true that at least some of the aspects of the Falujos' life style typify those which are generally emulated by others in society. All would admire their educational achievements. Most of the younger people, at least, seek recreation and entertainment of the sort the Falujos enjoy more easily — the Onadele, Ogunkoya, and Wahabi children go to watch television at friends' homes, Chief Ogunkoya and Bola Onadele have cars of sorts, and the international organizations, political concerns and discussions, and even the hair and clothing styles of which the Falujos partake in a major way have their reflections rather than alternatives in what many other people do.

Yet, despite the Falujos' economic superiority and the tendency of some to emulate their lives in one way or another, most people would not imitate their lives in every way, nor would they agree that all the Falujos' values are desirable. There are those few, for example, who *can* afford to live like the Falujos who have chosen instead to have their homes in the busy migrant quarters like Oke Ado rather than in the suburban housing estates, and to interact with their neighbors and fellow townsmen — to invest in people — much more than the Falujos do. For the many who cannot afford to emulate the Falujos in any case, a variety of the values and behaviors they pursue are foreign and even repugnant. These include the conjugal sharing of so many things from investment decisions to the dinner table, the brash spiritedness of the children, the shunning of kinship relations even in the choice of a house servant, the relative emphasis on material possessions, and the reliance on impersonal mechanisms of self-support like life insurance and business investments. In short, much of what the Falujo life style involves is *not* a model to which other urban Ijebu families aspire. In terms of respect and imitability, Chief Ogunkoya (at least at his peak), and not Victor Falujo, exemplifies the good life.

Social Class and "Westernization." If the Falujos and others like them do not form a full-fledged elite, do they then form a community apart, pursuing their own special interests and contented *not* to be wholly imitated? To an extent such a description is warranted. In the early days of colonialism, people who became Christian were sometimes driven from their homes. Working out a *modus vivendi* with local leaders, the mission compound made a virtue of its isolation, self-assured by the fervency of its faith and the industriousness of its will to survive. The break with the past was sharp, as people adopted English names, Western customs in education and religion, and the stern morality of their American fundamentalist or Victorian British pastors. Outside the mission grounds, life went on without the new Christians.

Some of this detachment persists among families like the Falujos. The isolation of the missions gave way with the lessening of their moral and spiritual rigidity, and now Christianity, having permeated normal Yoruba community life, is a force within it rather than outside. But some individuals continued to be thrown up who were quite highly "Westernized" in cultural style. Nearly all Christian, they were usually those who had managed to get to the old, church-run secondary schools (where foreign teachers remained longest), who had gone on to universities and acculturative experiences abroad, and who returned (as "Been-to's") to jobs which afforded them the chance to continue to enjoy the life style which they had learned. The Falujos fit this pattern extremely well. Perhaps if a majority of the educated and affluent people of Western Nigeria comes in the future from families that were less directly missionized, from schools with Nigerian teachers, and from universities at home, its partial isolation will be broken down just as the isolation of the Christians was many years ago. Yet this can only happen if recruitment is not simply from among the children of the presently affluent, for otherwise their isolation from rural kinsmen and poorer neighbors will grow.

Two conditions militate against the fuller indigenization of the "elite." First, expansion of its total numbers has slowed considerably, so that there are already enough children of the present elite to replace it in a new generation. Second, the presently wealthy have a further characteristic that the mission Christians never directly possessed — considerable power over the rest of the population. Victor Falujo has a direct role in economic policy-making for the ten million people of Western Nigeria; others like him head the courts, hospitals, universities, government ministries and commercial houses of the country. Such power seeks to ensure, among other ends, its own advantage. Indeed, the record of their control over rates and means of taxation (far lower than in many other countries for the affluent), the geography of development (largely tending to serve the cities), educational policy (favoring those who learn English early and well), foreign trade (encouraging exotic imports from cat food to Mercedes Benz automobiles), suggests that the present ''elite,'' acting cooperatively and consciously, initiates and perpetuates policies that grant it quite considerable privilege. Low rental rates for housing, for example, allowed Victor Falujo to accumulate capital to build another house which yields a high return to him; easy car purchase schemes permit Sade to keep a distant job she prefers; subsidies to private schools and a fairly high emphasis on curative medicine rather than preventive medicine make specialist services available to the Falujo children even though *no* services are available to many Nigerians, especially in rural areas but also in the cities.

Such a set of people, internally relatively homogeneous, aware of and acting for their own political and social interests, and competing with others for the rewards that society has available, is a ''social class.'' If the elite is a ''class,'' it is obviously an ''upper class,'' especially now that the colonial overseers have departed. Leonard Plotnicov, who studied the northern Nigerian city of Jos, has also argued (1970) that the modern elite indeed form a social class, though earlier writers suggested either that it was hard to envision an upper class since there was no correspondingly well-defined lower class (Lloyd 1966a:60), or that there was not enough cohesive activity among the elite to define it as a ''class'' in the usual sense (Mitchell and Epstein 1959; and see Dahrendorf 1959:25). If, for example, affluent families identify with and act for their ethnic communities as strongly as with their fellow ''economic superiors,'' it would be misleading to conceive the society as divided solely along *class* lines.

Ethnicity and Culture. A great deal of confusion surrounds the term ''ethnicity''. Some object to its use altogether, saying that it is only used to label Africans as ''backward'' or ''tribal.'' Yet there is little difference between the quality or significance of ethnicity in Nigeria and, say, in the United States or the U.S.S.R. Others argue that ''ethnic'' groupings may exist anywhere, but that they are archaic or anachronistic survivals of history, diminishingly important compared with stratification into more ''modern'' social classes. There is little evidence to support such views, for indeed the groups that struggle for political power in the contemporary world are as often based on shared ethnic membership as they are on shared class affiliation (Melson and Wolpe 1971). A poor man may, with or without justification, feel much more strongly that his chances in life will be radically improved if his own ethnic group achieves power than if "poor people" or "workers" in general achieve it. A rich man may decide that his chances of retaining his wealth are much better if he supports his fellow ethnics than if he supports other rich men in a struggle for political power. Ethnicity, in short, is a major *alternative* to social stratification as a principle underlying the organization of societal competition and conflict in the modern world.

Third, it is sometimes held by people who agree that ethnic conflict is currently widespread that ethnic groups are simply a special kind of social class, based on the sense of a historically distinct "community" but competing with other classes for societal dominance just the same. This position has two weaknesses: either it defines away the problem by making "class" a synonym for "group," or it erroneously assumes that there is just one set of values in a society, and that competition is therefore always a matter of relative access to a single set of "goods" like power and wealth that everyone defines in the same way. But ideas as to the valued behavior that is to be rewarded most highly can vary, and different groups may strive within a single society to control similar or different means in order to produce *different* ends. "Ethnic" groups, then, are groups which struggle to disentangle themselves from one another to pursue diverse sets of ideals, and these groups often cut across the horizontal stratification defined by reference to *one* set of goals. In Western Nigeria this series of ethnicities is based upon dialect areas and precolonial political boundaries, yielding "Ijebu," "Ẹgba," "Ekiti," and other labels. For Ijebu the goals discussed above with reference to Chief Ogunkọya are a major alternative to the meritocratic system of high personal achievement and material display of status that governs the Western-derived life-style in which the Falujọs visibly participate.

Are the Falujọs, then, involved in "ethnic" interests as well as in their more obvious "class" interests? Leaving aside for a moment the question of consciousness of such interests, it can be seen that the Falujọs participate actively in a system of ethnic relationships. Just as their "class" interests flow out of the intimate associations of school and job, but reach far beyond their friendships, so their "ethnic" interests flow from the intimate ties of kinship to a much broader embrace. It is perhaps incorrect to call "ethnic" such activities as Ṣade's support of her older sister's school-aged children (though it ought be noted that in some other cultures a socially-mobile person in her circumstances would turn her back on poorer relations), Victor's joining with nine friends (all but two of whom happen to be Ijebu) to purchase meat cooperatively at a good price, or even the couple's building a house in Ijebu Ode for eventual retirement (although again in other countries migration has simply left old settlements to die, not experience a building boom). These attachments to Ijebu and Ijebus are only a sort of infrastructure for ethnic relations.

Beyond them lie commitments which are not based on kinship at all. Seven of the eight partners in the fishing enterprise are Ijebu, and it is sited in Ijebu. The Falujos' closest friends are Ijebus, though of course there are exceptions — they are not any different from the other families we have met in this respect. Like the other families, too, the Falujos usually use Ijebus when they need services: the contractor for their house in Ibadan, their auto mechanic, and the lawyer they use are all Ijebu. Perhaps most importantly, Victor's resignation in 1964 from the research post he held had strong ethnic overtones, for three of the four people who resigned together were Ijebus, and the major reason for their decision to leave was what they considered to be the unfair firing of another man, who was also Ijebu, and his replacement by a man from the same town and political party as the then regional premier. (Saliu Wahabi, it will be remembered, almost lost his job during the same period.)

Some of this behavior relates to Ijebu as an ethnic group in the second, "class"-like, sense, for it seeks to advance Ijebu interests as against others in a competitive system. But at the same time it points away from class to values the Falujos share with the other families here on social investment, status display by generosity, and prosperity reflected through the esteem granted by others. Their Ijebu identity thus diverges from their class identity, and maintaining both is what at a wider level gives contemporary Nigeria part of its simultaneous Western and indigenous character.

Summary. The Falujos are, in a general way, not unlike the other families in our study except in the important attribute of income, and partly in consumption values. Their interest in preserving and increasing their economic position is parallel to the others'. Their "Ijebu-ness" is similar, too, based in the same sentiments and social relations as that of the Ogunkoyas or Odusanyas or Wahabis. And their own consciousness of either "identity" is neither stronger nor weaker, with overt references to class or ethnic group rare in their everyday life.

It is not surprising that this should be so. Victor and Ṣade Falujo, like the others in this book and like most adult Ijebu, were born in the provincial towns of Ijebu, in houses with dirt floors. They migrated to secure jobs and education. Had not their own cleverness and the aggregate resources of their families gotten them through higher education than they could find in Nigeria, their lives (and incomes) would even more closely match those of the other families. The "gap" between income levels has not yet, for the Ijebu families of Ibadan, translated itself into radical social and cultural estrangement, nor has the "gap" between ethnic communities translated itself into ghettoes and permanent distrust. These contrasting possibilities are still open for time and social policy to exacerbate or to reject.[3]

Footnotes

[1]The Falujos use about as much English as Yoruba at home, and it would become tedious to note which conversations are held in which language. Our notations are not always complete in any case. In general, discussion at the dinner table, concerning work or school or the hospital, and with guests of equal education is in English, while less formal interaction, or conversation about more mundane or intimate matters, is in Yoruba. Ṣade's older sister speaks little English; the children use English among themselves in much the same patterns as their parents. A host of intriguing problems in sociolinguistics remains to be researched carefully in Africa.

[2]On the other hand Victor's children rarely sleep at his brother's. This nonreciprocal relationship is continuous with age-old patterns of fostering children into families where moral exemplariness or economic prospects appear desirable.

[3]Discussion of the trends in these respects has been either speculative or ideological. Careful and extensive research, with the adult children or grandchildren of migrants, with the families of Nigerian-educated university graduates, with the adult children of men like Chief Ogunkoya, and so on, would yield exciting new information on value changes and social commitments.

CHAPTER XI

Conclusion: The Meanings of Migration

The seven households at which we have looked vary greatly in economic circumstances and domestic arrangements, and they are subject to varying degrees of internal and external stress. Yet the city itself, "urban life," has neither disoriented the psyches nor broken down the moral bases for social interaction of anyone we have met. Persistent imagery in popular literature on Africa[1] portrays "traditional," uncomplicated, backward-looking rural areas, "modern," buzzing cities, and the perils that confront those who dare to leap the "gap." No such cavernous duality threatens the Ijebus in Ibadan, nor does the "gap" theory apply to Ijebu society as a whole. Further discussion of attitudes and values in Ijebu migration will show more clearly how this is so.

Norms in Migration

Perhaps a fourth of all those people who now call themselves "Ijebu" live outside their home towns. "Migrants" include everyone from, say, teachers who room on the campuses of their schools a few miles away and return home every weekend, to those who have lived for years outside Nigeria without communicating or visiting home at all. The vast majority, however, are like the members of the families we have met, migrants pursuing economic opportunities where they can find them, and along the way maintaining strong links to their homes.

Importantly, migration is seen by Ijebu themselves as part of the way of life, decidedly not as an indicator of the breakdown of a way of life. Migration has become part of the system of social expectations — of norms — both at collective and individual levels.

At the societal level Ijebu is "totally" oriented to migration. That is, it is expected that virtually everyone who finds a better opportunity "abroad" (i.e., away from home) than he has at home will pursue it. In fact "society," in the persons of teachers, parents, and peers, urges him to look for such opportunities and aids him in the search. As a result, these days nearly every youth who grows up in a provincial town leaves home as soon as he or she finishes primary school. There are migrants from every age category, of course, but small towns appear totally depopulated of the young men, and most of the young women, who have had the benefit of primary education, which has been free of cost since 1955. And the young people in larger provincial towns are often themselves migrants from smaller places.

At the individual level a lifelong series of obligations and expectations binds migrants and their kinsmen and townsmen at home. The young migrant goes to live with a close relative or a parent's friend, who sponsors the youth by subsidizing his room and board until he is able to live on his own, by overseeing his adjustment to further schooling or a new job, and sometimes by providing the job as well. In direct return the migrant may only be able to offer housework, the tutoring of younger children, or errand-running. In this period as well rural parents usually expect to pay the actual monetary costs of the urban migrant. Tade Oyebanji, Bọla Ọnadele, and Chief Ogunkọya have participated in this process.

In a second stage, however, when the youth finishes school, or a craft apprenticeship, he begins the most independent period of his life, as the case of Tade Oyebanji shows. He may be a journeyman saving to buy his own tools, a junior clerk studying part-time for further certification, or he may actually be embarked upon a job he hopes to hold for many years. In any case money is freer now, and he becomes a consumer of clothes, phonograph records, beer, radios and many other items. He may continue to live with his sponsor, but usually gets his own room, where he entertains his friends, who may give form to their association by calling themselves the "Young Stars," the "Lovelies," or the "Rising Millionaires." In his lodgings he displays his own tastes and takes pleasure in his freedom. At the same time, he cultivates people of his town and/or of his profession so that he may have their aid in his future undertakings. He thus begins to act as an adult, but it is not expected that his obligations extend beyond himself.

Finally, at a point around the age of thirty for migrants of almost all degrees of education, what they themselves call "establishment" finally is achieved. A craftsman gets his shop and tools, a teacher has finished his training and much less actively than before seeks another occupation, an office worker is in a permanent position. By this time all are married, in nearly every case to a partner from the same home town or area. Children follow without delay. At this period migrants interact frequently with rural kin as each successive decision is made and as the events occur. Michael and Florence Odusanya are just beyond this threshold.

After this point, differences in skill, connections and backing, and sheer luck or fate start to be visible in a man's career. If his savings begin to grow, he will next think about building a house for himself in Ibadan. Not long ago he might have first considered building in his home town, but in recent years urban house owning has become such a lucrative investment that he starts there. At the same time his obligations to his kinsmen must begin to be repaid, and so the established man sponsors a junior relative or two, bringing the cycle of sponsorship full circle. In the vast majority of cases he is happy to repay these social debts: among Ijebu, only some of those trained in universities overseas try to break away from these patterns, as we noted above for the Falujọ family. At this time, he may also join his town's voluntary association, using it to extend the range of his close friends and potential supporters, and contributing more and more resources and time to it as he himself succeeds. The more affluent he grows, the greater the expectations are that he will play a full part in the political and social life of his migrant community and of his home town. Saliu Wahabi and Michael Odusanya exemplify two variations on this theme.

The highly successful are few in number, even if we include men like Chief Ogunkọya, whose present troubles are diverse. There are perhaps two or three hundred such men in the Ijebu community of Ibadan. But these "elders" of the migrant community wield profound influence in the city and at home in the province. They are, as we saw, the permanent leaders of their respective town's progressive associations, they provide the financial capital for many small businesses, they provide access to a great many jobs in Ibadan, they articulate the demands of their townsmen to the urban, regional, and national political systems. Almost all provide the services of dispute mediation, informal legal and medical advice, and sometimes even prayer leading for their compounds and neighborhoods. Many of them know one another and have associated with other men of their stature in politics, the economy, or fraternal organizations. Since, however, their positions are heavily dependent upon the quality of the relations they maintain with kinsmen and townsmen of lesser success than they, the set of leaders has little common consciousness of being a class apart from others.

Yet a man may, of course, not succeed. He may even lose (or never acquire) his tools and shop or a secure "white-collar" job. In such a situation an unestablished or disestablished migrant remains in many ways a youth, and the fact that he must struggle to raise his family anyway only compounds his sense of failure. He does not join, or drops out of, the town *egbé,* earns no influence over his relatives or townsmen, and often moves from one venture to another very different one in desperate attempts to achieve a sense of security. One man I know has tried carpentry and lottery ticket selling, another wheat farming and chalk making, a third perfume bottling and drum making. Bọla Ọnadele's many changes of occupation are a widespread strategy of coping with failure. Alice Bankọle has a relatively successful commercial career but many marital disappointments.

It is vital to realize that the urbanites we have met, and the thousands like them, thus behave according to role expectations that would pertain *even if they had not migrated at all*. With some circumstantial modifications, an ongoing system of roles and statuses has been extended geographically — to Ibadan in this case — as migrants pursue their careers. Within the structure, childhood dutifulness, the fostering of children with advantaged relatives and friends, youthful independence, the self-centeredness of the period of "establishment," the increased obligations of the successful to home town and urban neighbors (sometimes culminating in a chieftaincy), and the debilitations and social isolation of the unsuccessful — all these were norms of traditional Ijebu. As Ijebu move away from home, these phases of a person's career, and the behavior associated with them, continue to be both socially relevant and statistically prevalent.

The City As Farm

As the roles and behavioral expectations of migrant Ijebu remain closely tied to a specific community of origin, so do attitudes mirror these home-town commitments. Ijebu in Ibadan often sum up their feelings in the assertion that "the city is our farm!" There are many implications of the phrase. First, the metaphor itself has a purely economic referent: formerly "the farm," but now "the city" is the locus of extractive activities. A primary connotation is that just as the farm was a place of drudgery and deprivation from the good life of the traditional town, so migration and the city are ordeals necessary to the achievement of values still associated with the home town. Ijebus are not reluctant to be in Ibadan: wholehearted economic behavior is only realistic. But simultaneously every migrant hopes eventually to find a job at home, or at least to retire there with the fruits of his urban labors. Chief Ogunkọya has built a house at home, Victor Falujọ is about to, and the other younger migrants all express plans to do so. Although some of them will undoubtedly remain in Ibadan past active work life, others will indeed go home. In every rural town in Ijebu there are to be found retired men and women, and other returnees, many of them actively involved in public and family life at home. But even if some migrants do not eventually return home, the fact that they organize large segments of their occupational and leisure activities in terms of status achievement and political advancement among kinsmen and townsmen makes their "identification" (Mabogunje 1962:4) with their home a crucial determinant of their migrant adaptations.

A corollary of this continuing "identification" with the home town is the derision implicit in the equation of city and farm. Ijebu, that is, esteem Ibadan as little as they do farming, and Ijebu have never had that love of the soil which is incorrectly deemed true of farmers or peasants the world over. The low regard in which Ijebu hold Ibadan and its indigenous inhabitants is fully reciprocated by their hosts, who find Ijebu the most reprehensible of money-grabbing, miserly exploiters. Reinforced both by the traditional socio-political distinction between the "owners" of a place and "strangers" to it, and by a modern history full of provocative incitement by both sides, the Ijebu-Ibadan antagonism is a persistent feature of modern Yoruba politics (see, e.g., Sklar 1963; Mabogunje 1967:93-95).

Finally, the city/farm equation is a statement of the quality of contemporary Ijebu ethnic identity. Ijebu have no negative sense that their culture has been demolished or corrupted in the course of recent history. Anthropologists have too often given the impression that cultures contain an unchanging set of roles, and that hence to learn a new role is to begin to destroy a culture: in this view, a Yoruba farmer or a Yoruba elder are comprehensible terms but a Yoruba printer or a Yoruba TV-cameraman have some sort of incompatibility or strain about them. But just as the site of economic activity, farm or city, is separable from the center of Ijebu social gravity, so are specific roles only incidental to particular moments in Ijebu culture history. There is no contradiction, then, in being an Ijebu economist or an Ijebu builder, and no sense of cultural doom casts long shadows on a rapidly-changing Ijebu society.[2]

Social Versus Cultural Change

In fact, we have arrived at an apparent paradox. In many senses the Ijebu have obviously "changed" a great deal, but in other senses they have "changed" little, if at all!

Can the paradox be resolved? The facile "conclusion" that there is both "continuity" and "change" in African life has often closed accounts of African social change, but it explains very little. A second and more elaborate notion, that such people as the Ijebu are "transitional" between opposed poles of "tradition" and "modernity," is sometimes offered as a summary descriptive device for contemporary non-Western peoples. But this solution, too, is facile. For one thing, all real societies, as contrasted with ideal types, may be "transitional." Second, the term does not differentiate among the types of changes which may be occurring. Third, the presumed continuum from tradition to modernity introduces an unexamined and unjustified assumption that, among all the extant aspects of social life, some are anachronistic and must die, while others are the wave of the future and will endure. In the absence of detailed longitudinal studies we have no right to make such judgments. Besides, the holistic approach of anthropology leads us to expect that social life is more than an uneasy jumble of diverse elements.

A different distinction reduces the paradox of change in Ijebu. If we distinguish *social change* from *cultural change,* we get much closer both to the ways in which Ijebu think about their own situation and to an explanation of the "continuity" and "change" in their contemporary culture.

Social change may be recognized in the patterned, relatively enduring sums of actions taken by a number of individuals to cope with, modify, or take advantage of new opportunities and/or blockages they perceive to the attainment of goals, values, and ideals that they set themselves. *Cultural change* is evident in patterned sums of novel symbols, values, and ideals which make sense, for a group, of new but imperfectly perceived stimuli or situations. Both terms rest on an assumption that humans are goal-directed, but possess symbols and meanings as the critically human aspect of their species adaptation.

In these terms it is clear that the Ijebu Yoruba have undergone a great deal of social change but not much cultural change. In social terms the Ijebu we have met have obviously grasped a large variety of the methods, objects, and social symbols of Western industrial society, as they have taken examinations and earned certificates in schools, learned new and lucrative trades, gone to new houses of religion, migrated to new locations, engaged in novel forms of political activity, and learned a vast array of new techniques for attaining their goals. Evidence of all these changes abounds in the daily life of the families we have met.

Yet simultaneously these same people pursue goals and behave in full continuity with the ideals of social life of precolonial days: the idiom of kinship and community remains a vital source of norms for aid and support even as the content of the obligations changes; the system of seniority and deference structures social relations in new as well as old institutional settings; high value still obtains to the proper expenditure of income upon children, friends, followers, and in general upon people rather than upon things; ultimate peace of mind — and the good life — still come from having had the luck and skill to build a sturdy structure on the foundation of these values. In short, cultural stability has been maintained even as social change has been profound.

Of course it would be unrealistic to suggest that there has been *no* cultural change or *no* social stability in Ijebu life. The very continuities of the independent mercantile occupational system and of the patterns of kin ties are statements of social stability, while symbols of status and prestige such as the diploma and the automobile, and new values on education and personal security represent additions to or modifications of Ijebu culture. The Falujos, and other elite families like them, have changed their values and goals the most. Yet for the vast majority of urban migrant families, including many highly "successful" ones, the principle remains that innovation has been in social *means* and continuity has been in cultural *ends*.

The adaptation to new colonial and post-colonial conditions so pithily summarized by the phrase that "the city is our farm" thus encourages a wide range of experimentalism while it allows Ijebu to conceive of change as taking place on their own terms. Numerous observers of Yoruba society have remarked how, as Beier has said, "the old and the new . . . live side by side without tension . . . a typically Yoruba synthesis" (Beier 1968:154). How long this sense of reconciliation will last cannot easily be foretold: it holds out the possibility of a uniquely Yoruba, or Ijebu, form of modernity, but it may on the other hand be distorted or destroyed by changing social and political circumstances. It is to this larger arena that we must finally turn.

Individual Happiness and Cultural Freedom

An approach to Yoruba social change through an examination of the lives of seven families has certain inherent dangers. Concentrating on daily routines, one can see directly the humor and tension, the optimism and discouragement, the irony and the struggle which make human what are too often in social science literature only remote abstractions. Were our vision of Nigerian or of world society completely sanguine, it might be well to let it go at that.

To the contrary, unfortunately, there are events which overshadow the individuals we have met, even when they are participants in them. With a slight change in my research plans and strategies, the families in this book might easily have been Ibos rather than Ijebu Yoruba. If that had been the case, many of the people we have met, and especially the younger men and children, might be dead now, victims of the Nigerian civil war of 1967-1970.[3] Less spectacularly, job insecurity, questions as to the utility of education, purchasing power, the attainability of aspirations for oneself or one's children, and other matters which affect these Ijebu families' lives every day are all linked directly to events and decisions taken at national and international levels. The world economic and stratification system means that the price of a bar of chocolate or of a gallon of gasoline in North America incorporates the price paid to producers of cocoa and petroleum in Nigeria, and quite directly affects Nigeria's capacity to respond to the political and economic demands of her people.

We cannot overlook these relationships as we continue to develop anthropological perspectives on world society. A generation ago anthropologists who wanted to begin urban research were warned by colleagues reared on the rural village that they would find no order, no handle, in urban areas. As Leonard Plotnicov has recently reaffirmed, however, "urban life is complex but not disorganized" (1967:291). Indeed, urban anthropology has even enriched our understanding of rural communities which feed or are dominated by the cities in their midst. As we begin, despite new warnings by some colleagues, to unravel the dynamic of the world social system, we will similarly enrich our understanding of the ways in which urban and rural communities in the Third World feed their resources to and are molded by advanced industrial societies. In this new field some would argue that the blatant facts of worldwide stratification, and the urgency of its analysis and reform, override the need to focus at all upon individuals, families, or communities. Yet insofar as the task for action is still the traditional humanistic one of increasing freedom, we lose sight of the task of knowing about (and simply *knowing*) real human beings in the world system at their and our peril. In the final analysis Michael Odusanya, Tade Oyebanji, Bọla Ọnadele, Saliu Wahabi, Alice Bankọle, Abel Ogunkoya, Victor Falujọ, and their families are not just members of an exotic "other" culture but are members of the most deprived segment of our own.

Footnotes

[1]For an interesting summary of variable positions in Latin American urban research, on the paucity of the "gap" theory and the obscure psychology it involves, see Cornelius (1971), who suggests that "one is struck by the fact that studies by social anthropologists are perhaps the closest thing we have to a rounded portrait of migration and its impact on Latin American social and political life" (1971:118). Cornelius, it should be noted, is a political scientist.

[2]This is of course not to say that there are no strains or conflicts within Ijebu or Nigerian society. But the conflicts of one era are in the first instance only qualitative substitutes for those of another, and Ijebu as every other society has always had its conflicts. It is quite another and more difficult matter to argue that progress or decay are manifest in a comparison of two eras: here we simply cite Ijebus' own sense that there has been no decline from any glorious or glorified past.

[3]For studies of recent Nigerian politics and social change see Williams (n.d.), Luckham (1971), and Melson and Wolpe (1971).

EPILOGUE

December, 1972

Within two months of the completion of the fieldwork reported in this book, Nigeria burst into flames. Civil war between the Biafran secessionists and the federal forces racked the country for two and half years, from mid-1967 to January of 1970. The general outlines of the conflict need no recounting: by blockade, siege and occasional sharp attack, the federal noose slowly tightened around the necks of Biafra's defenders and bloated the bellies of its children. By the time Biafra surrendered, its people and its economy had been devastated.

Yet, despite its immense human wreckage, the war itself, like the massacres of Ibos in northern Nigeria in 1966, remained a distant set of events for people outside the main theaters. Often the war moved slowly, and the reporting of it in Nigerian newspapers was sporadic. Men enlisted, but there were rarely exploits, heroes, or deaths enough to raise widespread discussion. The national slogan, "To keep Nigeria one is a task that must be done," together with the insistence by the government that it was only punishing the rebellious leaders of a misled people, contributed to making the war an abstraction for those who could not hear the bullets.

Indeed, if the war was an illness of the body politic, most Yorubas were more deeply concerned as to whether there was enough strength left in the body to feed *them*. For a long period, there was some doubt. The diversion of enormous economic resources to build, outfit and sustain an army forty times its prewar size was to become a permanent demand on the national treasury. The postponement of political and administrative reforms, development projects, and even simple road maintenance, in areas well away from the war zones, while special taxes were *raised* for the war effort, drained the patience of the non-combatant farmers and urban workers. Shortages, local supply and demand distortions, and the restriction of many imports further aggravated Nigerian civilian tempers. And the reports of official corruption at a scale unmatched even by the deposed politicians' venality, but this time with no threat of eventual accountability, produced a mixed reaction of contempt and awe about all government.

Some segments of the population articulated their grievances forcefully enough to be heard above the din of war. In 1968 and 1969, some of the poorest farmers around the city of Ibadan, and then farmers in many other areas, rose in revolt against the combination of added taxes, harassment by local officials, and disappearance of visible returns for the taxes being levied. Before the Western State government capitulated, one hundred and sixty people had been killed in widespread clashes between farmers and police (Western State of Nigeria 1969). At the same time, urban workers' wages were reviewed by a national government commission, which found them to be so inadequate that immediate increases of up to thirty per cent were ordered into effect, just to catch up with the rising cost of food, accommodation and other essentials (Federal Republic of Nigeria 1971).

By late 1972, when I made my first return visit to Nigeria since the fieldwork for this book, it was thus possible to frame my questions not simply as "what had become" of the seven households we have met, but as "what had been the toll" of all these forces and events on them.

II

None of the families was hard to find. All were still in Ibadan: four lived in the same places they had nearly six years before, and the three others were easily located through friends or former neighbors. Further, and more surprising, almost all reported themselves distinctly better off than they were in 1967.

The Odusanyas. Michael Odusanya had voiced fears that the huge number of apprentices in the carpentry trade would soon choke the market, but it had not happened yet. His old apprentices had found jobs, and he had taken new ones on. On the other hand, when the man from whom Michael rented his shop site raised the rent, in one jump, to three times what he had been paying (and one full year's rent due in advance), Michael moved to a less prominent but much cheaper location nearby. So much in demand were shops in Ibadan in 1972 that his landlord had no trouble finding a new tenant.

The Odusanyas lived in the same house as before, but had taken an extra room. Rent had tripled for each room, and now the landlady was threatening further increases. So, after fifteen years, Michael finally bought a plot of land near Liberty Stadium, in an area almost all built up. Building plots in new tracts farther from downtown cost only £150 to £200, but Michael paid £500 ($1,500 at current exchange rates) for his central location. He hoped to begin building his house within the next few months.

Ma Deji still worked alternate shifts at the cigarette factory. But instead of hiring a house girl, the Odusanyas relied on Michael's younger sister, who had lived with the family for eight years, and had begun to trade in petty items outside the front door, to look after the house and the children when Ma Deji was away.

Deji was attending secondary school at a small new school on the outskirts of Ibadan: the fees there kept Michael from starting his building sooner. Deji would have a broader education than his parents, but it is likely that his school had neither the staff nor the facilities to ensure that many of its graduates would win places in the universities. Ṣọla, Wọle and Olu, his three younger siblings, were still in primary school, and were likely to follow the same route as Deji.

There had also been two new children. The first, born in 1968, died just before her second birthday, while the family was on a visit to Michael's home town — she came down with a fever, fell asleep, woke quietly in the middle of the night and managed to set fire, as if by announcement, to her clothes which were stored under the bed, then climbed back into bed and fell asleep and died. Ma Deji missed her, and was consoled only by the memory that, when she was married and went to a prophet for blessing, she was told that she would have many children, but that the fifth would die. In 1971, another girl was born, and had been quite healthy so far.

When Ma Deji's grandfather died in 1970, her younger brother, a private in the army, refused to contribute toward funeral expenses. Ma Deji spent over £300 on the funeral, herself. In their decisions to make expenditures such as this, in the continued support of relatives in their house, and with rising prices offsetting their increased income, it is not difficult to understand why the Odusanyas had not yet upgraded their own living standards very substantially.

Tade Oyebanji. When the new Water Corporation hived off from the Ministry of Works, Tade refused to go along unless he was given executive training. Turned down, he stayed at the Ministry, and, with a promotion there, he was using far more of the Trade Centre education he had. An Assistant Technical Officer, he reviewed plans and estimated the costs of the government's share of water connections for private and public buildings. His salary was two and a half times what it had been six years before.

With the increased wages as means, he had settled down. When his friend and roommate, Tunde, took a job in Lagos, Tade moved to a busy house on the main road. Savings went for furniture, a radiogram and records, a table fan and other household items. But time was still spent in romantic pursuits. One shop in the new house was kept by a girl from a larger town near his own, who sold bottled cooking gas and provisions. In 1971 they were married, and within a year their first child was born. They currently rented three and a half rooms in a quiet house near Tade's brother's place.

Tade still had career plans beyond the relative safety of his civil service job. Two friends and he had formed a joint plumbing contracting company. Already he had taken on one apprentice, although the jobs to date were only occasional and the boy was doing more housework than plumbing. Tade hoped that the business would develop to the point where he could leave his government job altogether. Toward that end, the three partners were putting nearly all their profits into a bank account to further capitalize the business, rather than simply use the work to supplement their current incomes. Tade's thrift was of long standing. When he took his savings from the ẹsusu in 1967, he gave the money to his brother, Pa Yẹmi, who had turned from running his small taxi fleet, to being a sales agent for a major importer of Japanese taxicabs. Tade got informal "dividends" from this investment in his brother's business. It might be a long time before his own private enterprise could replace his current salary, but Tade was optimistic. "We are an underdeveloped country," he said, "and we must join together to work to improve it, and not rely only on the government." Added Pa Yẹmi, "Capital is the most important thing!"

The Ọnadeles. After the fieldwork reported here, things went from bad to worse with the Ọnadele family. First, the university lecturer reneged on payment for Bọla's work — only five years later did Bọla recover it by taking the case to court. The lull in building contracts deepened, and Bọla's only income, for a year and more, came from selling some building plots he had bought as an investment several years before. Quarrels with Ma Lara continued, and in mid-1968 she finally took the children and moved home to her parents' house across the city. Neither side sought reconciliation, although in 1969 Bọla sued Ma Lara in the Customary Court to retrieve her or the money he had given her before they married. Ma Lara's family argued simply that there had never been even a formal marriage by "customary law," and the case was dismissed.

Thus rejected, Bọla sought isolation. He went to consolidate his title to the large piece of property on the edge of town that he had been buying piecemeal from various members of the Ibadan family who kept surfacing with claims to part-ownership. To take possession, he built a tool shed on the land and moved into it. Then, in 1969, he bought a small concrete block-making machine, and began to turn out blocks, one by one, with which to begin his own house. He said that people came to joke about how long it would take him at that rate to put up a house, especially in such an area where rich men were putting up large houses within a few months. But he persevered, reselling the rear area of his tract of twelve acres to a poultry farmer nearby, and moving into a back room of the new house as soon as it was roofed. Two years later, the ground floor, five rooms, of his house were nearly finished, and he was about to furnish them and begin to live comfortably.

Living at this new site, Bọla began to pick up new building jobs nearby. He was also in a strategic location to watch the real estate development in this rapidly-growing part of town. With his cousin the lawyer, Bọla had bought and resold several small building plots, making up to one hundred per cent profit, even after only a few months. Not infrequently, he could parlay an option to purchase from a potential seller and a deposit from a potential buyer into a substantial profit, with no money of his own involved at all. Now he had his eye on land along a new highway that would soon be built — the exact location had not yet been published, but Bọla had met the surveyors! There had, in six years, been an intensifying commercialization of land in Ibadan, and, if Bọla's investment decisions were judicious, he might yet realize one of his schemes for getting rich.

His private life still troubled him, however. His son Ṣegun had come to live with him and do house chores. In Primary 3, Ṣegun did not care much about school, although he stayed there all afternoon playing because there was no one at home for company. Otherwise, Bọla was neither seeing nor contributing to the support of his three other children. Ma Lara had a small canteen across town where she cooked and sold food, helped by one employee and by Lara, who had dropped out of school, but Lọla, the youngest, had been staying with Ma Lara's elder sister. Living in a room nearby, Ma Lara seemed determined to be on her own.

Meanwhile, without prospect of reconciliation with Ma Lara, and with little stomach for further permanent entanglements with any other woman, Bọla persisted in a self-centered solitude that other Yoruba find eccentric.

The Wahabis. In continued contrast to the Ọnadele family, Saliu Wahabi's social status and family solidarity had steadily grown. In 1968, Mama Olobi, Saliu's mother, fell ill. Earlier, the old woman had been hostile to Mama Ẹbun, the separated second wife, but now, seeking favor, Ma Ẹbun came to tend her mother-in-law dutifully, until she died a few months later. That was demonstration enough; the estranged wife returned to the house permanently, despite Saliu's laugh that "she is still a troublesome woman." More children followed, now numbering nine in all, with the tenth due soon. Saliu had some hope, but probably not much expectation, that his family would now be complete. His central concern was to be able to give them all good education. Indeed, the older ones were progressing well in school: Yinka was at a good secondary school (run by the Catholic Church) already, and Ẹbun would follow the next year.

Saliu had no difficulty with the school finances. In 1969 he finished the upper floor of his house, moved his own family upstairs, converted his former sitting room into a shop by altering the front wall, and began collecting rapidly-rising rents from eight rooms. The rents, a promotion at work, and the wage increases of the Adebo Commission award made Saliu's monthly income almost £90 ($270 at current exchange rates), double what it was in 1967. In addition, the substantial farmland his mother left him brought income in the form of a share of his tenant's proceeds.

With the house finished, Saliu was able to use his savings to enhance his status in other ways. He gave his mother an expensive funeral. He began supporting two young cousins from Ijebu Ode, who came to school in Ibadan. But, most importantly, in January of 1971, he made his Hadj, the pilgrimage to Mecca which is enjoined upon all devout Muslims. One among over 10,000 pilgrims from Western Nigeria, he paid almost £300 for the chartered flight, accommodation and incidental expenses. But the personal experience, he said, was moving, and this status as an Alhaji had clearly reinforced and given a powerful religious dimension to the prestige he already enjoyed as a wise counsel and mediator. He was now fully committed as well to the Ansar-ud-Deen modernist Islamic movement, and he was one of the elders at its local mosque.

Now Saliu was beginning to plan a house at home in Ijebu Ode. "I think a man needs only these two houses," he argued, denying that he would build more houses in Ibadan. Depending on educational expenses for his children, the next project would be to buy a car. Saliu had no idea he would prosper as he had done when he began to teach himself to type twenty-two years before.

Madam Bankole. Of the seven households here described, Madam Bankole's had changed least in the passage of five years.

She lived in the same room and traded from the same stall in Dugbe market. The contents of each place had changed little, nor had Mama's living patterns. Healthier than in the immediate period of our study, she stayed at Dugbe from nine in the morning until after dark at seven, six days a week. But on Wednesday in the late afternoon, and on Sunday for most of the day, she went for prayers and social gatherings in the Anglican church. She had not pursued further status among her townsmen or in market political affairs, but lived her life quietly among her neighbors and friends at work, in church, and at home.

Not so, this lack of change, in her daughter's life. Soon after their return from study in the United States, Ayo and her husband broke up their marriage permanently. With her M. Ed. in hand, however, Ayo won a lecturer's position in one of the best teacher training colleges in the state. But she was unwilling to take her son to the small town where it is located, and instead, Biodun, currently finishing primary grade four, was at a new but high-standard boarding school in Oshogbo.

Chief Ogunkoya. Chief Ogunkoya's troubles had abated. First, he and his fifth wife reconciled their differences, and she returned, reasserting authority over her children. Second, of course, the children had all grown, among other things in reasonability, and there remained only four under the age of twelve —

and those had their mothers present to control them. Third, the oldest children had begun to contribute to the family (Yetunde and Nikẹ sending money), while the next oldest set were in various places which gave their father pride (Bisi doing a dental technician's course in Lagos, Kẹhinde studying science at the University of Ibadan, Fẹmi working but also about to try to gain university admission, and Kọla, Wale, Banji and Modupẹ, all in first-rate secondary schools). Finally, the Chief himself, who had just passed his sixtieth birthday, had begun to have lapses of memory, and while the condition was bothersome at times, he was basically content to follow his doctor's advice that he remain close to home, avoiding pressure.

Chief Ogunkọya had thus begun his old age. He had sold his car, and no longer sought new investment possibilities. His house in Oke-gan, damaged during the last, violence-ridden days of civilian politics, had been only partly repaired, as he realized that he would continue to live in Ibadan rather than go home in retirement. He did not keep alive many of his old associations with the politicians, some of whom, as he remarked, were still powerful, and some of whom had become avaricious and conniving shadows of their former selves. His one remaining extra-domestic activity was the Reformed Ogboni Fraternity, where he was now a senior officer. For some people, Lodge membership is an active political forum, but Chief Ogunkọya downplayed this aspect, preferring the warm and long-standing conviviality to the equally possible calculation of social advantage.

With the first of his grandchildren at his knees, the Chief was secure in his own large family. His children may not be at all like him later on, however, for they were all having long western educations and were taking roles in the new bureaucracies of Nigerian society. Whether they valued their father's decisions about family composition, residence arrangements, financial means, and so on, enough to live the same kind of life remained to be seen.

The Falujọs. Under military rule, life had become even more comfortable and stable for the Falujọ family, and for others like them. While interpersonal tensions still flared in government offices, as anywhere else, the high drama of arbitrary political incursion from outside and of continuous internal intrigue had subsided.

With the promotion of his friend and colleague to the second most senior position in the ministry, Victor Falujọ had become chief of his section. A larger, more centrally-located house came with the position, though Victor had apparently not tried also to obtain the plusher furnishings that he might have gotten if he had demanded them. Ṣade's routine had been made easier by the fact that, in the State reorganization of schools, she had been transferred from her former school to another newer one much closer to home. Although she missed her erstwhile colleagues and students, she was relieved that she had only a five-minute drive to work instead of the forty-minute cross-town trek that the rapidly-accelerating traffic congestion in Ibadan had produced.

Both Victor and Ṣade benefitted from the Adebo salary awards. Their savings had enabled them to erect a spacious ten-room house in Ijebu Ode, formally opened in November of 1972 to an impressive party of half a dozen clergymen and over three hundred guests. Though they doubted that they would be "home" for more than one weekend each month, they were proud to thus reestablish their old roots in Ijebu. In addition, the Falujọs were currently supporting two young relatives in their house in Ibadan ("Mama," Ṣade's elder sister, returned to her husband's home in 1969), and were sending money to various relatives at home.

Contrary to many of their elite friends, Victor and Ṣade did stop at four children. Gbenga was in the third grade and Akin, fully recovered from his liver disease, was in the sixth grade of a private primary school with an excellent reputation. Tọla and Bandele attended perhaps the best girls' and boys' secondary schools in Ibadan, and they lived in the boarding houses there.

Bandele would soon have to think about university. In the summer of 1971, Victor took the whole family on a cross-country tour of the United States while he was visiting small-business research programs in American universities. Along the way, Bandele determined that he would follow his father's footsteps to higher education in the States. Victor was reluctant, though; he was twenty-six years old at the time he went abroad, and was not sure that sixteen-year old Bandele should be on his own just yet. There was still a year before the decision must be made. But, whatever the outcome, finances would not hinder the Falujọs' ability to gain any advantage open to contemporary Nigerians.

III

The paradox persists. In terms of world society, reasons abound to make one believe that in Nigeria the material and even perhaps more intangible conditions of peoples' lives are worsening. Yet at the micro-level, at least insofar as the seven families here are concerned, material circumstances and personal pride and satisfaction are waxing.

There are at least three possible ways of explaining the paradox. My data and interpretations may be wrong, and the people we have met may simply be poor, oppressed and headed for more and more disappointment, their desperateness counterbalanced only by the fact that as they *as individuals* get older, their savings and incomes allow a slightly enhanced standard of living. Second, however, the macro-level materials may be wrong, relying too heavily on incomplete or inaccurate data and compounding errors with pre-conceived biases; in short, perhaps life *is* getting better for Nigerians. Third, perhaps both horns of the paradox are correct, and the resolution is that while *some* segments of Nigerian society, including the subjects of this study, are benefitting from changes taking place, other and larger segments are losing ground. In fact, each of these explanations invites reflection.

Are the Ijebu families we have met in fact poor and exploited? By any international standards, yes. Except for the Falujọs, the value of the labor of working adults is measured in small coins — from perhaps a shilling to three or four shillings per hour. Diets, though plentiful in calories, do not have much protein content. Rooms are crowded; adults sleep on mats on springs, most of the children on the floor. Simple tasks — cooking, getting water — are arduous. The cost of urban living is high and growing higher, and the families can accumulate savings for major expenditures like furniture or schooling only very slowly. Social services, from police protection to old age assistance, are virtually non-existent, requiring individuals to cover themselves against every contingency. (Investment in other people is a positive response to these threats, but, of course, it is not determined by them). Nor do educational facilities provide opportunity for the recognition or encouragement of individual potential, or health facilities for the efficient treatment of other than routine ailments. In all of these circumstances, there is no room for miscalculation in school choice, financial affairs, exposure to illness, or a hundred other ways. This inability to relax one's vigilance is itself a form of oppression.

Furthermore, it is clear that this poverty is not to be blamed on the poor. Colonialism, draining resources and reinvesting no profits; neo-colonialism, continuing the old patterns with the cooperation and reward of a minor but vastly powerful ruling segment of Nigerian society; and indigenous apathy to dedicated reorientation of society; all these external sources of poverty and its persistence do indeed constitute exploitation. Tade Oyebanji, Bọla Ọnadele, Victor Falujọ, Florence Odusanya and others all see in their work situations the magnitude of differential rewards, inequities and corruption in the award of contracts or the allocation of jobs, or the costs of verbal criticism. Life is free for those who will toe the line!

Is there improvement, or deepening distress? It was evident in 1972 that life was getting better for the families we met (although perhaps not as fast as life improves for families in Europe or North America). There was more schooling, more health during childhood, higher real incomes and consumption levels, more money passing through the hands of these Ijebu families than in 1966 and 1967. And while part of the difference for these families was simply concomitant to their advance through their life cycle, living standards in Oke

Ado in general were higher, as evidenced at least by the much greater variety of goods available in local shops, or by the new ubiquitousness of motorcycles and the spread of television viewing. The literature on urban African socioeconomic conditions errs badly in failing to assess adequately the productivity, rewards, and multiple sources of income of town dwellers outside the wage bills of industry and government (there is, for example, no substantial work on the incomes of small traders and craftsmen, little attempt to measure total family income from all sources against long-term expenditures). In this light, the data arrayed here, and the optimism of the actors, must be taken as genuine, and as a plea for further elaboration of aggregate measures of the real and variable conditions of urban life. In rural Nigeria, Polly Hill (1972), and in Ibadan, Rolf Güsten (1968) and Michael Koll (1969), have made much the same point and have contributed other perspectives.

Does the improvement noted here obtain only to a small portion of Nigerian society, these Ijebus and a few others? As many authors have pointed out, urban workers in Africa are ''privileged'' in social services and opportunities, and probably in income, relative to the overwhelming proportion of the population which still lives in rural areas. In a sense, then, all the families in this book are part of a Nigerian ''middle class,'' sharing in whatever expansion and redistribution of wealth is taking place.

Yet to persist in the most pessimistic frame, making of our families only exceptional cases, or arguing that the evidence here ''proves'' the aristocracy of the urban condition over rural destitution, would be a distortion, too. For one thing, the range of families we have met is wide, and an even wider sample of occupational levels and family types would show, I can only assert here, similar optimism and improvement. Second, the families here come from a rural area which is itself growing more wealthy and diverse — for example, these families have helped to support the rural construction industry, weaving and dyeing, pottery and basketmaking, fishing and milling, and other skilled rural trades, all this over and above the direct financial contributions they make to rural relatives and the obvious interdependence of town and country for food production. If we do stretch the notion of middle class privilege to include all of these people, urbanites and rural dwellers, we can hardly speak of growth benefitting only a *tiny* elite. Nonetheless, there are many areas of Nigeria with no export crops, few migrants in the urban economy, and little individual or collective power to channel resources in their direction.

To resolve these dilemmas conclusively, of course, we need much more sophisticated studies of living conditions throughout urban and rural Nigeria, conditions which change more slowly than regimes and individual economic factors. A rehabilitated anthropology, with its intensive community study methods but a perspective on national social structure rather than individual cultural difference, might add greatly to our present understandings. Meanwhile, myths of an undifferentiated Africa, or of an urban or rural population undifferentiated except by tongue and ethnicity, do little to advance real understanding of the positive and the tender points of social change. Worse, mechanistic studies of customs rather than conditions dehumanize Africans in the abstractness of their categorizations. If Yoruba and others are to think about and act in their society, their own concerns must remain in full view. The Ijebu families in this book have pleaded, each in its own way, for a positive struggle for a better life for all: it is to *their* human condition, not The Human Condition, that social scientists, development planners, and political leaders must respond.

References Cited

Abernethy, David B.
1969 The Political Dilemma of Popular Education: An African Case. Stanford, Stanford University Press.

Adams, John
1823 Remarks on the Country Extending from Cape Palmas to the River Congo, Including Observations on the Manners and Customs of the Inhabitants. London, G. and W.B. Whittaker.

Ajayi, J.F. Ade
1965 Christian Missions in Nigeria 1841-1891: The Making of a New Elite. London, Longmans, Green and Co., Ltd.

Ajayi, J.F. Ade and Robert Smith
1964 Yoruba Warfare in the Nineteenth Century. London, Cambridge University Press.

Aronson, Dan R.
1970 *Review of* The Yoruba of Southwestern Nigeria, by William Bascom, *and of* Yoruba Towns and Cities, by Eva Krapf-Askari. Africa Report 15, no. 6:38-39.

Awe, Bolanle
1967 Ibadan, Its Early Beginnings. *In* The City of Ibadan. P.C. Lloyd, A.L. Mabogunje, and B. Awe, eds. London, Cambridge University Press. Pp. 11-25.

Ayandele, E.A.
1966 The Missionary Impact on Modern Nigeria 1842-1914: A Political and Social Analysis. London, Longmans, Green and Co., Ltd.
1970 The Changing Position of the Awujales of Ijebuland Under Colonial Rule. *In* West African Chiefs. Michael Crowder and Obaro Ikime, eds. Ile-Ife, University of Ife Press. Pp. 231-254.

Ayantuga, O.O.
1965 Ijebu and Its Neighbours 1851-1914. Unpublished Ph.D. Thesis. University of London.

Bascom, William R.
1942 The Principle of Seniority in the Social Structure of the Yoruba. American Anthropologist 44:37-46.
1944 The Sociological Role of the Yoruba Cult Group. American Anthropologist Memoir 63.

1951a Social Status, Wealth and Individual Differences among the Yoruba. American Anthropologist 53:490-505.

1951b Yoruba Food. Africa 21:41-53.

1951c Yoruba Cooking. Africa 21:125-137.

1952 The *Esusu:* A Credit Institution of the Yoruba. Journal of the Royal Anthropological Institute 82:63-69.

1969 The Yoruba of Southwestern Nigeria. New York, Holt, Rinehart and Winston.

Bauer, P.T.

1954 West African Trade. London, Cambridge University Press.

Beier, H. Ulli

1968 Contemporary Art in Africa. London, Pall Mall Press.

Biobaku, Saburi O.

1957 The Egba and Their Neighbours 1842-1872. Oxford, Oxford University Press.

Bowen, Elenore Smith

1954 Return to Laughter. New York, Harper & Brothers.

Callaway, Archibald

1967 From Traditional Crafts to Modern Industries. *In* The City of Ibadan. P.C. Lloyd, A.L. Mabogunje, and B. Awe, eds. London, Cambridge University Press. Pp. 153-171.

Clignet, Remi

1970 Many Wives, Many Powers: Authority and Power in Polygynous Families. Evanston, Northwestern University Press.

Cohen, Abner

1966 Politics of the Kola Trade. Africa 36:18-36.

Custom and Politics in Urban Africa. Berkeley and Los Angeles,
1969 University of California Press.

Coleman, James S.

1958 Nigeria: Background to Nationalism. Berkeley and Los Angeles, University of California Press.

Cornelius, Wayne A., Jr.

1971 The Political Sociology of Cityward Migration in Latin America: Toward Empirical Theory. *In* Latin American Urban Research, Vol. 1. Francie F. Rabinovitz and Felicity M. Trueblood, eds. Beverly Hills, Sage Publications. Pp. 95-147.

Dahrendorf, Ralf

1959 Class and Class Conflict in Industrial Society. Stanford, Stanford University Press.

Diamond, Stanley

1967 The Anaguta of Nigeria: Suburban Primitives. *In* Contemporary

Change in Traditional Societies. Julian H. Steward, ed. Volume I.
Urbana, Chicago and London, University of Illinois Press. Pp.
361-505.

Epstein, A.L.
1961 The Network and Urban Social Organization. The Rhodes-
Livingstone Institute Journal 29:29-61.

Fadipe, N.A.
1970 The Sociology of the Yoruba. Ibadan, Ibadan University Press.

Federal Republic of Nigeria
1971 Second and Final Report of the Wages and Salaries Review
Commission, 1970-71. Lagos, Federal Ministry of Information.

Forde, Daryll
1951 The Yoruba-Speaking Peoples of South-Western Nigeria. London,
International African Institute.

Geertz, Clifford
1962 The Rotating Credit Association: a Middle Rung in Economic
Development. Economic Development and Cultural Change
10:241-263.

Goldschmidt, Walter
1969 Kambuya's Cattle: The Legacy of an African Herdsman. Berkeley
and Los Angeles, University of California Press.

Gugler, Josef
1969 On the Theory of Rural-Urban Migration: The Case of Subsaharan
Africa. In Migration. J.A. Jackson, ed. Cambridge, Cambridge
University Press. Pp. 134-155.

Gulliver, P.H.
1969 The Conservative Commitment in Northern Tanzania: The Arusha
and Masai. In Tradition and Transition in East Africa. P.H.
Gulliver, ed. London, Routledge & Kegan Paul. Pp. 223-242.

Güsten, Rolf
1968 Studies in the Staple Food Economy of Western Nigeria. Munich,
Weltforum Verlag.

Gutkind, Peter C.W.
1967 The Energy of Despair: Social Organization of the Unemployed in
Two African Cities: Lagos and Nairobi. Civilisations 17:184-214,
380-405.

Hill, Polly
1972 Rural Hausa: A Village and a Setting. Cambridge, Cambridge
University Press.

Hodgkin, Thomas
1956 Nationalism in Colonial Africa. London, Frederick Muller, Ltd.

Hopkins, Anthony G.
    1964   An Economic History of Lagos: 1880-1914. Unpublished Ph.D.
            Thesis. University of London.
    1973   An Economic History of West Africa. London, Longmans & Co.
Howell, Joseph T.
    1973   Hard Living on Clay Street. Garden City, N.Y., Anchor Books/
            Doubleday.
Johnson, Samuel
    1921   History of the Yorubas. Lagos, C.M.S. (Nigeria) Bookshops.
Karve, D.D., ed.
    1963   The New Brahmans: Five Maharashtrian Families. Berkeley and
            Los Angeles, University of California Press.
Koll, Michael
    1969   Crafts and Cooperation in Western Nigeria. Düsseldorf, Ber-
            telsmann Universitätsverlag.
Kopytoff, Jeàn Herskovits
    1965   A Preface to Modern Nigeria: The "Sierra Leonians" in Yoruba,
            1830-1890. Madison, University of Wisconsin Press.
Krapf-Askari, Eva
    1969   Yoruba Towns and Cities. London, Oxford University Press.
Langness, L.L.
    1965   The Life History in Anthropological Science. New York, Holt,
            Rinehart and Winston.
Leighton, Alexander H., T. Adeoye Lambo, Charles C. Hughes, Dorothea
    C. Leighton, Jane M. Murphy and David B. Mackin
    1963   Psychiatric Disorder among the Yoruba. Ithaca, Cornell University
            Press.
LeVine, Barbara B.
    1962   Yoruba Students' Memories of Childhood Rewards and Punish-
            ments. Occasional Publication No. 2, Institute of Education,
            University College, Ibadan.
LeVine, Robert A.
    1966a Dreams and Deeds: Achievement Motivation in Nigeria. Chicago
            and London, University of Chicago Press.
    1966b Sex Roles and Economic Change in Africa. Ethnology 5:186-193.
Lewis, Oscar
    1959   Five Families. New York, Basic Books.
    1961   Children of Sanchez. New York, Random House.
    1964   Pedro Martinez. New York, Random House.
    1965   La Vida. New York, Random House.

Little, Kenneth
    1973   African Women in Towns: An Aspect of Africa's Social Revolu-
           tion. Cambridge, Cambridge University Press.
Lloyd, Barbara B.
    1966   Education and Family Life in the Development of Class Identifica-
           tion among the Yoruba. *In* New Elites of Tropical Africa. P.C.
           Lloyd, ed. London, Oxford University Press. Pp. 163-183.
Lloyd, P.C.
    1954   The Traditional Political System of the Yoruba. Southwestern
           Journal of Anthropology 10:366-384.
    1962   Yoruba Land Law. London, Oxford University Press.
    1965   The Yoruba of Nigeria. *In* Peoples of Africa. James L. Gibbs, Jr.,
           ed. New York, Holt, Rinehart and Winston, Inc. Pp. 549-582.
    1966a Introduction. *In* The New Elites of Tropical Africa. P.C. Lloyd,
           ed. London, Oxford University Press. Pp. 1-65.
    1966b Class Consciousness among the Yoruba. *In* The New Elites of
           Tropical Africa. P.C. Lloyd, ed. London, Oxford University
           Press. Pp. 328-341.
    1966c Agnatic and Cognatic Descent among the Yoruba. Man (n.s.)
           1:484-500.
    1967a Africa in Social Change. Harmondsworth, Penguin Books, Ltd.
    1967b Introduction. *In* The City of Ibadan. P.C. Lloyd, A.L. Mabogunje,
           and B. Awe, eds. London, Cambridge University Press. Pp. 3-10.
    1967c The Elite. *In* The City of Ibadan. P.C. Lloyd, A.L. Mabogunje,
           and B. Awe, eds. London, Cambridge University Press. Pp.
           129-150.
    1971   The Political Development of Yoruba Kingdoms in the Eighteenth
           and Nineteenth Centuries. Occasional Paper No. 31. London,
           Royal Anthropological Institute.
Lloyd, P.C., A.L. Mabogunje, and B. Awe, eds.
    1967   The City of Ibadan. London, Cambridge University Press.
Luckham, Robin
    1971   The Nigerian Military: A Sociological Analysis of Authority and
           Revolt 1960-1967. London and New York, Cambridge University
           Press.
Mabogunje, A.L.
    1962   Yoruba Towns. Ibadan, Ibadan University Press.
    1967   The Ijebu. *In* The City of Ibadan. P.C. Lloyd, A.L. Mabogunje,
           and B. Awe, eds. London, Cambridge University Press. Pp. 85-95.
    1968   Urbanization in Nigeria. London, University of London Press.

McClelland, D.C.
    1961   The Achieving Society. Princeton, Van Nostrand.
Melson, Robert and Howard Wolpe, eds.
    1971   Nigeria: Modernization and the Politics of Communalism. East
            Lansing, Michigan State University Press.
Mitchell, J.C. and A.L. Epstein
    1959   Occupational Prestige and Social Status among Urban Africans in
            Northern Rhodesia. Africa 29:22-40.
Onakomaiya, S.O.
    1965   Primary Occupations in Oṣunmaiyegun District. Ijebu Province.
            Unpublished essay. University of Ibadan, Department of Geog-
            raphy.
Ottenberg, Simon
    1959   Ibo Receptivity to Change. *In* Continuity and Change in African
            Cultures. William R. Bascom and Melville J. Herskovits, eds.
            Chicago, University of Chicago Press.
Plotnicov, Leonard
    1967   Strangers to the City: Urban Man in Jos, Nigeria. Pittsburgh,
            University of Pittsburgh Press.
    1970   The Modern African Elite of Jos, Nigeria. *In* Social Stratification in
            Africa. Arthur Tuden and Leonard Plotnicov, eds. New York, The
            Free Press. Pp. 269-302.
Schwarz, Walter
    1968   Nigeria. New York, Frederick A. Praeger, Inc.
Sklar, Richard L.
    1963   Nigerian Political Parties. Princeton, Princeton University Press.
Smith, Mary F.
    1954   Baba of Karo. London, Faber & Faber.
Smith, Robert S.
    1969   Kingdoms of the Yoruba. London, Methuen & Co. Ltd.
    1971   Nigeria — Ijebu. *In* West African Resistance: The Military
            Response to Colonial Occupation. Michael Crowder, ed. London,
            Hutchinson & Co., Ltd. Pp. 170-204.
Southall, Aidan
    1960   On Chastity in Africa. Uganda Journal 24:207-216.
Teriba, O. and O.A. Philips
    1971   Income Distribution and National Integration. Nigerian Journal of
            Economic and Social Studies 13:77-122.
Turnbull, Colin M.
    1962   The Lonely African. New York, Simon and Schuster, Inc.
    1972   The Mountain People. New York, Simon and Schuster, Inc.

Western State of Nigeria
    1969   Report of the Commission of Inquiry into the Civil Disturbances which occurred in certain parts of the Western State of Nigeria in the month of December 1968, and other matters incidental thereto or connected therewith. Ibadan.
    1971   Annual Digest of Education Statistics Vol. X, 1970. Statistics Division, Ministry of Economic Planning and Reconstruction, Ibadan.
Williams, Babatunde A.
    n.d.   Political Trends in Nigeria 1960-1964. Ibadan, African Education (1965) Press.
Winter, Edward H.
    1959   Beyond the Mountains of the Moon: The Lives of Four Africans. Urbana, University of Illinois Press.